TRANSIT

The Story of Public Transportation in the Puget Sound Region

by Jim Kershner

SOUNDTRANSIT

King County METRO
Moving forward together

LMN   Parametrix
ENGINEERING. PLANNING. ENVIRONMENTAL SCIENCES   WSP

HistoryLink / Documentary Media
Seattle, WA

TRANSIT
The Story of Public Transportation in the Puget Sound Region

Previous spread: Link light-rail commuters bustle through University Station in Seattle not long after its opening in 2016.

HistoryLink
93 Pike Street, Suite 315B
Seattle, WA 98101
206.447.8140
www.historylink.org
admin@historylink.org

Documentary Media
3250 41st Ave SW
Seattle, WA 98116
books@docbooks.com
www.documentarymedia.com
206.935.9292

First Edition
Printed in China

By Jim Kershner
Editor: Chris Boutée
Image Editor: David Koch, HistoryLink
Production Assistants: Edward Daschle, Tori Smith
Book Design: Paul Langland Design
Editorial Director: Petyr Beck, Documentary Media

ISBN: 978-1-933245-55-3

Distributed by the University of Washington Press
uwapress@uw.edu
206.543.4050

Library of Congress Cataloging-in-Publication Data
Names: Kershner, Jim, 1953- author.
Title: Transit : the story of public transportation in the Puget Sound Region / by Jim
    Kershner.
Description: Seattle, WA : Documentary Media, [2019]
Identifiers: LCCN 2018050398 I ISBN 9781933245553 (soft cover)
Subjects: LCSH: Local transit--Washington (State)--Puget Sound Region.
Classification: LCC HE4487.P84 K47 2019 I DDC 388.409797/7--dc23
LC record available at https://lccn.loc.gov/2018050398

Contents

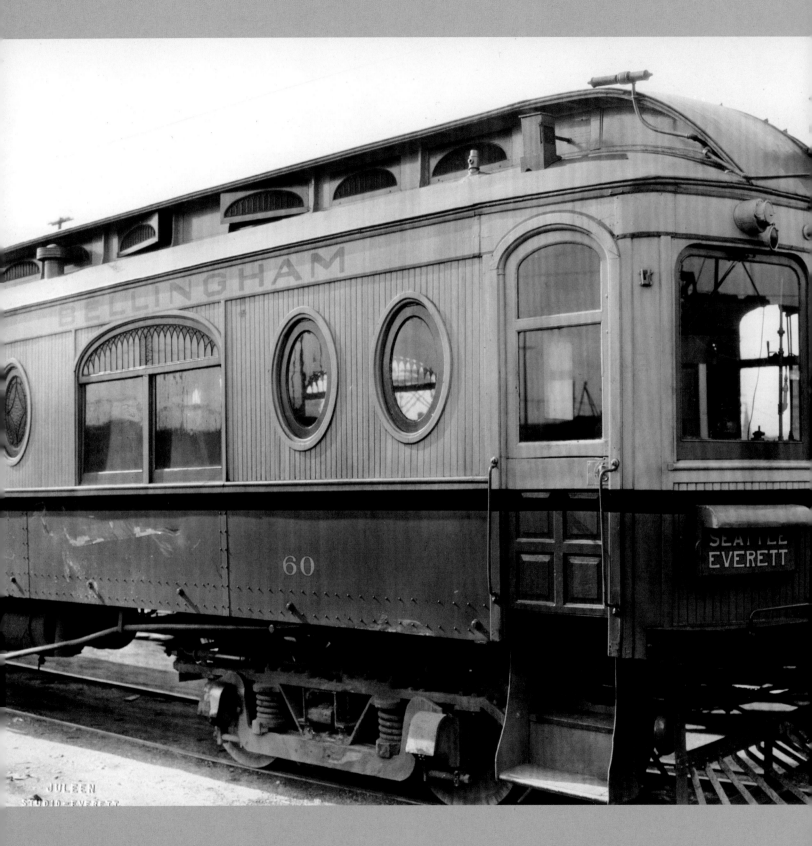

A Long, Strange Ride

• • • • • • • • • • • • • • • • •

The Puget Sound region has the dubious distinction of owning five of the nation's worst traffic bottlenecks. So perhaps the next time you are stuck in one of these jams, you might have an hour or two to ponder this question: How did we ever get *into* this mess?

Or perhaps the next time you find yourself sitting in a Link light-rail car, zipping past this same traffic jam, you might have a few minutes to ponder a question of a different stripe: How did this region manage—finally—to forge a path *around* this prodigious mess?

This history sets out to answer both questions. The first can be answered in simple terms: The population grew and grew until there were too many people, in too many cars, attempting to squeeze through too many choke points. The second question can be answered simply as well: We dismantled one rail transit system, waited 60 years, and then started building a system that looks, in some ways, like the one we tore up.

The full story, however, is nowhere near that simple. It is filled with high political drama and the making and breaking of Seattle mayors. It is the story of momentous turning points, none more disastrous than the defeat of the Forward Thrust rail transit system in 1968, and none more startling than the 1996 vote authorizing Sound Move—the results of which are speeding along tracks today.

Left: An interurban car, circa 1928, on the Pacific Northwest Traction Co. line, which ran from Seattle to Everett until 1939.

An all-too-common Seattle scene in 2003: a traffic snarl on the Alaskan Way Viaduct.

The old Mosquito Fleet—one of Puget Sound's first forms of mass transit—at the Colman Dock.

Because this is a mass transit history, not a general transportation history, it cannot describe in detail all of the freeway dramas that have played out in the region for nearly six decades—although the term "Mercer Mess" will make an appearance. Nor will it attempt to describe in detail the region's long ferry history. That's a topic big enough for its own book. However, the story will begin with the region's first mass transit conveyances: canoes and steamboats.

Mainly, this history will describe how Seattle, Tacoma, and Everett built their own street rail and interurban railroad systems in the late 19th century. It will describe what life was like during this "golden age" of street rail—and why that age wasn't as golden as it sounds. (It was, in significant ways, a train wreck.) It will examine the streetcar's surprisingly sudden decline. And it will chronicle the era of rubber-tired transit—buses and trackless trolleys—when mass transit entered a slow decline, and hit rock bottom when voters in 1968 defeated a Forward Thrust transit bond that would have rebuilt a complete rail system.

From there the story will examine the region's transit renaissance, beginning in 1973, as a regional agency named Metro created King County's first truly successful transit system—resulting in the construction of a controversial bus tunnel directly under downtown. Finally, it will discuss the dogged determination necessary to create Sound Transit, an agency that began to redeem the opportunities lost in the 1968 bond defeat.

The Sound Transit story is filled with the kinds of ups and downs usually associated with a slightly more terrifying form of rail transit—the roller coaster. This particular thrill ride includes a period known as "The Dark Days," followed by a more exhilarating period in which Sound Transit managed to fulfill some of the visions once dreamed of by a forward-thinking civil engineer named Virgil Bogue almost a hundred years earlier.

This history is not strictly about buses and trains. It's also a story about how the entire Seattle–Tacoma–Everett region developed. Transit has always been one of the drivers of how and where the Puget Sound population grew. To put all of these stories into perspective, we need to start at the very beginning—back in the days when mass transit meant hopping into a really big canoe.

*Sound Transit's
University Station,
with the University of
Washington's Husky
Stadium looming
overhead.*

CHAPTER ONE

The Coming of the Streetcar

• • • • • • • • • • • • • • •

For thousands of years, the canoe was the most efficient—if not only—form of mass transportation in what is now called the Puget Sound region. Land transportation by foot or by horse through dense forest was slow and laborious for the region's native tribes. They faced the same topographical challenges that confound Puget Sound transportation planners even today: Passage in almost any direction was blocked by a steep hill, a tidal flat, a lake, a ravine, a salt marsh, a river, or even an entire mountain range. As a result, native tribes traveled largely by canoe—and some of those canoes were huge. A typical canoe used for family transportation weighed up to three tons and carried 15 people or more.[1] These canoes cruised the Puget Sound shorelines and connected villages and tribes throughout the area. They weren't fast—these trips sometimes took days—but traveling by canoe was faster than going by foot. Canoes were, in essence, the transit vans of their day.

Left: Seattle's original horse-drawn streetcar, making one of its first test runs on September 23, 1884. It switched its route to Second Avenue after Front Street merchants complained that it might scare wagon traffic.

After American and European pioneers arrived in the mid-1800s and the fledgling villages of Seattle and Tacoma were established, water was still the predominant mode of transportation. Steamboats, fast and reliable, proliferated into a swarm of "Mosquito Fleet" ferries.[2] These steamboats got their name because they were so numerous that people said they resembled "a swarm of mosquitoes."[3]

Meanwhile, the Washington Territorial government began building crude roads to accommodate an influx of new arrivals. Still, as late as the 1880s, land travel was restricted almost entirely to a few muddy wagon tracks and foot trails.[4]

Large tribal canoes may have been the first true mass transit vehicles on Puget Sound.

Getting anywhere by land was a challenge in steep, muddy, pioneer Seattle. This is Commercial Street (today's First Avenue South) looking north, in 1865.

In Seattle, city streets remained slippery and steep. Getting anywhere outside the small downtown district was time-consuming. With the Seattle population mushrooming—it would grow from under 4,000 in 1880 to 42,837 in 1890—a better way to move masses of people became necessary.

That better way soon arrived: street railways. These would later take many forms, but at first they combined rails with an ancient power source, the horse. In 1884 Frank Osgood, a Seattle entrepreneur, proposed the first horse-drawn streetcar in Seattle. It would go down Front Street, the city's main street (today's First Avenue). The Front Street merchants worried that the clattering of the streetcars would scare away wagon traffic, so Osgood was forced to switch his proposed route to Second Avenue.[5] He obtained financing from several of Seattle's leading citizens and began laying track. On September 23, 1884, the Seattle Street Railway carried its first passengers up and down Second Avenue. The fare was a nickel.[6] It was the first street railway in Washington Territory—Tacoma and

Spokane would not get their first streetcars until four years later. "It was no mean achievement for a town of 6,000 to have inaugurated the first streetcar line in Washington Territory," wrote streetcar historian Leslie Blanchard. "... The Seattle Street Railway was more than a mere local convenience or source of civic pride. It was a weapon in the struggle for survival. Rivalry between Seattle and Tacoma was bitter and intense, with each city battling with every resource at its disposal to become the principal community of the Pacific Northwest."[7]

A horse-drawn streetcar in 1886, looking north from about First Avenue and James Street.

This little horse-drawn streetcar was the precursor to a coming street railway boom. Despite the fact that the horses occasionally bolted or failed to slow down at a curve, the Seattle Street Railway proved popular from the start. Osgood soon extended his streetcar line to the southern shore of Lake Union.

Horses were soon pulling streetcars down Tacoma streets, as well. This city was almost as populous as Seattle and had the distinct logistical advantage of being the western terminus of the Northern Pacific railroad. On May 30, 1888, the first streetcars of the Tacoma Street Railway rolled down Pacific Avenue, from the wharf to 17th Street.[8] Horses pulled bright yellow, 14-passenger streetcars with upholstered seats.[9] On the same day, a steam motor (a method of streetcar propulsion promptly abandoned) began propelling streetcars on the C Street line. Another horse-drawn line started up on Tacoma Avenue. Riders flocked to these lines, which were quickly extended. Other tracks were hastily laid. When the

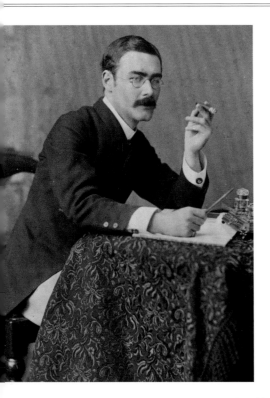

Young British poet and writer Rudyard Kipling was mostly unknown when he described Tacoma's street rail lines in 1889.

young, but soon-to-be-famous, British author Rudyard Kipling visited Tacoma in 1889, he was unimpressed with Tacoma's new streetcar infrastructure: "Down the muddy, grimy [unpaved] thoroughfare ran a horse-car line—the metals three inches above road level. Beyond this street rose many hills, and the town was thrown like a broken set of dominoes over all. A steam tramway—it left the track the only time I used it—was nosing about the hills."[10]

However, new technologies were about to supplant the horse and the steam motor. The cable car—a streetcar pulled by an underground cable powered by a central steam power plant—had already been developed in San Francisco. J.M. Thompson, a San Francisco cable car pioneer, immediately recognized that steep, hilly Seattle would be a perfect candidate for cable car service. In 1887 he and local investors built the Lake Washington Cable Railway (later renamed the Seattle City Railway Company). It ran from Pioneer Square due east to Lake Washington, along the line of Yesler Way (or Mill Street, as it was known then) with the return route along Jackson Street. This was an incredible—and borderline frightening—feat of engineering, requiring a pair of rickety 500-foot-long trestles to span a forested ravine. The Yesler trestle was 200 feet above solid ground at its highest point. Occasionally, winds caused the trestles to sway, terrifying the paying customers and causing cars to derail. In fact, the Jackson Street trestle was abandoned in 1900 for safety reasons, and the Yesler trestle was then used in both directions. The public decided that the convenience and speed were worth the risk, and people flocked to the new cable car service.

Savvy street railroad entrepreneurs soon learned that building an attraction at the far end of a streetcar line was good for business—they could sell tickets even on Sunday afternoons—so the company later created Leschi Park at the Lake Washington terminus, complete with "expanses of well-manicured lawn, fountains, scenic walkways, bathing beaches, bandstands, greenhouses, dancing pavilions and a menagerie of carefully selected animals," in Blanchard's words.[11]

The Jackson Street trestle of the Lake Washington Cable Railway was massive, rickety, and often terrifying. It's shown here under construction in 1888.

Within a few years, more cable car lines were built, dragging cable cars up Madison Street, James Street, and to and from the West Seattle ferry terminal at Duwamish Head.[12] Meanwhile, the merchants of Front Street (First Avenue), overcame their initial qualms about a streetcar line. The Front Street Cable Railway Company commenced operations on March 1, 1889, on a route that went up Front Street from Yesler to Pike Street, jogged over to Second Avenue, and continued

The advent of electric trolleys, like this one from 1893, was greeted with cheers from crowds who went "half wild" in Tacoma.

farther north to Depot Street (today's Denny Way). It would be extended in 1890 up Queen Anne Hill. Around the same time, Tacoma also acquired a cable car line—its first and only. It ran from the waterfront up a steep hill and connected the east and west sides of the city.

Also in 1889, an even newer technology—electric traction—arrived in Seattle and would soon become dominant. It had already proven to be an efficient way of moving streetcars in Richmond, Virginia. Osgood proposed scrapping the horses altogether and electrifying his Second Avenue streetcar. However, electricity was still new and frightening. "This plan was greeted with great skepticism and even alarm," wrote historian Walt Crowley in *Routes*, his essential history of Seattle public transportation (from which much of this early history is derived). "Detractors warned of runaway bolts of electricity arcing through Seattle's rainy skies and zapping innocent pedestrians," wrote Crowley. "Others doubted if the new machines could master Seattle's slopes."[13] One businessman appeared before the Seattle City Council and warned that Seattle's rain would "wash all of the electricity off the wires" and that electricity was so unpredictable it would "make the cars jump off the tracks."[14] So when the electric service began on March 30, 1889, crowds gathered to scoff. Those hoping to witness a debacle were disappointed. The cars of the renamed Seattle Electric Railway and Power Company "zipped up James Street's 11 percent grade without a hitch".[15] Occasionally, sparks flew. Yet there were no rogue bolts of electricity shooting through the air. The public quickly overcame its qualms about electric streetcars, and it wasn't long before many other electric streetcar lines fanned out from downtown. These electric streetcars required "trolley pole" apparatuses on the roofs that attached to overhead power lines—which is why electric streetcars quickly gained the nickname "trolleys."

These street railways would soon transform the city itself. Most early street railways were built by private developers, not because of an altruistic desire to make people's lives easier, but to help sell homes outside the city center. Before the advent of street railways, housing was crowded in close to downtown because people were loath to face a lengthy walk or horseback ride to work or shop. The streetcar opened up new opportunities for developers, who could now build in "far-flung" places such as Lake Union and Fremont. Developers often built streetcar lines before they even started construction on the homes because it was far easier to sell lots that had streetcar service. Thus Seattle began expanding outside its old downtown and started to take its present shape, with houses sprouting up in places like the Lake Washington shorefront, Georgetown, and Queen Anne. As Crowley wrote in *Routes*, "public transportation is almost always a means to other ends."[16]

In Tacoma, the streetcar lines quickly abandoned the horse as well. The city's first electric streetcar zipped down Pacific Avenue on February 10, 1890, and "the people went half wild," according to early Tacoma historian Herbert Hunt. "Crowds in the restaurants left their meals, the saloons disgorged, the games of pedro, poker, and faro were deserted and within ten minutes the avenue was crowded with people who cheered again and again."[17] The next Sunday, more than 4,000 passengers jammed the new electric streetcars. New lines began springing up all throughout Tacoma.

The electric streetcar was more than a transportation phenomenon. It was the beginning of an entirely new endeavor that would profoundly shape the entire 20th century: the electric power industry. At this early date, streetcar companies had to build their own small generating plants because nobody else was making electricity. These fledgling streetcar companies would soon evolve into power

One of David Denny's Rainier Power and Railway Company rail cars, 1892.

utility giants, eventually meeting the demand for streetlights and household electricity. In fact, the streetcar was the seed from which today's Puget Sound Energy would grow.

In 1890, according to Blanchard, "Seattle possessed three separate and more or less unrelated street railway systems: the Lake Washington Cable Railway, the Front Street Cable Railway, and the Seattle Electric Railway and Power Company. … The corporate growth, already too lush to be economically borne by a city of less than 50,000, had only just begun."[18] Now a baffling tangle of "organizations, reorganizations, consolidations, receiverships, and incorporations" ensued, none of which requires detailed historic scrutiny, except to note the sheer scope of the confusion.[19] Here's the way Blanchard described it: "Lines were built from the center of town to the outlying districts. They were usually built independently of one another by concerns having no corporate connection. Very often they were built without any real intention of meeting the legitimate needs of transporting

The cars of the Lake Washington Cable Railway, at the line's terminus on Lake Washington in 1890.

people and goods, but merely as adjuncts to land speculation."[20] By 1892 Seattle had 48 miles of electric street rail and 22 miles of cable railway.[21] (By comparison, King County in 2019 would have only 20.4 miles of completed light-rail.)

Many of these lines landed in immediate financial trouble, partly because of the national economic panic of 1893, partly because land sales flopped, and partly because there simply weren't enough riders in Seattle to support the number of lines built. However, most of the lines struggled along, sometimes by stimulating traffic with amusement parks, such as the one at Leschi Park. They were a hodgepodge that utterly changed the way people moved through the city. People jammed the streetcars to get to work, to shop downtown, and to enjoy a Sunday afternoon at a beachfront park. They grumbled about having to buy tickets to transfer to another line, they grumbled about the bumpy ride, and they grumbled about uncoordinated schedules and routes. Yet they rode in droves. An 1896 map of Seattle's street railways shows 16 separate lines, mostly radiating from downtown, with fingers stretching north, east, and south.

An even more ambitious southern route, the Rainier Avenue Electric Railway, had begun clattering down the brand-new thoroughfare of Rainier Avenue in about 1891, all the way to the little sawmill town of Columbia.

Seattle's tangle of competing street railways stretched north to Green Lake by 1896.

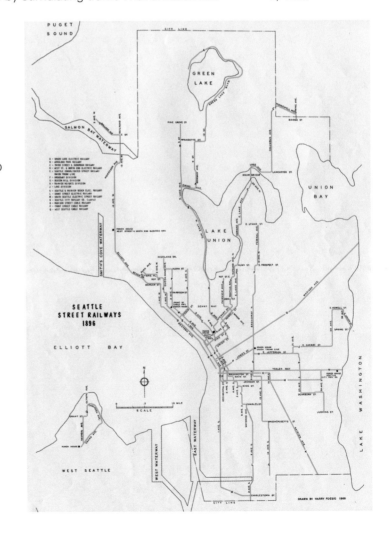

SEATTLE STREET RAILWAYS 1896

In 1896 it changed its name to the Seattle and Rainier Beach Railway Company and extended its lines all the way to Renton for a total distance of 12 miles, making it "the longest electric railway in the state."[22] It had pushed into what Blanchard called "the almost uninhabited wilderness that was Rainier Valley in those early days and inaugurated the freight and passenger service which catalyzed the growth of the region."[23] It changed it's name again to the Seattle and Renton Railway Company (and even later, to the Seattle, Renton and Southern Railway) and became an indispensable lifeline into downtown for a huge swath of country people south of the city limits.

Meanwhile, over in Everett, horse-drawn and electric streetcars were rolling by 1893. The electric street railways and other utilities in Everett were owned by a private land and improvement company. In 1894 the company found itself in financial trouble and offered to sell its water works, electric works, and street railway to the city of Everett. Voters rejected the offer, and the city missed a chance "it would not have again," wrote Everett historian Norman H. Clark.[24] Missed chances would become a running theme of mass transit for the entire Puget Sound region.

The Seattle, Renton and Southern Railway, originally called the Rainier Avenue Electric Railway, was at one time the longest electric railway in the state, covering 12 miles from Seattle to Renton. It is shown here in its 1910 heyday.

By the turn of the century, Everett had developed a modest network of electric streetcars, including these at the intersection of Hewitt and Colby Avenues.

CHAPTER TWO

From Counterbalance to Interurban

The streetcar had entered its most vigorous era—later called its Golden Era by those recalling it through a glow of nostalgia. It was, in fact, a boisterous and exciting time, in which nearly everybody in urban Puget Sound relied on mass transit. "Developers platted new neighborhoods clustered around compact business districts at street railway intersections, built broad avenues such as Westlake, Madison, and 15th Northwest, and opened attractive parks at Golden Gardens, Alki Beach, and Guy Phinney's former Woodland Estate to lure residents and riders," wrote Crowley.[1]

New innovations popped up. In 1901 the cable line up Queen Anne Hill was converted to a "counterbalance," an ingenious way for an electric trolley to barrel its way up a steep slope. A tunnel was dug directly underneath the surface tracks. A second set of tracks was laid in this tunnel. An underground railcar, loaded with concrete, rolled along those tracks, connected to the trolley by a strong cable and pulley system. When the trolley was headed uphill, the underground railcar was headed downhill. The weight helped pull the trolley up. When the trolley was headed downhill, the railcar headed uphill, serving as a brake. People in Queen Anne referred to this steep portion of the streetcar line as, simply, the Counterbalance. Even today, nearly 80 years after it has ceased to exist, the old Counterbalance continues to exert a pull on the identity of the neighborhood, which boasts Counterbalance Park and the Counterbalance Barbershop.

Left: Trolley passengers, circa late-1930s.

Electric streetcars would never have been able to safely navigate the 17 percent grade of Seattle's Queen Anne Hill without a counterbalance system, hidden in tunnels beneath the tracks.

Yet the profusion of competing tracks in Seattle had become baffling and grossly inefficient. Ten different companies were operating tracks. A passenger transferring from one line to another needed a new timetable, a new fare, and a new ticket. Some neighborhoods were over-served, while others were not served at all. "Street railway entrepreneurs, who had once thought of trolley lines primarily

as a means of building land values, were beginning by this time to realize that real estate speculation and good investment from a traffic standpoint did not always go hand in hand," said Blanchard.[2] The situation had come to a head. The choice, said Blanchard, "was between consolidation and chaos."[3]

Some halfhearted attempts at consolidation had already been attempted in the late 1890s, all of them unsuccessful. Then, in 1900, a national engineering and investment firm known as Stone & Webster cast its eye upon Seattle. Charles A. Stone and Edwin S. Webster were graduates of the Massachusetts Institute of Technology, and they had already created an empire of street railways and power utilities on the East Coast and in other parts of the country. The Northwest soon became the "last to fall within reach of Stone & Webster's tentacles," in Crowley's words.[4] They proposed a plan to consolidate the city's 10 lines and soon bought up six of them in anticipation of winning the exclusive street railway franchise. When Seattle's progressives learned of Stone & Webster's ambitions, they warned darkly of monopoly—not just of the street railway, but also of electric power, since almost all of Seattle's generating plants were included in the deal. They pushed for municipal ownership.

The Seattle City Council granted only one major concession to the progressives —it scaled back the term of Stone & Webster's proposed franchise from 40 years to 35. Stone & Webster also promised to spend $1 million to improve the slapdash system and pay off the original street railway investors. These promises helped sway a divided council. In the first of the crucial turning points in the region's transit saga, the Seattle City Council approved the Stone & Webster franchise on March 8, 1900, setting the course for decades of turmoil.

Queen Anne Counterbalance chief attendant W.W. Wiley inspects one of the counterbalance cars in the tunnel below Queen Anne Avenue.

The new, consolidated company was named Seattle Electric Company and it was granted exclusive rights to operate the city's street railways until 1935 (although it would not survive that long). Stone & Webster quickly snapped up the city's remaining four lines, making the firm's Seattle streetcar monopoly complete by 1903. Two years later Seattle Electric owned and operated more than 103 miles of track in Seattle. The deal also had far-reaching ramifications beyond transportation because the company had essentially acquired a second vital Seattle public service: "a substantially complete power generating and distribution system."[5] On the electric side, the controversial deal had the effect of galvanizing Seattle progressive opinion. It resulted in Seattle's 1902 vote to create the municipally owned Seattle City Light to compete with Seattle Electric. The Seattle Electric Company would later evolve into Puget Sound Power & Light Company, which

A trolley shares Second Avenue with horse-and-wagon traffic in 1905.

would become today's Puget Sound Energy.[6] Seattle City Light and Puget Sound Power & Light would vie for decades to supply the Puget Sound region with electricity.

On the street railway side, Stone & Webster had designs on a region-wide monolith. The company bought nearly all of the various Tacoma lines: City Park Railway Company (the Point Defiance line); the Tacoma Traction Company line to Puyallup and Wapato; Tacoma Railway and Motor Company; and Tacoma & Columbia River Railway Company. All of these lines were folded into one Stone & Webster company called the Tacoma Railway & Power Company, which was incorporated in 1899 and would hold the Tacoma street railway monopoly until the demise of the streetcar in 1938— and the bus monopoly after that. The consolidation was considered a positive step at the time, since the old railways had been "in bad order," wrote Tacoma civic historian Herbert Hunt in 1916. "The buyers at once began a general reorganization and upbuilding, and soon gave the city excellent service," said Hunt.[7]

The Rise of the Interurbans

In addition to cable cars and electric streetcars (trolleys), one other primary form of rail transit sprang up in this era: the electric interurban railway. The interurban railway was like a super-sized electric street railway, running from city to city instead of neighborhood to neighborhood. It was, in essence, the 1900s equivalent to commuter rail. By this time Seattle had its share of major commercial steam railroad lines, including three that already connected Seattle to Tacoma.[8] However, as the 1900s began, demand had built for a high-speed electric interurban railway, in order to avoid what interurban historian Warren W. Wing called "the whims of the steam railroads, who were not above charging high fares and exorbitant freight rates."[9] An interurban railway promised to be cheaper, faster, and run on a much more frequent schedule than the big steam railroads. This idea appealed tremendously to people in all three large Puget Sound cities and the suburbs in between.

A few street rail lines had already ventured beyond the city limits, notably the Seattle and Renton Railway. But the first line to fully embrace a true "interurban" concept was the Seattle–Tacoma Interurban Railway, which launched on September 25, 1902. It began with a train that ran between downtown Seattle and downtown Tacoma every two hours—via Georgetown, Kent, Auburn, Fife, and other intermediate stops—and later increased to a train every hour. The *Seattle Times* quoted a railway official on opening day as saying that "it will add to the growth of both Seattle and Tacoma, … the small farmers along the line are brought into direct communication with the large cities."[10] The 36-mile trip took 90 minutes, or 75 minutes if you took one of the twice-daily "limited" trains—express trains without any stops along the way.[11] The Seattle–Tacoma Interurban Railway was soon acquired by Stone & Webster. Its name was changed to the Puget Sound Electric Railway in November 1902, reflecting its ties to Puget Sound Power & Light, the larger Stone & Webster company that also owned the Tacoma Railway & Power Company and operated the street railways in Tacoma. It was under the name Puget Sound Electric Railway that this interurban would become legendary over the next three decades.

An interurban car zips along the Pacific Northwest Traction Company line through Echo Lake in 1938–not long before this Seattle–Everett interurban met its demise.

The Puget Sound Electric Railway was an immediate hit and crowded with passengers. It also spurred a real estate boom along the route in places like Riverton and Pacific City, small burgs in South King County. The Puget Sound Electric Railway even advertised the fact that it could also furnish electricity for these new housing developments. "What's the use? Why worry over trimming lamps and using inflammable explosive gas when you can have ELECTRIC LIGHTS?" said one ad.[12] Meanwhile, the Puget Sound Electric Railway was also extolling its advantages over the big steam railroads: "Hourly Service … Baggage Checked Free … Low Rates … Fast Time … No Cinders … No Smoke," said its timetable brochure.[13]

A map of the northern half of the Seattle–Tacoma interurban route.

The Puget Sound Electric Railway was also faster than the steam railroads, with speeds reaching 60 or even 70 miles per hour on the 12-mile stretch of straight track between Renton Junction and Auburn.[14] Steam railroads ran next to the interurban tracks on that section. If an interurban train and a steam train happened to be heading the same direction at the same time, the engineers saw it as a challenge to race. The electric train invariably won, leaving the steam train puffing in its wake.[15]

The *Seattle Post-Intelligencer* grasped the significance of this new line within weeks, saying, "The day the first car ran, Kent and Auburn were lifted from the country-side right into the suburbs of two cities and [the residents] fully appreciate what that means to them. It now means that Kent is as close to downtown Seattle as Ballard and Green Lake."[16] Greater metropolitan Seattle was coming into being.

A similar phenomenon was occurring to the north with the Everett and Interurban Railway Company, which had dreams of running from Seattle to Everett. This electric interurban line was launched in 1902. By 1905 it had completed 14 miles of tracks from its Ballard terminus to Hall's Lake,

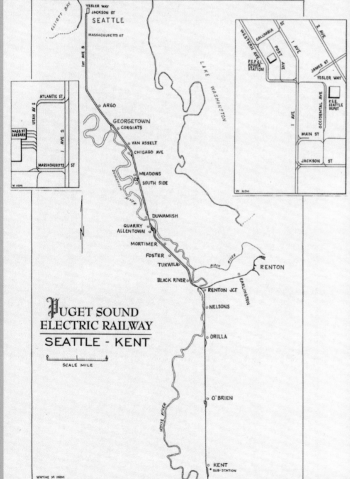

in today's Lynnwood. Northbound passengers boarded the interurban at Ballard Avenue and 15th Avenue Northwest. The land north of the Seattle city limits was still forested and sparsely populated, so in these early days the interurban carried more freight than passengers. People traveling south into Seattle disembarked in Ballard and hopped on streetcars to continue downtown.[17]

The line changed its name in 1907 to the Seattle-Everett Interurban Company, changed it again to the Seattle-Everett Traction Company after being acquired by Stone & Webster in 1908, and then again to the Pacific Northwest Traction Company, the name that stuck. The Seattle portion of the route was shifted eastward in 1910 through Fremont—near where the 1978 sculpture, *Waiting for the Interurban* now stands, and not far from where Fremont Brewing today makes its flagship Interurban IPA. It continued into downtown Seattle on tracks shared with the streetcars. In 1910 the tracks finally made it all the way to downtown Everett. From there passengers could then connect to another small interurban line, the Everett–Snohomish Interurban, to go to the town of Snohomish.

Yet the Pacific Northwest Traction Company had even bigger dreams. It intended to establish a giant interurban route all the way north to Bellingham. The company started work in Bellingham and succeeded in building a line from Bellingham to Mount Vernon. But the connection between Mount Vernon and Everett was never completed.

The Puget Sound Electric Railway barrels through Kent in 1909 on the Seattle–Tacoma interurban route. These cars could reach 60 or 70 miles per hour on this stretch of straight track. The raised "third rail" is visible alongside the tracks.

What was it like riding the big interurban trains? An account written by railway historian Wing described some of the sights and sounds of the Puget Sound Electric Railway's route:

We climb on board as the conductor steps into the telegraph office for his orders. Although we're going all the way to Tacoma, we take a seat in the lead car, which is usually reserved for local passengers. Our car is composed of baggage-express, smoking, and coach compartments, with a swinging glass door between the smoker and coach sections. Fares are collected and rung up on huge registers at the front of the car. … The conductor gives a three-bell signal that a passenger will be getting off at Orillia. The motorman gives his answer with two shots on the whistle. We stop briefly, then two pulls of the bell cord and we head out again. … Our big overhead bell is ringing steadily as we cross a busy thoroughfare and gradually come to a stop at Kent Station. … At 13th Street (in Tacoma) we stop for the cable line; it has rights over the Interurban at this intersection, but at 11th the Interurban has the right of way. At Ninth, we turn right one block and then a left turn takes us to the depot on A Street. Our conductor yells, 'Tacoma' and picks up the little stool and steps off as the train makes its final stop.[18]

One old-timer from Renton, who had the choice of riding the Puget Sound Electric's interurban or the more streetcar-like Seattle and Renton Railway line, said, "I much preferred the interurban since it seemed more train-like and rode better."[19] The entire greater Seattle area—Seattle, Tacoma, and Everett—was now connected by fast, frequent electric interurbans. The impact was so large that the most venerable form of Puget Sound area transportation—the Mosquito Fleet—was losing passengers and slashing fares.[20] The boats would prove resilient, however, and some would eventually outlast the fast and flashy interurban trains.

In Seattle's Fremont neighborhood, the Waiting for the Interurban *sculpture evokes the days when residents relied on the Pacific Northwest Traction Company interurban.*

The Everett Railway, Light & Water Company's city streetcar system also passed into the hands of Stone & Webster. In 1907 the local company leased its streetcar franchise and its other utility operations to a Stone & Webster enterprise, Puget Sound International Railway & Power Company. Stone & Webster now "controlled, through a 999-year lease, the street railway, the water supply, and practically all of the electric lighting and power business in the city of Everett," according to Puget Power historian Arthur Kramer.[21] Stone & Webster's monopoly on mass transit in all three main Puget Sound cities was now complete.

The period between 1900 and 1910 was destined to become the high point of the region's street railway era.[22] "Almost any place within the city limits worth visiting could be quickly and conveniently reached via a five-cent trolley ride," said Blanchard. "Cars were available at very reasonable rates for picnickers, excursionists, and sightseers; and for many citizens in those halcyon days uncomplicated by the automobile, the acme of holiday or weekend pleasure-seeking was to be found in a trolley car ride through the wilds of West Seattle to Luna Park, through the scenic splendor of Woodland Park, or over Shilshole Bay to Ballard Beach; or perhaps over the steep gradients of Madison Street or Yesler Way to Madison or Leschi Park, both rides affording unparalleled scenic vistas of Seattle and the surrounding countryside."[23]

It was not exactly a risk-free way to travel. Streetcars had their share of bang-ups and derailments. Gongs clanged at every intersection to warn horses, pedestrians, and the occasional auto to clear the way. Cable cars occasionally lost their grip and careened downhill while riders jumped to safety.[24] Small boys greased the tracks as a joke on Halloween, causing streetcars to lose traction.

Occasionally, the failures were catastrophic. On July 4, 1900, a Tacoma streetcar, jammed with holiday revelers, lost traction in the rain, slid out of control on an incline, and plunged off a trestle into a deep ravine. "[The streetcar] apparently turned over and over with its load of humanity in the 100-foot fall from the top of the trestle to the ground below, finally striking top downwards," said the *Seattle Daily Times*. "The people inside were smashed to the ground head downwards. Agonized cries rent the air."[25] A total of 43 passengers died and dozens were injured.[26]

This was by far the worst tragedy—but by no means the only one. On April 30, 1910, a runaway coal car hit a Seattle, Renton & Southern streetcar at 40 miles per hour, killing two and injuring 15.[27] Interurban trains also had numerous fatal

A transfer coupon for the Seattle Municipal Railway's Ballard Beach route.

accidents, often at high speeds on dangerous crossings. The Puget Sound Electric Railway included long stretches in which an electrified "third rail" replaced the overhead power lines. This third rail was out in the open, without any protection. Horses, dogs, and sometimes people were electrocuted by merely touching it.[28]

By 1910, however, the agents of street rail's demise were chugging along every street. The auto was no longer newfangled and no longer a rarity. Autos and streetcars were now jammed together on city streets—sometimes meeting in a crunch of metal at intersections. Nevertheless, the streetcar was still the undisputed king.

A Fremont-area trolley with special UW football service, circa 1920s.

By the end of this decade, Seattle's streetcars would be carrying a staggering 117 million passengers a year.[29] The supremacy of the streetcar was seemingly embedded even in the common nomenclature of the day. When people used the word "car," they meant a streetcar, never an auto.

However, the "golden age" of the streetcar was already past, even if people did not yet realize it. Some of the problems were slow and irreversible, such as the steady increase in auto sales. Others were unique to Seattle and might have been avoided, or at least mitigated. At the top of the list was the fact that the city had granted a 35-year monopoly to a private corporation over which it had little control. While some of the lines—especially the interurbans—were models of modern efficiency, the bulk of the neighborhood streetcar lines were in poor repair and operated by an indifferent and underpaid staff. The Stone & Webster promise to pour money into upgrading the system had not been kept. What's more, the streetcars had "become a source of daily irritation for local commuters," said Crowley.[30] The municipal ownership faction within city politics had been defeated a decade earlier, but it was still powerful and gaining adherents among all of those fed-up streetcar commuters. It was also gaining strength because of larger social forces at work in the Northwest. "Labor unions and social activists criticized the long hours and poor pay meted out by such firms as Stone & Webster and even economic conservatives such as the Chamber of Commerce became uneasy with the power of the railroads in dictating the pace and direction of Seattle's development," said Crowley.[31]

In 1916, a Seattle snowstorm marooned streetcars at Fourth Avenue and Pike Street.

In 1911 the Seattle City Council embarked on its first step toward changing that situation. It presented an $800,000 bond issue to Seattle voters to purchase the Seattle, Renton & Southern Railway—the Rainier Valley line. Voters passed the bond issue, but the entire scheme fell apart when the railway owners raised the price to $1.2 million. The city backed out of the deal but still had $800,000 to spend on a street railway. So it used the money to build its own line, dubbed the Seattle Municipal Railway, which began construction in 1912 and finished in 1914. This was a four-mile line from downtown Seattle up the west shore of Lake Union to the Lake Washington Ship Canal. It was derided by skeptics as "the line that began nowhere, ran nowhere, and ended nowhere."[32] Yet it was the beginning, however modest, of a Seattle municipal street rail system.

It was certainly modest by the standards of a progressive plan sponsored by Seattle's Municipal Plans Commission and drafted by civil engineer Virgil Bogue in 1911. His *Plan of Seattle* called for a new Civic Center, a new park encompassing Mercer Island and, crucially, an astonishing "91 miles of new street railways, including an interurban tunnel from Seattle to Kirkland, beneath Lake Washington."[33] He also proposed another 36 miles of rail outside the city limits, for a total metropolitan system of 127 miles. About 33 of those city miles would have been subways; 27 more would have been elevated. "Business men, and workers generally, cannot be served by a surface street railway system, over lines stretching out six or seven miles, with stops at every street crossing, consuming from thirty minutes to an hour each day," wrote Bogue in his *Plan of Seattle*.[34] As for that Lake Washington tunnel, he pointed out that "ferry service will not wholly meet the needs of the distant future" and that "development of the district beyond Lake Washington cannot be expected so long as nearly half an hour must be spent in reaching the lake shore."[35]

This breathtaking plan envisioned a Seattle rapid transit system that would have created advantages reaching far into the future. In 1995 Ross Anderson of the *Seattle Times* looked back at Bogue's plan with chagrin at what could have been. "The transit technology would have become dated, but the public would own

the rights-of-way, a complex network of corridors that would continue to serve as a skeleton for future development."[36] About 100 years later, these rights-of-way alone could have saved taxpayers millions, if not billions, of dollars. However, Seattle voters in 1911 were unimpressed by the plan's audacity—and especially by its unspecified, but clearly enormous, price tag. In another key turning point in the mass transit story, voters rejected it by a two-to-one margin. It failed to carry even a single ward.

Meanwhile, Seattle's tiny municipal railway system was growing, although at a far less ambitious pace. In 1913 the owners of the Highland Park and Lake Burien Railway, which ran from Spokane Street in West Seattle south to the small village of Burien, offered to donate the entire line to the city. The line had been conceived as a real estate venture to develop "the thinly settled region north of Lake Burien."[37] It had begun service in June 1912, but on November 8 of that year, a massive land-slide swept away nearly a mile of track.

Right: This map from the 1911 Bogue Plan laid out an ambitious future for Seattle's transit system. Voters overwhelmingly rejected it. It would take nearly a century for a transit plan of similar proportions to emerge.

Workers clear a devastating mudslide in West Seattle on the former Highland Park and Lake Burien Railway line. The Seattle Municipal Railway took over the line, cleared it, and reopened it in 1914.

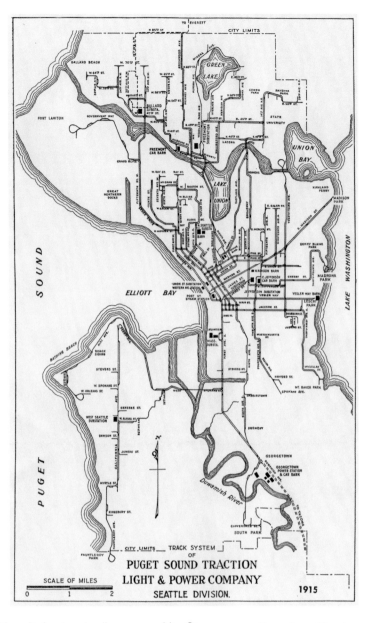

Puget Sound Traction, Power & Light owned and operated most of Seattle's street railways in 1915, but the City of Seattle would purchase the entire network in 1919.

Without the money to repair it, the owners chose to gift the entire line to the city. The city formally took over the line in May 1914, rebuilt the wiped-out sections of track, and designated it as Division C of the fledgling Seattle Municipal Railway. The rebuilt line accomplished its original goal of stimulating development in West Seattle, all the way down through White Center into Burien. With various connections and spur lines, people in Burien could ride 14 miles of track into downtown Seattle.

Despite these advances, Seattle Electric continued to own the vast bulk of the city's street railways, and its Stone & Webster allies also owned the systems in Tacoma and Everett. In Tacoma, competing streetcar lines had been consolidated under Tacoma Railway & Power, a Stone & Webster-controlled company. In 1912 Stone & Webster organized all of its holdings in the region—streetcars and electric utilities—under one new centralized company: the Puget Sound Traction, Power & Light Company.

In Everett, impatience with Stone & Webster boiled over. The streetcar workers of Stone & Webster's Everett Railway, Light & Water went on strike on New Year's Eve in 1910 for higher wages. The company brought in strikebreakers to operate the cars. The people of Everett had little love for the Stone & Webster monopoly and crowds threw bricks at the cars and threatened to overturn them. Hundreds of people chose to walk, sometimes for miles, rather than ride.[38] The company granted the wage increase after a week of turmoil. *The Everett Daily Herald* declared the outcome a victory for public opinion. In 1916 the city of Everett took over the water plant from Stone & Webster—but not the street railway.[39]

The word "traction" was not destined to last much longer in the name Puget Sound Traction, Power & Light. By the middle of the decade, the headaches were beginning to mount for the company, many of its own making. When it had snapped up all of Seattle's lines, the company inherited many ill-conceived and redundant routes with low ridership and low profits. It gradually stopped pouring maintenance money into these lines, which only made the situation worse. "Complaints about slow, undependable, and erratic service were deluging the city council and the columns of local newspapers," wrote Blanchard. "… Capitalists and monopolists were the currently favored whipping boys in almost every stratum of the population; and traction companies, along with steam railroads, were generally regarded—not entirely without reason—as the most corrupt and sinister of the detested moneyed interests."[40]

Two new blows hit the company hard in the latter half of the decade. The first came in the form of the "jitney," which was essentially a private automobile or van.

The angled trolley pole, connecting to overhead wires, is what gave the electric streetcar its nickname. Pictured below is a Seattle Municipal Railway trolley in 1914.

Owners of autos quickly realized they could make good money by offering passengers a ride for a small fee. Many jitneys went directly after the streetcar market by driving along the popular streetcar routes ahead of the trolleys and picking up passengers at the stops. They found no shortage of willing customers, because they could undercut the streetcars on fares. This was having a sudden and disastrous effect on streetcar business all over the U.S., and Puget Sound was no exception.

Puget Sound Traction Power & Light retaliated by going to federal court in 1917 and asking for a ban on jitneys as a "nuisance and a menace to other users of the streets."[41] Some of the company's arguments sound similar to the ones used by 21st-century taxi companies against Uber and Lyft. The jitneys, complained the company, were enjoying a free ride without paying taxes, licenses, and city franchise fees. Also, the jitneys were not obligated to serve the whole city but were instead free to operate only on the most popular routes and at the busiest times,

Jitneys, like this one in Seattle, circa 1919, were eating into the profits of street railways, hastening a financial crisis.

thus "skimming the cream" off the streetcar company's profits.[42] A federal judge agreed and instituted a full ban on jitneys. A jitney operator's consortium succeeded in getting a stay on the ban, pending an appeal—but other events soon took precedence.

A strike by 1,500 streetcar employees on July 17, 1917, was the biggest blow. Nearly the entire Seattle railway workforce of Puget Sound Traction, Power & Light walked out. They had joined the Amalgamated Association of Street and Electric Railway Employees (which later evolved into today's Amalgamated Transit Union) and their grievances were many, including low wages and long hours. However, what precipitated the strike was the company's barely disguised union-busting strategy. It had fired two employees who joined the union and threatened to fire everyone else who joined. The indignant workers marched out en masse, paralyzing most of Seattle's street railway system.

Seattle's pro-labor mayor, Hiram Gill, demanded that the company resolve the strike and restore service, or he would revoke the company's franchise. The company was unfazed; it dug in its heels and threatened to fire all of the strikers unless they returned to work by a certain deadline. The company also brought in strikebreakers, recruited from its light and power divisions, and tried to run the streetcars with replacements. On July 21, 1917, two of these streetcars rolled slowly into downtown, with nervous strikebreakers at the controls. A waiting crowd of strikers and sympathizers showered the cars with rocks and bottles. A melee ensued, with police wading in with batons. In the end, 20 people were injured, about 20 were arrested, and the two thoroughly wrecked streetcars had to be hauled back to the barns.

Undeterred, Puget Sound Traction, Power & Light dug its heels in even harder and requested federal troops. That plea was quickly rejected, so the company began recruiting strikebreakers from the East Coast, hundreds of whom soon arrived at the Georgetown shops, where they were given a crash course on how to operate a streetcar. They never had a chance to complete it. The U.S. was involved with World War I and the streetcar strike was having a deleterious effect on wartime production in Seattle. The federal government leaned hard on the company to end the strike. Meanwhile, Mayor Gill threatened anew to revoke

Stone & Webster's franchise. The company saw which way the wind was blowing. On August 1, 1917, it reached a tentative agreement with the union and the two-week strike was over. The sound of trolley gongs once again filled Seattle's streets. The two union members got their jobs back and the company agreed to stop its union-busting activities.

For these and other reasons, the Puget Sound Traction, Power & Light streetcar system was injured and limping in 1918. The city of Seattle was increasingly frustrated and impatient—especially since it now saw the company as a competitor to its own fledgling streetcar system. A burst of wartime production had also created an influx of new workers, all of whom needed to get to and from their shipyards and airplane factories. The old Stone & Webster transit system was not up to the challenge and was handling "twice the traffic it was built for."[43] Also, many of its employees had been called off to war. One streetcar crew, in trouble for crashing into a switch mechanism near First Avenue and Columbia Street, simply abandoned the car and hung a sign on it saying, "We have gone to enlist in the Navy."[44]

This jitney driver protested what he saw as the greed of the Stone & Webster street rail monopoly in 1918.

The city attempted to fill some of the transit demand by building a massive elevated railway on Railroad Avenue, today's Alaskan Way, to serve the busy shipyards, but the war ended before it was finished in 1919.

In May 1918 Puget Sound Traction, Power & Light met with the city and attempted to get relief from two of its biggest problems. First, it wanted to raise the five-cent fare that had been imposed with the original franchise agreement, and which had been in effect since Frank Osgood's first

horse-drawn streetcar. Second, it wanted to be freed from the tax obligations it owed to the city, at least for the duration of the war. The city was reluctant to budge on these issues. Actually, "reluctant" is a massive understatement. Seattle Mayor Ole Hanson wrote an outraged scream of a letter to the Seattle City Council in which he accused the company of backing the public "into suffocating, dirty, unsanitary cars like bananas in a bunch. … Conditions are all but unbearable, and the service unspeakable." He said the only kind of peace the company wanted to negotiate was the "same kind of peace the Kaiser desires to make with the world"—and the German Kaiser was currently waging furious war with the U.S.[45]

The City of Seattle built this elevated railway in 1919 to serve the shipyards on what is now Alaskan Way. It proved unprofitable and was torn down in 1929.

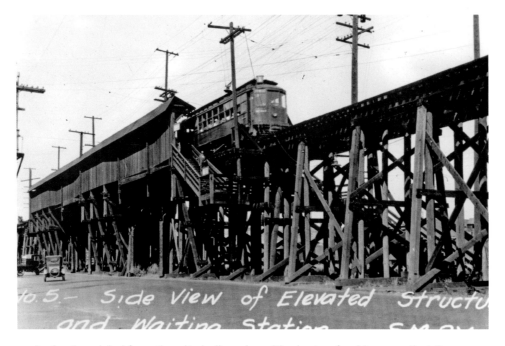

As for the nickel fare, the city believed—with plenty of evidence—that the public would be appalled by any fare increase. When the Seattle, Renton, and Southern Railway had tried to raise fares about eight years earlier, a "near riot" resulted and passengers simply refused to pay it.[46] Instead, the city made some demands of its own. It wanted the company to live up to its franchise agreement and pay for paving between its tracks. It was essentially asking Stone & Webster to pave many of Seattle's streets. This was becoming an increasingly important issue, since more autos were sharing the roads.

At the same time, the federal government intervened by implying that if Seattle's transit mess wasn't cleared up, it would yank its Seattle shipbuilding contracts. Faced with all of this pressure, Puget Sound Traction, Power & Light was ready to wash its hands of the streetcar business altogether and remove the word "traction" from its name. It offered to sell its entire transit system to the city for $18 million.

Stone & Webster management claimed that $18 million was a bargain, since it had spent $19 million fixing up the system. Hanson came back with a figure of $15 million, extrapolated roughly from how much the city had just spent, per mile, to build its own municipal lines. Puget Sound Traction, Power & Light accepted the $15 million offer with startling alacrity, which only increased public suspicion that this was no bargain even at $15 million. These suspicions were correct. Hanson's estimate was based on the faulty assumption that the old system's dilapidated tracks and equipment were worth what the city had just paid for its own brand-new tracks and equipment. One city council member estimated that the true value of the system was only about $5.5 million. The *Seattle Post-Intelligencer* estimated the value at $11.7 million. The influential *Seattle Times*, however, somehow estimated the true figure at $16.1 million, which implied that the city was getting a great bargain.[47] Voters apparently cared less about the price tag and more about the opportunity to rid itself, once and for all, of the Stone & Webster transit monopoly. They approved the $15 million offer by more than a three-to-one margin on November 5, 1918.

This was only an advisory vote, however. The Seattle City Council still had to pass an ordinance and come up with $15 million, which it did not have. The second of Seattle's momentous turning points arrived after an extended bout of city council dickering and infighting—complete with angry charges of corruption and bribery. On March 31, 1919, the city of Seattle became the sole owner of its entire transit system.[48] The council had agreed to issue a 20-year utility bond to pay for the system, which meant Seattle's new possession was saddled with debt from day one. Since the deal did not include the electrical generating plants to run the system, the city also had to agree to one other unfortunate provision: It had to purchase power from Puget Sound Power & Light.

This might have seemed like a happy ending for advocates of municipal ownership, yet history has been unkind to this transaction. It inaugurated 20 years of fiscal chaos. Seattle street railway historian Blanchard believed it would have been better if the city had simply let the franchise expire in 1935 and send Stone & Webster packing. Then the city could have spent far less than $15 million to upgrade the system to modern standards. If this had been done, wrote Blanchard in 1968, "the history of public transportation in Seattle might well have made entirely different reading. … Seattle might, in fact, have been spared the dubious distinction of being one of the earliest American cities to junk its trolley system in toto, in favor of buses."[49]

Walt Crowley concluded that the city's system was "crippled from the beginning, by the debt of the system's purchase, which cost $833,000 a year in interest alone."[50] In 1991 Seattle civic historian Richard C. Berner went even further. He concluded that the sale was "an almost satanic calamity for the city" with repercussions far into the future. Two decades of system decline and brutal political warfare would ensue. Nobody benefited except one particular entity. Berner uncovered an internal letter from a top Stone & Webster executive, who called it "a bully good trade for the company."[51]

Next page: Seattle Mayor Ole Hanson takes over the controls of a streetcar in 1919 and celebrates the city's acquisition of the entire street rail system. This would later prove to be no cause for celebration.

CHAPTER THREE

Derailed

Not included in the city's deal were the two big interurban railroads. The Puget Sound Electric Railroad (linking Tacoma to Seattle) and the Pacific Northwest Traction Company (linking Everett to Seattle) were both owned by Stone & Webster subsidiaries, but they were more profitable and better regarded by the public. These two interurban lines had healthy ridership in their first decade, partly because of a phenomenon that the interurbans themselves made possible: More people were moving to the suburban and semirural areas north and south of Seattle.

Left: This trolley on Spokane Street lost its brakes and smashed into a pillar. Three died and 60 were injured.

Yet the first harbingers of trouble had arisen even for the interurbans. Paved highways were being built throughout the region. Beginning in 1913, motorized "stages," or "coaches," began operating north and south of Seattle. That nomenclature hearkened back to the old horse-and-wagon days, but these were actually the first primitive gasoline buses. By 1919 two different stage lines were

By 1919, motor stages had begun to cut into ridership on interurban lines.

running between Auburn and Seattle, one which advertised "30 stages a day."[1] Buses immediately began eating into the interurban ridership. Within two decades, they would kill them off entirely.

The depot at A Street and Eighth in Tacoma served as a stop for both rail and rubber-wheeled transit in 1925. Electric interurbans were competing with—and increasingly losing out to—the intercity motor coaches.

Farther south, the Tacoma Railway & Power Company (a Stone & Webster holding, tied to Puget Sound Power & Light) was the city's dominant streetcar company. In 1916 it extended a line to Steilacoom, replacing another company's line that had gone bankrupt. This line barreled through deep forest. The conductor reported that "his car had killed about a dozen deer, and a bear once pursued his motorman."[2]

The city of Tacoma began to take small steps toward having its own municipal line in 1914 when it laid tracks across a bridge to the tideflats industrial area. The city partnered with Tacoma Railway & Power to operate the service, but the line lost money, partly because there were no true fare collection boxes. An old joke at the time ran: "The five-cent fare was on the honor system, but no one honored it."[3] About one-third of the riders rode free.[4] On January 1, 1919, Tacoma Railway & Power dropped out of the partnership, and the city of Tacoma officially owned the line, which was renamed the Tacoma Municipal Railway (renamed again in 1925 as the Tacoma Municipal Belt Line, or simply, Belt Line).[5] It carried freight by locomotive and passengers via trolley. In 1920 it operated 38 streetcars.[6]

At its inception, the new city-owned Seattle Municipal Street Railway consisted of 195 miles of electrified rail, 8.6 miles of cable railway, 540 streetcars of varying types, and roughly 1,500 employees.[7] For riders, city ownership brought one advantage. They no longer had to pay two fares to transfer between the public and private lines. Even so, the extent of the problems that the city had inherited became obvious within mere months.

First, there was the labor problem. The former traction company employees demanded the same, higher pay that the city had been paying its municipal line employees. The city and workers eventually settled on a compromise, which increased the system's expenses. Plus many of the traction company employees chose to stay with Puget Sound

Interurbans connected the Puget Sound region from Everett through Tacoma with fast, frequent service— but their reign would prove to be short-lived.

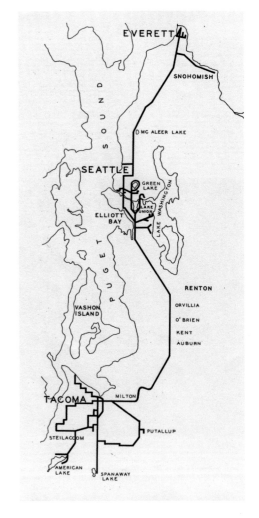

Power & Light as power utility workers, which meant that the Seattle Municipal Street Railway faced an immediate shortage of experienced car operators and maintenance workers.

Second, the city's debt obligation to Stone & Webster—$833,000 a year—was almost comically larger than the system's annual income, which was estimated at around $120,000 per year. The system superintendent suggested boosting the traditional nickel fare to six cents to help lift the system out of debt. This sugges-

Motor coaches like this one, running from Seattle to Index, became more popular as the region's highways improved.

tion was roundly rejected—the nickel fare remained politically sacrosanct. As a result, the Seattle Municipal Street Railway finished its first year with a half-million-dollar loss.[8] Of course, this meant that no money was available for badly needed maintenance and repair.

Third, the jitneys returned with a vengeance after the end of World War I, and jitney drivers had cynically chosen to interpret the court ban as null, because the ban referred only to the old Stone & Webster system. Once again, the jitneys cruised the most popular streetcar stops and skimmed off the most lucrative business. It wasn't until 1921 that the jitneys were banished by the courts, once and for all.

These labor, maintenance, and budget problems contributed to the fourth and most shocking problem of all—a safety crisis. On October 28, 1919, a streetcar on the Queen Anne Counterbalance lost its brakes and careened down the steep hill at 35 miles per hour. It was jerked to a sudden halt by its counterbalance cable, which tore the rear truck assembly clean out from under the trolley. It skidded another six feet minus its rear wheels. One passenger suffered a serious leg injury and 20 were severely shaken up. On January 5, 1920, a more deadly accident occurred when a car in the Woodland Park area took a curve too fast, derailed, tipped over, and slid into a telephone pole. One passenger died and 70 were injured. The motorman blamed defective brakes, and the *Seattle Times* ran a front-page editorial calling for new safety precautions. During one stretch of weeks following the city's acquisition of the system, five runaway accidents occurred.

This all fed into a fifth and highly sensational problem: The system had become a political football, and everyone was kicking it around. The streetcar system had become not just *an* issue of city politics, it had become *the* issue, ultimately making and breaking mayors. Hugh Caldwell ran for Seattle mayor in 1920 largely "on a promise to investigate the purchase of the street railway."[9] The public, increasingly disgusted with the new system's insolvency and safety problems, swept Caldwell into office. He launched a six-month investigation into the city's acquisition of the system. Investigators sought, but failed to uncover, proof of graft and corruption by Mayor Hanson's administration. But it confirmed what most of Seattle had already concluded: The city had paid about three times too much for the system. The investigation mainly revealed that the street railway had been unprofitable as a private system and was now equally unprofitable as a public system. City officials tried to solve this problem in several spectacularly unsuccessful ways.

70 HURT IN GREEN LAKE CAR WRECK!

In December 1920 the city decided to use money from its general fund to cover some of the street railway's debt. An outraged Seattle taxpayer named S.B. Asia and 14 other Seattle taxpayers sued the city to prevent it. Ultimately, the State Supreme Court ruled in favor of Asia, a ruling which blocked all government subsidies for public transportation for decades.[10]

Then the city announced in 1921 that it would hold back workers' wages to pay the annual bond payment, which immediately raised the prospect of a strike by angry workers and a complete shutdown. Fortunately, the workers and local banks came up with a plan in which the banks would honor the workers' warrants— essentially, IOUs. This plan worked for a year, but by 1922, the banks had lost patience. Catastrophe was averted only because the workers agreed to become creditors to the railway system. This, they reasoned, would be better than shutting the system down. It was hardly a long-term solution.

Finally, Mayor Caldwell revived the idea of raising fares—in fact, he doubled them to 10 cents in July 1920. The riding public reacted with a "roar of disapproval."[11] This may have been the fiscally responsible thing to do, but it was certainly not politically prudent. The nickel fare was an ingrained tradition, dating back to that very first horse-drawn streetcar in 1884. This move caused Dr. Edwin J. Brown to launch a Seattle mayoral campaign in 1922, largely on a promise to restore the nickel fare. Brown won the election and briefly kept his promise, but even he had to boost the cost of some fares that included transfer privileges. By the end of 1922, it was obvious to nearly everyone that the Seattle Municipal Street Railway was lurching from crisis to crisis.[12]

In 1922 Alton Leonard, the general manager of Puget Sound Power & Light, wrote a private memo to his Stone & Webster superiors, describing the problems that Seattle's system faced. "The trouble with the carlines is that they have no friends, no voice with which to reach the public," he wrote. "The mayor has been a critic; the council have been destructive rather than constructive; the newspapers have been critical rather than helpful, and the citizens don't understand the problem."[13] He predicted, with admirable accuracy, that the system would become "the waif of municipal politics."[14] In short, Leonard was a man thrilled to no longer own Seattle's street railways.

As dreary as the system's prospects seemed, they were destined to get worse, mainly because of a larger social trend that people still only faintly grasped. By the middle of the 1920s, autos were no longer toys for the affluent. They were jamming the streets of Puget Sound cities. Autos were at first regarded as weekend excursion vehicles, as opposed to commuter vehicles, but that had gradually changed. In June 1923 authorities finally took the unavoidable step of raising fares.[15] The nickel fare was now a dime (although riders could still buy discounted tokens at three for a quarter). Riders squawked, but everybody in Seattle knew that the street railway was broke, and they finally had to accept the inevitable. The fare increase failed to reverse the system's deficit and may have exacerbated another ominous trend: decreasing ridership. Between 1925 and 1926 streetcar usage dropped 4.6 percent on weekdays and even more on Sundays.

Seattle streetcar superintendent Clark R. Jackson was tellingly defensive and more than a little resentful of autos. "The automobile owner should be very appreciative of the streetcar," he wrote in a 1926 report.

The nickel fare was a sacrosanct feature of Seattle transit—but even a dime was not nearly enough to pull the city's system out from under crushing debt.

"We furnish him with 'ready to serve' transportation for 18 hours a day and 365 days a year. When his automobile breaks down or the snow and ice prevent its use, he gets his usual opportunity of giving our transportation system a few sledge-hammer blows, because he does not arrive home as early as he would had he driven his car. … He never stops to realize that it is this same automobile which contributes to a large degree to his delay. Next day he will proceed to double park his machine while he buys a cigar, perhaps delaying 200 people for a period of one minute while a line of cars passes around his parked machine."[16]

City officials tried to cope with the system's financial woes by dropping underused and redundant lines. The elevated waterfront railway, intended to serve World War I shipyard workers on Railroad Avenue (today's Alaskan Way), was torn down in 1929 after ten years of unprofitability. A new mayoral regime under Bertha K. Landes did its best to keep the trolleys running, but it was a nearly hopeless battle. In 1928 Landes sent a bond issue to voters to raise $1.5 million for badly needed line maintenance and new cars.[17] It passed. But this did nothing to alleviate the original problem, the $833,000 annual debt payment. In one ironic twist, Stone & Webster offered to either take the system back or refinance the original bonds, if Seattle City Light would supply electricity for the streetcars at a loss.[18] The city rejected it, knowing this would have made a bad deal even worse.

Meanwhile, the city was experimenting with a new solution—buses. At this point, they were using van-like gasoline vehicles strictly as "feeder buses," meaning they "fed" passengers from outlying areas into the nearest trolley stops. The question arose for the first time: Can buses replace the trolleys? In Everett, the answer was already yes. In 1923, it became "the first of the larger cities of the United States" to tear out the tracks on its main business streets and replace trolleys with "large automobile buses."[19] Buses could provide something trolleys could not: curbside service. However, Everett was an outlier, and a small one at that. It had only about seven trolley lines total, and not all of those were torn out. In Seattle, and the rest of the country, the answer was still no. The buses of the era were, in Blanchard's words, "small, light, primitive, and ill-equipped to handle large numbers of passengers."[20]

Buses began to run a few routes by the 1920s, yet it wasn't until 1941 that buses finally supplanted streetcars in Seattle. The buses below are in a Seattle repair shop in 1942.

The street railway system continued to limp its way through the 1920s, under-funded and increasingly unloved. Longtime Rainier Valley resident Elmer Yates recalled what a ride was like on one rickety spur line that the locals had nicknamed "the Toonerville Trolley," after the comic strip streetcar. "The conductor had to stop at any block along the route where somebody might be waiting," wrote Yates. "The brakes being applied often caused the wheels to squeal on the rails before they brought the car to a complete stop. The steel tracks were anything but smooth and I dare say that no doubt some of the regular riders knew how many lengths of rail there were between their station and the end of the line. They would be able to count the clickity-clacks as the trolley passed over rail connections."[21]

In 1928 Seattle mayoral candidate Frank Edwards won the election after he "hinted that he had a solution to the railway mess."[22] This sounded promising, except for one problem. He did not, in fact, have one. The system staggered along in even worse shape, and as the decade closed, the inevitable happened. The city began defaulting on its debt payments.

H.L. Purdy of the University of Washington soon launched a study to answer the question of whether the blame lay with municipal ownership, as some private-util-ity backers claimed. His answer was a resounding no. The main problem—the auto—would have been the same under any ownership. "The passenger trend is largely beyond the control of management. Advertising might possibly increase the number of passengers, but it is extremely doubtful that it would have sufficient effect to pay for its cost, and no other effective instrument exists," wrote Purdy.[23]

Even the formerly popular interurbans were having serious troubles. Stage lines—or bus lines—had proliferated to the point where Stone & Webster (which still owned the interurbans to both Tacoma and Everett) decided it was better to join them than fight them. In 1927 Stone & Webster snapped up some of the competing stage lines and started a new company called North Coast Lines, with bus service directly competing with its own interurbans both north and south of Seattle. In 1927 and 1928 the new Highway 99 (Pacific Highway South) was mostly paved, providing the fastest route yet for buses and autos. By the beginning of 1928, Stone & Webster was taking out newspaper ads in Auburn that barely mentioned the Puget Sound Electric interurban, formerly the queen of the region's interurbans. Instead the ads touted multiple bus departures on the North Coast Lines to Seattle. The interurban was relegated to an afterthought in the small print.

In January 1928 the Puget Sound Electric line was bleeding money so badly that its parent Stone & Webster company, Puget Sound Power & Light, refused to advance additional funds to bail it out. Puget Sound Electric subsequently announced that it would suspend its interurban operation at the end of the year.

The Auburn newspaper noted sadly that the interurban had for decades been considered a "godsend to valley residents" and that "many old timers are loath to believe it had been abandoned."[24] Soon they had to accept the truth. The last car on the Seattle–Tacoma interurban line rumbled into the Kent yards on December 31, 1928.

Some residents, consumed with love for the old interurban, refused to give up. They organized the Interurban Confederated Community Club in Fife, with the goal of bringing it back from the dead. They agitated for a while, but the company's response was to simply rip up the tracks. Clinton H. Betz of Renton, who rode the Puget Sound Electric interurban hundreds of times, described his conflicted feelings: "The arrival of the automobile brought better roads and the public flocked to the new convenience—THIS WAS PROGRESS! In my case, I was no longer confined to a rigid schedule, waiting for or hassling heavy packages on crowded cars. Like so many others, I embraced the convenience of the automobile, and in doing so, contributed to the demise of the interurban."[25]

The Seattle and Rainer Valley Railway had been a vital lifeline to Renton since 1896, but it was replaced by gasoline bus service in 1936.

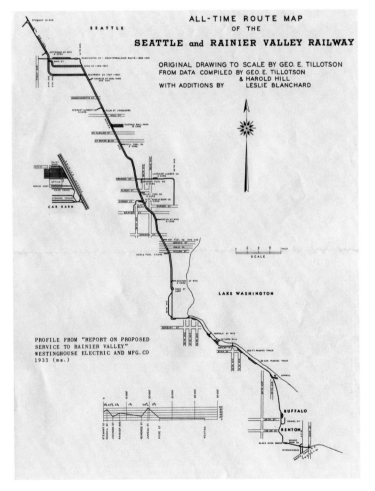

The interurbans had a powerful emotional appeal, soon to be magnified by nostalgia. But nostalgia was no match for practicality. Buses were simply more flexible. Routes could be added and altered whenever necessary. Buses also required less infrastructure investment—they took advantage of the new highways that local governments were paving all over the Puget Sound region. Why not run rubber-tired buses and let the taxpayers pay for the infrastructure?

A similar story played out up north with the Seattle–Everett interurban, the Pacific Northwest Traction Company. In 1930 Stone & Webster merged Pacific Northwest Traction with their North Coast Lines, which turned this interurban into the neglected stepsister of the company's bus lines. The interurban already accounted for an ever-diminishing fraction of the North

Coast Lines' income and ridership. In a telling omen, Highway 99's Aurora Bridge opened in 1932—without any provision for tracks. The Seattle–Everett interurban line managed to hang on more than a decade longer than the Seattle–Tacoma interurban, but ridership dwindled every year. The line met its final demise in 1939 after it became obvious that the Seattle Municipal Railway was preparing to tear out the tracks it shared with the

interurban in Seattle.[26] The *Everett Herald* struck a bittersweet note on the line's last day, February 20, 1939: "Tuesday morning the sun will beat down on two parallel steel rails winding south from Everett, shiny and still. Another monument to man's winning of the West will be hushed, the last remnants to be slowly dulled by rust and buried from sight by the encroachment of nature."[27]

Suddenly, the name Stone & Webster, which had been at the heart of civic controversies for 34 years, vanished forever from the region's utilities scene. In 1934 the federal Securities and Exchange Commission had taken antitrust action against the company and ordered it to divest itself of Puget Sound Power & Light and other utility holdings. Stone & Webster's utilities had finally been "regulated out of existence."[28] However, Puget Sound Power & Light retained many of the same corporate officers and many of its old holdings, including Tacoma Railway & Power and the North Coast Lines.

In the 1930s the privately owned Seattle and Rainier Valley Railway Company, the quasi-interurban that had been trundling down Rainier Avenue to Renton since 1896, was also in trouble. It had flirted with bankruptcy in the past. The city once attempted to purchase it, but voters quashed that idea. In 1934 the company applied for a new franchise, but angry motorists opposed it, claiming that the unpaved area between the tracks had turned Rainier Avenue "into a thoroughfare of death."[29] The city refused to renew the franchise. Nevertheless, the company blithely kept the trolleys running, franchise or not, until the end of 1936, when the city replaced service with Seattle Municipal Railway's gas buses and private Lake Shore Lines buses to Renton.

Stone & Webster acquired several stage lines and merged them into the North Coast Lines. This Seattle-bound bus, circa 1929, competed directly with the company's own interurbans.

By this time the Seattle Municipal Street Railway was dying a slow and agonizing death. The city negotiated a temporary moratorium with Puget Sound Power & Light on some of its debt payments. Some of the routes were actually profitable—although not remotely profitable enough to pay off its still-massive debt. As of 1935, the Seattle Municipal Street Railway had "one of the worst revenue-to-debt ratios of any transit operation in the country."[30] It still had $8.3 million in bonded debt, which meant that over the space of 17 years it had worked its way through less than half of its original $15 million debt.[31]

The Great Depression and competition with autos only exacerbated its problems. By the middle of the decade, the system was in desperate need of extensive modernizing—or tearing up the tracks and starting over. If the city had held out long enough, the old Stone & Webster franchise would have expired in 1935, and the city could have acquired the system, modernized it, and saved tons of money and heartache. Unfortunately, that option was long gone and few other good alternatives existed. General Motors stepped in with a self-serving offer: It tried to talk the city into selling off the system "to a private company that would buy buses"—made by General Motors.[32] However, Seattle was not willing to go back to private ownership, nor was it quite ready to commit to buses. At the time, buses remained a secondary part of Seattle's system. In the mid-1930s Seattle operated 410 streetcars and only about 60 buses.

Seattle's system stood at a turning point. By 1935 the city and Puget Sound Power & Light were working together to find a way to pay off the railway debt once and for all. The power company was struggling in the depths of the Great Depression and wanted the city to float new bonds and retire its old debt. The power company even offered to shave more than $3 million off the $8 million outstanding debt and accept $5 million. Yet the company knew that no financiers would touch these bonds if Seattle didn't have a sound plan for modernizing and revamping its old street railway system.

By 1933, Seattle's street railway network was in worse financial shape than ever, and the city began seeking a way out.

The red ink kept growing for the Seattle Municipal Street Railway.

EXHIBIT VII
INCOME BY YEARS SEATTLE MUNICIPAL STREET RAILWAY

	Revenues	Misc. Gains	Operation and Maintenance	Bond Interest	Taxes	Depreciation and Amortization	Misc. Losses	Gain	Loss	Cumulative Net Income
1918										$ 60,705.95
1919	$4,158,153.20		$3,568,729.27	$605,110.32		$499,173.39	$ 2,314.01		$517,175.79	577,879.74
1920	5,463,392.84	$11,515.50	4,915,031.05	858,752.06		677,178.65	260,230.18	$236,568.29	1,236,283.60	1,814,163.34
1921	6,347,175.46	55,833.39	4,431,766.15	859,938.79		680,629.20	304,086.42	$236,568.29		1,587,575.05
1922	6,228,102.81	31,210.07	3,953,302.05	828,624.46		685,114.32	82,188.12	710,083.95		877,491.10
1923	5,742,148.64	2,831.55	4,090,283.60	797,114.47		685,114.32	280,335.94		107,868.14	985,359.24
1924	6,173,907.10	22,440.63	4,172,250.10	759,299.27		685,114.32	210,253.26	369,430.78		615,928.46
1925	5,999,938.05	18,480.79	4,392,806.37	718,868.45		683,556.64	197,441.37	25,746.01		590,182.45
1926	5,791,315.62	8,562.12	4,353,136.27	691,932.61		701,766.00	157,014.24		105,971.38	694,153.83
1927	5,758,291.95	58,143.79	4,072,081.07	691,196.21		728,493.68	168,073.95	156,590.33		537,563.00
1928	5,682,933.30	15,925.50	4,086,755.95	640,174.36		744,390.60	601,898.33		374,360.44	911,923.44
1929	5,602,294.06	21,881.36	4,002,408.85	605,486.04		747,245.60	61,938.98	207,097.95		704,825.49
1930	5,291,068.58	12,677.84	4,056,868.18	569,891.81		748,520.40	120,643.72		172,177.69	877,003.18
1931	4,754,206.52	10,336.62	3,819,146.44	559,529.16		741,924.00	230,141.55		586,198.01	1,463,201.19
1932	3,879,771.28	5,150.04	3,350,760.01	558,665.34		744,691.20	56,757.19		825,952.62	2,289,153.81
1933	3,675,182.86	3,454.08	3,244,012.26	555,026.22		790,360.00	2,534.89		875,296.43	3,164,450.24
1934	3,983,459.91	337,280.38	3,415,319.85	556,745.64		742,152.00	55,597.33		449,072.53	3,613,522.77
1935	4,002,575.07	5,724.77	3,233,365.88	553,540.95	$805,076.70	767,844.00	54,364.26		665,891.95	4,279,414.72
1936	4,188,065.44	5,880.55	3,400,763.77	528,593.28	65,822.42	756,084.45	45,526.30		602,844.23	4,882,258.95
1937	4,502,629.74	601,671.60	4,175,400.04	529,349.19	68,764.75	637,084.08	105,934.04		412,230.76	5,294,489.71
1938	4,387,944.73	117,711.99	4,004,114.88	509,753.19	72,147.41	702,526.66	99,680.60		882,566.02	6,177,055.73
*1939 to 8-25.	2,807,757.84	29,841.69	2,581,429.81	294,850.40	45,620.00	473,937.20	12,387.98		570,625.86	6,747,681.59

Adjustments affecting Deficit August 25, 1939 to December 31, 1944. .... $ 2,465,131.28

Deficit resulting from operations and liquidation of Fixed Assets to August 25, 1939. (To Exhibit VI) $4,282,550.31

* August 25, 1939 marks closing of books at time of installation of Seattle Transportation Commission.

SEATTLE MUNICIPAL STREET RAILWAY
TRACK MAP
APRIL 1933

The power company hired a respected engineering firm, the John C. Beeler Organization, to study Seattle's street railway system and create a new, modern Seattle transit plan. This would allow the city to "start anew with a clean slate," said Puget Sound Power & Light's president, Frank McLaughlin.[33]

When the 1935 Beeler Report came out a few months later, it recommended relatively modest changes—at least compared to what was about to come a year later. It recommended keeping most of the street railway system intact but replacing the streetcars themselves with sleeker, modern-looking models. The report also suggested changing the routes through downtown to be more efficient, dumping the city's three outmoded cable car lines—the Madison, Yesler, and James lines—and replacing them with "modern, super-powered buses."[34] Another recommendation: replacing the bus feeder lines with express bus routes "to, and frequently through and beyond" downtown.[35] Finally, the report advised replacing several of the existing streetcar lines with buses—but only a few.

In general, the 1935 Beeler Reported proposed a combined rail-bus system—familiar in outline to systems that would be proposed 70 years later. The plan would reduce the total railway mileage just a touch—from 225 to 195 miles. The whole thing might be financed, or so the report hoped, by a $7 million federal New Deal loan. The report firmly rejected one modern advance—the rubber-tired "trackless trolleys," electric vehicles which dispensed with tracks, but not with overhead trolley wires. The Beeler Report said the trackless trolley was "impracticable" for Seattle because of its much higher initial outlay. Trackless trolleys required two overhead wires, instead of the streetcar's one, which would make the initial cost "three or four times" greater than the plan Beeler proposed.[36] Also, the trackless trolley—constrained by its wires—would be no more "adaptable" than the existing fixed-route street railways.

The workers of the streetcar men's union liked the plan. They could keep their streetcar jobs and finally get their IOUs paid off. However, the federal government proved unwilling to issue a New Deal loan and instead offered only a small grant, which was insufficient.[37] The plan languished for a year.

In 1936 the city, the power company, and Beeler cast their eyes toward New York bankers in hopes of getting a much bigger loan, as much as $12 to $13 million, financed by a bond issue, to pay off the debt and completely modernize the Seattle transit system. That August, Beeler issued a new and far more controversial report. This one called for scrapping the street railway system entirely. It proposed the purchase of 240 trackless trolleys ("trolley coaches") and 135 gasoline buses. Why did Beeler do such a sudden and complete about-face on trackless trolleys?

In 1939, the Seattle Municipal Street Railway ceased to exist, and the Seattle Transit System was born. Shown is a Seattle Transit badge, circa 1940s.

The New York financiers insisted on it. They refused any plan that attempted to merely revamp the outmoded street railway system.

"This is declared to be the only program which the banking syndicate and equipment manufacturers are willing to support," said city councilman David E. Lockwood. "We have only the alternatives of accepting it or of trying to keep on with our present dilapidated system, which has about reached its limit and is losing $500,000 to $600,000 a year. By accepting the syndicate's plan, we would have all new equipment and better service which the people would patronize, no rail lines and broken-down cars to maintain at huge annual cost, and for all of this we would owe only about $1,500,000 more than we do now for a bunch of junk."[38]

Seattle Mayor John F. Dore and the Streetcar Men's Union continued to push a plan that would retain most of the street railways, but the bankers stood firm. One of those bankers, Guy C. Meyers, succinctly outlined the case against streetcars: "Streetcars, cumbersome and slow, will not weave in and out of modern traffic. They force passengers to go into the middle of busy streets to climb aboard. This factor … is corrected by the trackless trolley buses and gasoline buses."[39]

In 1937 this trackless trolley demonstrator raced a streetcar up the Queen Anne Hill Counterbalance—and "embarrassed" the old streetcar, by making it to the top twice as fast.

The rubber-tired trackless trolley was controversial— Mayor John F. Dore compared it to a "pig"—but in 1940 hundreds like it began replacing the old streetcars. Trackless trolleys remain a key part of Seattle's transit scene even today.

The council eventually settled on a $12.5 million bond issue, which would pay off the old debt, the IOUs to the streetcar workers, and leave $5 million or $6 million for purchasing a brand-new rubber-tired transit system. Beeler issued an updated report in January 1937, mostly reiterating the August 1936 plan and claiming that the entire changeover from rails to rubber could be accomplished in 12 months.[40]

This kicked off a furious public debate leading up to the March 9, 1937, bond issue vote. Dore continued to oppose it, siding with the Streetcar Men's Union, which believed that it would cost its members jobs. Dore acidly pointed out that Beeler had previously declared trackless trolleys "impracticable" for Seattle, not to mention financially unsound, and "then he [Beeler] gets hired by these people [the financiers] and so now he says the trackless trolley is the only thing for Seattle."[41] On the other side, proponents of the plan printed elaborate brochures calling it a vote for modernization. "Horse Car Days Are Gone," they declared in a headline.[42]

The pro-streetcar forces were certainly not helped by the events of January 8, 1937, when a streetcar on the Fauntleroy line in West Seattle slid out of control. "The car, roaring into the hairpin, with its air brakes apparently frozen after descending the Avalon Way hill, pitched off the tracks onto a heavy concrete pillar," reported the *Seattle Times*.[43] A headline screamed, "Shattered Vehicle Totters on Edge of Guard Rail With Its Screaming Load of Dying and Injured Passengers." Three passengers died and 60 were injured. It was the worst streetcar tragedy in Seattle's history.

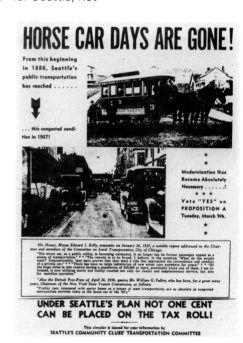

The campaign culminated in a debate—often more of a shouting match—on the day before the election between Mayor Dore and city councilman Arthur B. Langlie. About 6,000 people jammed the Civic Auditorium to cheer, boo, catcall, and heckle. Dore went on the attack. He called the plan a "wicked swindle" and said it was "so crooked it smells in high heaven."[44] He called it a scheme propagated by New York banks, not Seattle. He said the trackless trolley "is all right in its place; so's a pig."[45]

Langlie retorted that the only person who had been swindled was "Honest John," a sarcastic reference to Dore. Langlie suggested it was better to take the old, dangerous streetcars and burn them in a bonfire, rather than "burn them up on the Eastlake line, loaded with passengers."[46] Both men were greeted with jeers and applause. But in an omen of what was to come at the polls, Dore's applause was louder.

In a 1937 vote, proponents of a new rubber-tired transit system said a yes vote was a vote for progress. Voters were not swayed and rejected the $12.5 million plan.

Mayor John F. Dore was a champion of the streetcar and a resolute opponent of the trackless trolley, but he was swept out of office in 1938 and died the same year.

On March 9, 1937, Seattle voters rejected the $12.5 million plan by a solid majority of 53,501 against versus 39,069 in favor. Dore relished the triumph and announced preliminary plans for a modest rehabilitation of the Seattle Municipal Street Railway, involving replacing streetcars as needed, "piece by piece."[47] Dore even floated a vague idea for subways in the congested areas, but admitted the money did not currently exist for that pipe dream. One new councilman, Hugh DeLacey, was swept into office by dredging up that ever-popular Seattle idea: the return of the nickel streetcar fare.

This bit of wishful thinking was spectacularly unsuited to the situation, since the Seattle Municipal Street Railway's finances were worse than ever. Bankers continued to reject all loan proposals that included keeping the street railway intact. The system finally went bankrupt and the city defaulted on its loan payments. Facing no good options, Dore was compelled to "confiscate" dimes and nickels directly out of the fare boxes to meet the workers' payroll.[48] Dore still vowed to prevent the demise of the street railway system, but, as fate would have it, Dore met his demise first. He was defeated in the February 1938 primary and died on April 18, 1938. His old debating foe, Arthur Langlie, became mayor.

In 1939 the last tickets were punched for the Seattle Municipal Street Railway.

Langlie immediately set out to revive an old idea: financing a complete transit revamp by asking the federal government for a low-interest New Deal loan. This time the government's answer was yes. In June 1939 Seattle secured a $10.2 million loan from the Reconstruction Finance Corporation, a New Deal recovery agency. The loan allocated $4.5 million to retire the system's debt, $3.25 million of it going to Puget Sound Power & Light. That was only about 40 percent of what

the city truly owed, but the power company agreed to this bargain price because of a "desire to give constructive aid in this situation," according to a Puget Power historian—or possibly because, after 20 years, getting something was better than nothing.[49] The rest went to the system's other main creditor, the union workers.

That left $5.7 million to purchase a whole new transit system. Some observers noted that this was about 38 percent of what the city had paid for its old transit system in 1919—without even factoring in inflation.

As one of the loan's prerequisites, the Reconstruction Finance Corporation insisted on removing corrosive city politics from Seattle's transit management. It demanded that the system be put under the control of an independent three-person transportation commission appointed by the mayor and council, yet not subject to the control of the city. In 1939 the Washington State Legislature duly passed an enabling act creating the Seattle Transportation Commission, "legally bound only to carry out the requirements laid down by the Reconstruction Finance Corporation."[50]

The rickety old Yesler cable car—the same cable line that thrilled and frightened the customers in 1888—made its final run in August 1940.

Beeler issued one more report that year, laying out the plan for the new system. It called for scrapping the rail system, buying 235 trackless trolleys and 102 buses (for a total of 175 buses, counting the ones the city already owned). The 1939 Beeler Report put to rest the debate over rail versus rubber, seemingly once and for all. The new report, like the one from 1936, opted for trackless trolleys because it said they were more economical and had the advantage of loading at the curb. Beeler said they could easily handle the passenger volume in Seattle. During this time, the number of buses more than doubled and became a key part of the plan. The report further noted that trackless trolleys were the best fit for many of Seattle's steepest routes—including the old cable car routes—because no "self-propelled vehicle (bus) can exert a sustained tractive effort comparable to that of a vehicle of equal weight drawing its power from an electric power station."[51] This is one reason why Seattle would retain its trackless trolleys to the present day, especially on steep routes.

The 1939 report set in motion the next great turning point in Seattle's transit tale: the utter demise of Seattle's entire street rail system. Beeler's 12-month window for converting from rails to rubber proved a little optimistic, but not by much. New trackless trolley coaches and gas buses began arriving at the beginning of 1940. Exactly $1 million had been allocated to stringing new trolley wires to accommodate the two-wire trackless trolleys. Route by route, the new trolleys and buses began taking over, and the old trolley cars were trundled off to the wrecking yard. "A common sight on many a summer evening in 1940 was a long string of orange cars being hauled to the boneyard in Georgetown," recalled Blanchard.[52] That spring and summer, the three old cable car lines—Madison, James, Yesler— along with the Queen Anne Counterbalance, were disassembled.

Sometimes, the final runs were celebrated with raucous "last mile" revels— in the case of the Counterbalance, far *too* raucous. A "mob" of 70 Queen Anne youths stormed the final trolley, pelted the passengers with corn cobs and tomatoes, broke every window, and tossed the seats into the streets. Police rounded up 20 of them on vandalism charges, and the Counterbalance car limped into history. By spring of 1941 the changeover was almost complete. On April 13, 1941, nothing remained except the final streetcar on the final rail route, the 8th Avenue Northwest.

"Compressed air sighed in the shadows at Second Avenue South and Main Street 1:02 o'clock this morning," wrote a *Seattle Times* reporter that day. "The jaundiced bulk of the last streetcar to be operated in Seattle groaned, stirred, and moved uptown, starting and stopping slowly as if the lights hurt her eyes. Out in the dark suburban districts, she began going faster, waltzing tipsily on the old rails with a spurious jauntiness, like a tired dowager remembering her youth. But at the end of the 8th Avenue Northwest line, she groaned wearily again, and ground her lonely way to the Fremont car barns and the end of her career, like the dinosaur going off to die."[53]

Most of the dinosaurs were headed to the Northwest Steel Rolling Mills, where they would be junked for scrap. The *Seattle Times* indulged in a modest spread of nostalgic trolley photos, but also noted that "the city will engage

Seattle ripped out its entire network of street rail tracks in a remarkably short time. By 1942, few rails remained.

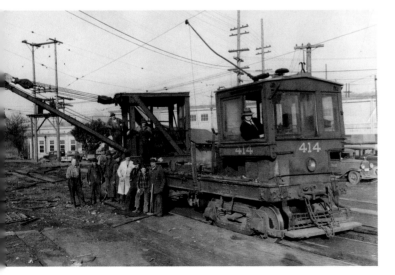

in no official weeping."[54] In fact, the Seattle Chamber of Commerce declared it to be Seattle Transit Progress Week.

No trace remained of the old system, not even the name. It became the Seattle Transit System. Soon even the rails would be ripped from the streets. In the words of Walt Crowley, "After scrimping for more than a generation to secure clear title to its own street railway system, Seattle promptly dismantled it."[55]

The old and new existed side-by-side briefly in 1940, but streetcars would disappear by April 1941.

A rails-to-rubber denouement had also played out in Tacoma. At the end of 1937, Tacoma Railway & Power placed orders for 85 motor coaches (buses) to replace the entire 76-mile streetcar track system.[56] The company made the conversion to an all-bus system in the middle of 1938. The passenger service of the city-owned Tacoma Municipal Railway (the Belt Line) followed suit. Tacoma residents chose to celebrate the final streetcar day on June 11, 1938, with a series of boisterous citywide parties, many taking place right inside the old cars. *Life* magazine photographers showed up to document the merriment, which included a barbershop chorus version of "The Old Streetcar Ain't What She Used to Be," led by Tacoma Railway & Power president Curtis Hill.

There was a whiff of bittersweet nostalgia amidst the revelry. "Because for nearly half a century, Tacoma's trolley cars have been a beloved institution as well as dependable transportation, Mayor John C. Siegle declared the day of their demise a public holiday to be celebrated with appropriate rites," reported *Life*.[57] Partygoers "were allowed to detach as souvenirs anything they could detach with their bare hands"—including the trolley bells and gongs. They stripped 21 streetcars in two hours. After a Gay Nineties dance at the Winthrop Hotel, revelers jumped on the last

Some old street-cars were "suitably cremated with public ceremony."

streetcar and rode it to the car barns, where the old trolley was, in the words of the mayor, "suitably cremated with public ceremony."[58] Many of the 10,000 celebrants looked on, "sentimentally sobered for the moment."[59]

CHAPTER FOUR

Forward Thrust and a Shift into Reverse

The new and independent Seattle Transportation Commission now managed Seattle's sparkling new rubber-tired transit system. It was no longer politically controversial, primarily because the main bone of political contention—the crippling debt—had been removed. Meanwhile, larger world events combined to boost ridership and revenues through the roof. The U.S. entered World War II at the end of 1941, and almost overnight Seattle became a huge wartime industrial center. Tens of thousands of workers poured into the Boeing Company's airplane plant and Puget Sound shipyards. Mass transit was more vital than ever. People flocked—gratefully—to the modern buses and electric trolleys. Few gave wistful glances backward to the slower and clunkier streetcars. The Seattle Transit System opened a "huge new terminal at Airport Way and Atlantic Street" early in 1942 and noted that "the city's increased passenger travel necessitates the use of all available coaches during the peak hours."[1] The new terminal had space for 350 coaches—both buses and trackless trolleys.

With the transit system now routinely operating at 100 percent of its capacity, the Seattle Transit System faced a new problem: overcrowding. In the spring of 1942, officials of the War Production Transport Commission launched an ongoing "battle against Seattle's nightmare of traffic congestion," in the words of the *Seattle Times*.[2] Its main weapon was the

Left: The trackless trolleys ruled Seattle's downtown streets in the 1950s and beyond.

Seattle's new fleet of trackless trolleys and buses are lined up at the Jefferson Street yard in December 1940.

Seattle Transit System Jefferson Yard No. 1 12-15-40

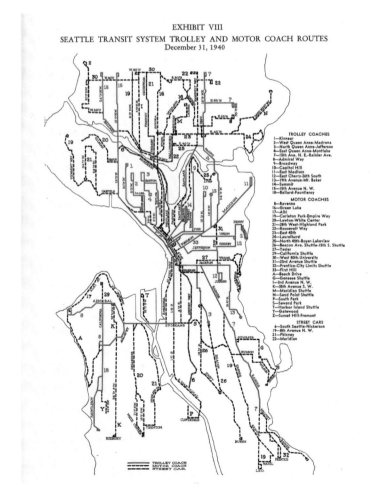

EXHIBIT VIII
SEATTLE TRANSIT SYSTEM TROLLEY AND MOTOR COACH ROUTES
December 31, 1940

The influx of World War II workers created an all-time high demand for transit in Seattle. Even old buses were drafted into service.

staggered work shift, intended to "level off rush-hour peaks and distribute traffic volume evenly throughout the day," said Kenneth B. Colman of the commission.[3] Lloyd P. Graber, Seattle Transit System manager, said "there is no doubt that the staggered-hours program is beginning to alleviate rush-hour crowding of transit vehicles." But he also warned that the "transportation picture is changing so rapidly" he couldn't be certain if that would be sufficient.[4] Colman predicted that before the year was out, staggered hours would affect every family in Seattle. This turned out to be true. Company after company shifted their hours to later in the day in order to free up the morning rush-hour bus space for war workers.

As the war ground on, gas rationing further boosted mass transit use, to the point where authorities warned that any further gas rationing would cause people to abandon their autos and overwhelm the Seattle Transit System.[5] In fact, in late 1942 Graber worried publicly that the Seattle Transit System might have to resort to ride rationing. He called it a "last resort," and, ultimately, one he would never have to implement.[6] Instead, people were encouraged to ride share in autos, or, to use a newly coined term, "carpool." But new cars were nonexistent and so were new tires. In 1945 Seattle Transit ridership peaked at 131.2 million revenue-paying passengers, its all-time high.[7]

After the war ended, a 1946 study by the Municipal League of Seattle, a good-government group, concluded that the switch from rails to rubber—had "enabled the system to stand up under abnormally heavy traffic during the war."[8] As of 1946 the Seattle system averaged 368 rides per year, per capita—a little more than one ride per day—which was well above

By the end of 1940, the trackless trolley coaches (shown in red) were taking over and the streetcar lines were nearly phased out.

the national average of 305 rides. The system had 48 miles of transit routes, far more than the national average of 30. Yet its vehicles were less crowded than the national average, at seven passengers per bus-mile, compared to 8.6. The report noted that with the war boom over, revenues were starting to decline. So was ridership, which plummeted to 117.7 million in 1946 and was about to drop

Fares went up to a flat 10 cents per ride in 1947.

below 100 million, never to recover. The Municipal League concluded that "if Seattle Transit is to continue paying high wages and giving good service with modern equipment, fares will have to be increased."[9] In 1947 Seattle Transit took that advice. The three-for-a-quarter tokens were retired, and the fare was now a flat 10 cents per ride.[10]

Intercity transit between Tacoma, Seattle, Everett, and the growing suburbs was now operated almost entirely by privately owned gas and diesel stage bus lines. Lake Shore Lines, which already operated a route to Bothell and the old Rainier Avenue route to Renton, acquired the Black Diamond Stage Company in 1946, giving it control of the Green River Valley routes. Most of the other intercity stage lines were still controlled by North Coast Lines (also called North Coast Transportation Company). By 1947 it was running 165 buses along the corridor from Portland to Vancouver, B.C. It was no longer accurate to call this a Stone & Webster company, since Stone & Webster was long gone. But North Coast Lines remained a Puget Sound Power & Light

subsidiary, and it still had the old Stone & Webster taste for monopoly. It actually owned one of its only major "competitors," Independent Stages. Federal antitrust investigators took notice and forced Pugot Sound Power & Light to sell both North Coast Lines and Independent Stages to Greyhound in 1947. This, wrote Crowley, "closed the book on more than a half-century of hegemony over the region's public transportation."[11]

A West Seattle trackless trolley was the star of this 1947 promotional poster.

That was true in Seattle but not necessarily in Tacoma. Tacoma Railway & Power changed its name in 1941 to Tacoma Transit, yet it remained essentially the same company that had first laid tracks in Tacoma before the turn of the century.

The name change was for the most obvious of reasons: The company "no longer operates trains or sells electricity."[12]

The postwar boom became an auto boom, as new cars were available and cheaper than ever. Seattle commuters seemed to be relatively happy with their bus-and-trackless-trolley system. Its use remained well above the national average, but like the rest of the country, people were even happier driving their own cars. The Seattle Transit System ridership declined to 77.8 million in 1951 and auto use was spiking—a trend that would continue to accelerate. This resulted in chronic traffic jams in downtown Seattle, a problem that was exacerbated by

Traffic congestion was already a serious problem in 1939, as this downtown Seattle scene attests.

the city's geography. North-south traffic was squeezed into a bottleneck near downtown because of the city's hourglass shape. Traffic on Highway 99 or State Highway 2 or any of the other north-south routes was funneled directly into the jammed downtown. The Washington State Highway Department (later known as the Washington State Department of Transportation) had begun studying downtown Seattle congestion as early as the 1930s, and in 1946 conditions were becoming so bad that it launched a major study, the 1946 Origin and Destination Survey, to determine where to build a north-south expressway. The survey made the extent of the problem clear. The average traffic speed through downtown Seattle was 10–15 miles per hour. It wasn't much better just south of downtown, at 15–20 miles per hour.[13] The survey focused on autos, but the city's buses were forced to crawl as well. As a result of this study, planning began immediately for what was called a North-South Expressway—which would later evolve into Interstate 5.

The entire region was growing fast—alarmingly fast, from a transportation perspective. Between 1950 and 1960 Seattle's population shot from 467,591 to 557,087. King County had grown even faster, from 732,992 to 935,014. Most of that growth was in the burgeoning suburbs to the east and south of the city. In 1950 Seattle accounted for nearly two-thirds of King County's population, but by 1960 that percentage was down to 60 percent and soon less than half. Perhaps the most ominous statistic was this: The county's auto registrations nearly doubled between 1950 and 1960, to 373,000 vehicles.[14] Seattle Transit ridership dropped to half its wartime high, with only 64.7 million riders in 1953.[15] Ridership and fare box revenues continued to decline. In 1955 the Seattle Transit Commission (formerly known as the Seattle Transportation Commission) asked for, and eventually received, a subsidy from the city's general fund.[16] A 10-day bus driver strike during the 1956 Christmas shopping season did not help matters.

Facing these issues, the state and county governments embarked on what seemed, at the time, to be a logical approach. They began to plan more and bigger highways. The Alaskan Way Viaduct was completed in 1953, taking some of the pressure off the jammed downtown streets (but also, as Crowley noted, effectively "walling off" downtown from the waterfront).[17]

Highway planners in 1953 were debating a new route over Lake Washington. The route labeled "State Recommended Route" would be similar, but not identical, to the eventual route of the Evergreen Point Floating Bridge.

The Alaskan Way Viaduct (right) was under construction in 1952. The goal was to take some of the pressure off the surface streets.

Planning continued for the North-South Expressway, originally intended to be a toll road. By the early 1950s the route—similar to today's Interstate 5—was selected. Meanwhile, King County Engineer D.L. Evans proposed another audacious solution to the city's traffic congestion. In December 1953 he unveiled a $33 million scheme to drill a mile-and-a-half-long tunnel northeast from downtown, through Capitol Hill toward Laurelhurst, in order to create a new highway route connecting with planned bridges across Lake Washington. Evans envisioned his project as a toll highway, but he also included a transit component, proposing that auto drivers could park in big, new lots near the University of Washington and then take "express buses" through the tunnel and arrive downtown in five minutes.[18] In what would become a common pattern with other forward-thinking transportation ideas, this proposal was destined to go nowhere.

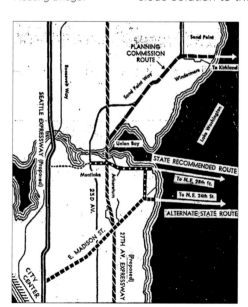

PROPOSED TUNNELS: This system of toll tunnels and viaducts, extending from the central business district to Laurelhurst, was proposed today by County Engineer D. L. Evans. The system, expected to cost $33,-000,000, would connect with either of the proposed sites for a new Lake Washington bridge. The plan calls for a 1½-mile tunnel under Capitol Hill, a viaduct and new bridge across the Ship Canal and a tunnel under high ground of the Laurelhurst shopping center.

County engineer D. L. Evans offered an audacious proposal in 1953 to create a toll tunnel from downtown to beyond the University of Washington—not far from where Sound Transit would eventually dig a light-rail tunnel.

As traffic grew worse, people in Seattle began to grapple with the implications of the auto explosion. On December 23, 1953, the *Seattle Times* ran an editorial, quoting a *Chicago Tribune* piece about traffic congestion. "The problem exists because, among many other reasons, the ordinary automobile is a most inefficient vehicle for transporting large numbers of people in a limited area. The automobile wastes power and more particularly, it wastes space. A city bus will seat as many passengers as will be found in 30 motor cars … and will occupy only about twice as much pavement as one of them." Highway and parking improvements would only mean that "more automobiles will be attracted and the trouble will reappear anew." The *Seattle Times* agreed with this view, saying, "The *Tribune* could have been discussing problems right here in Seattle. Seattle looks forward to relief in some far-distant future through such improvements as an expressway—a very vague hope—or by the tunnel plan recently proposed by County Engineer Evans." But what good are superhighways "if they funnel their traffic into a hopeless downtown tangle?"[19] The *Times* concluded that both Seattle and Chicago had "the simplest of solutions in their own hands, if they would only apply it: making more general and more regular use—*much* more general and much more regular—of municipal transit facilities."[20]

However, the region's commuters failed to embrace this apparent "simplest of solutions." Seattle Transit bus ridership continued to plummet, from 59.5 million in 1954 to 39.3 million by 1961. Transportation planners also failed to embrace the idea of mass transit—especially rail transit. When the U.S. Congress passed the Federal Aid Highway Act in 1956, the north-south Expressway plan turned into the Interstate 5 plan. The Seattle Transit Commission had urged the Washington State Highway Department in 1953 to include a 50-foot median in the new freeway as a future rail right-of-way. The state rejected the rail plan. It would entertain only express bus service on its new freeway.[21] Again in 1957 Seattle brought up the concept of incorporating rail into the Interstate 5 project. The rights-of-way alone would have cost $16 million. Once again, the state said no.

As transit ridership declined, Seattle Transit came up with creative efforts to convince people to take the bus in 1959.

YOU DON'T HAVE TO PARK A TRANSIT BUS

"I RIDE TRANSIT ….hate to park reindeer"

Let our driver fight traffic for you…

These passengers have no parking problems.

Argue Politics… *not right-of-way*

WATCH OUT for pedestrians… especially little ones

The North-South Expressway plan evolved into Interstate 5—which would eventually include bus-only express lanes.

To the south, the privately owned Tacoma Transit was struggling and looking for a way out. Its franchise was ready to expire, and it was losing money. The company had even entertained the idea of selling out to the city of Tacoma. In 1954 the employees themselves entered the discussion, with the Motor Coach Employees Union making an offer to buy the company. The union secretary said that the employees decided "that a cooperative ownership would be preferable to municipal ownership, which has been discussed."[22] The management, many of whom were held over from the old Tacoma Railway & Power days, including president Curtis L. Hill, said they believed that "cooperative ownership might solve Tacoma's transit problems." In December 1954 a deal was struck and the union members agreed to buy out the company stock at $6 per share, for a total of $2 million. For their $2 million, the union members would be acquiring 115 buses and the company's real estate property, putting an end to the final vestiges of the Stone & Webster transit legacy.[23]

A Tacoma bus driver shows Daffodil Princess Elisa Peterson how to use a new route in 1962.

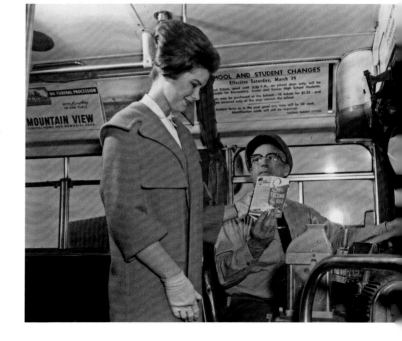

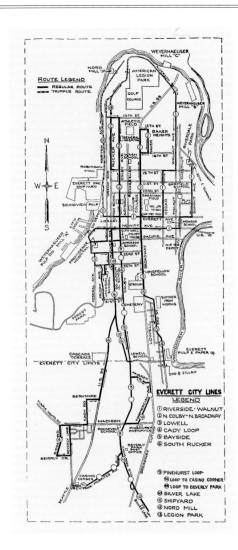

An Everett City Lines route map from 1953, showing its 13 bus routes.

The union estimated it would take until 1960 to consummate the deal, because it was purchasing all of the stock in increments through payroll withdrawal. Unfortunately, by 1960 the employees' payments were lagging behind. The company threatened to foreclose on the union, so the city of Tacoma stepped in. It offered to buy Tacoma Transit for $750,000, because "if the council fails to act—and soon—Tacoma may end up without a bus system."[24] Tacoma voters, worried about going bus-free, approved the purchase. On February 1, 1961, the city of Tacoma officially took over the Tacoma Transit Company, and the name was changed to the Tacoma Transit System. With this move, Tacoma became only the second city in the state, after Seattle, with a publicly owned transit system.[25]

Everett's small bus system was also moving toward municipal ownership. In 1961 a private bus company owned by former bus driver Clyde Hammond bought the city's bus system. Hammond's Everett Transit System (sometimes called the Everett Bus System or Everett City Lines) soon became awash in deficits. By 1969 it had reached a crisis and in September of that year, Mayor Robert Anderson announced that Everett was seeking voter approval to "go into the transit business."[26] He said that Clyde Hammond had "approached city officials and asked them to save the business." The entire system consisted of only 16 buses, all more than 20 years old. The city's proposal included a "modest" tax increase, because the mayor proclaimed that the "system must stand on its own feet." On November 4, 1969, Everett voters approved the sale. At long last, Everett owned its own transit system.[27] The fight over public-versus-private transit ownership had been going on since the beginning of the 20th century, but finally all three large Puget Sound cities owned their bus systems.

Seattle Transit's guidebook cover, circa 1950s.

Unfortunately, civic ownership did not go well for Tacoma, at least initially. By 1964 the Tacoma bus system had lost nearly a half-million dollars. The problem? Dwindling ridership. The system had 7.5 million passengers in 1960 but only 6.2 million in 1964.[28] This was a problem that was affecting all bus systems, including Seattle's.

The Seattle Transit Commission recommended stemming the bleeding in Seattle by scrapping the costly rubber-tired electric trolleys and converting to an all-bus system. Trolley fans, organized as the Committee for Modernization of Electric Transit, or COMET, responded with a ballot initiative to save the trolleys. It turned out that trolley fans—although passionate—were not particularly numerous. The initiative was defeated by a vote of 106,159 to 54,726. Ironically, the Transit Commission would soon commute the death sentence for trolleys, partly because the city did not have the money to replace them. The rubber-tired trolleys continued to zing along Seattle's streets. Yet the system as a whole now required an annual subsidy from the city's general fund just to keep going.

In the first three months of 1964 alone, the Seattle Transit System reported operating losses of more than $250,000, a trend that would only worsen. Both Seattle and Tacoma city attorneys were investigating new legislative proposals to allow either a vehicle tax or a "direct transit charge on city utility bills." Tacoma city manager David Rowlands predicted that the time was coming when the rest of the cities in the state would have to decide whether "to step in and keep the buses operating."[29] In a desperate attempt to keep Seattle's transit system funded, the Seattle City Council voted at the end of the decade to impose a transit tax of $1 per household. This tax was immediately repealed by voters.

Metro would eventually take over transit operations for all of King County. Here, an AM General trackless trolley rolls through downtown Seattle.

Meanwhile, stronger political winds were gusting from another quarter. King County's suburban sprawl had grown so large and unwieldy that a few forward-thinking leaders, spurred by the Municipal League of Seattle and King County, became convinced that the region's sewage, water, and transportation problems could no longer be tackled piecemeal by 180 competing jurisdictions. Seattle lawyer James R. (Jim) Ellis and other leaders of the progressive Municipal League urged the creation of a regional government structure, which would encompass Seattle, the suburban cities, and the unincorporated areas of King County. They called this new, still-imaginary entity, the Municipality of Metropolitan Seattle. We know it today as Metro.[30]

The original idea called for this new "Metro" government to handle six basic services for the entire metropolitan area: sewage treatment, solid waste disposal, water supply, regional parks, comprehensive land-use planning, and yes, mass transportation. Still the concept was fought bitterly by many of the surrounding suburbs because of fears that they would be "dominated and controlled" by Seattle.[31] An initial vote to create Metro was defeated in spring of 1958. Metro backers scaled back the idea and concentrated on one main issue: cleaning up the shockingly polluted Lake Washington by consolidating and modernizing the region's sewage treatment. This proved to be a winning issue. When voters went to the polls in fall 1958, Metro was born.

Transit was not included—at least, not yet. But as the 1960s dawned, it became increasingly obvious that if there was one issue that demanded a regional, not strictly Seattle, solution, it was mass transit. Commuters were coming into downtown not just from Laurelhurst and Ballard, but from Bellevue and Auburn, too. The Seattle Transit System was unable to serve most of these commuters. The private suburban bus line, the Metropolitan Transit Corporation, was barely serving most of them as it was. The transit line had consolidated several small ones—the Suburban Transit System in Edmonds, Lake Shore Lines, and Overlake Transit Service in 1962 and then snapped up the suburban Greyhound lines in 1965. By the end of the decade Metropolitan Transit owned nearly all of King County's suburban lines, yet it still operated only 83 buses, carried only 2.3 million passengers a year, and was bleeding money by the minute.[32]

Metro scaled back its proposal in fall of 1958 to one issue: cleaning up Lake Washington. Voters approved.

This 1959 Metropolitan Transit Corporation bus was later lovingly refurbished to mint condition, but when Metro first acquired the suburban bus company in 1972, the entire fleet was best described as ramshackle.

In 1960 an even broader intergovernmental body, the Puget Sound Governmental Conference, commissioned a report called the Puget Sound Regional Transportation Study. However, the study director refused to include rapid rail transit, despite requests from the Municipal League. This stubborn insistence on making transportation planning synonymous with highway planning was becoming a common theme. A huge "political mass" was now allied behind private auto transportation, which included many powerful blocs: auto makers, road contractors, building trade unions, trucking companies, and the Teamsters Union, according to Crowley.[33] They were strengthened by perhaps the most powerful bloc of all: the region's ordinary auto drivers, who loved the freedom of the private car and showed little enthusiasm for mass transit of any kind. Rail transit had a comparatively small political constituency, possibly because older Seattle residents still had less-than-fond memories of the old streetcar system, but more likely because rail simply seemed old-fashioned in this Chevy Impala era.

Seattle did build one decidedly futuristic "rail" line in April 1962: the Seattle Monorail. It was built to whisk people quietly and stylishly from downtown to Seattle's Century 21 Exposition, aka the Seattle World's Fair at Seattle Center. This 1.3-mile line cost $3.5 million and was intended (although somewhat vaguely) to be expanded after the fair, possibly to the airport. It never was, although it survives as one of the most visible reminders of the World's Fair. (See sidebar on page 144 describing Seattle's attempt to expand the monorail system.)

Seattle Transit came up with a creative way of reminding riders of the fare rules in 1960.

Consequently, the most significant transportation development of the mid-1960s was the completion of Interstate 5 through Seattle. The freeway included no mass transit component, beyond the obvious benefit of providing a quicker route for buses. But even this modern freeway was not up to the demands of a growing city. Interstate 5 was designed to meet projected 1975 traffic volumes, but those projections proved to be way off. On the day Interstate 5 fully opened through Seattle in 1967, some stretches were already exceeding their designed capacities.[34] The freeway was intended to move traffic more quickly through Seattle's bottlenecks, and it often did. However, its design laid the foundation for thousands of traffic jams to come. The term "Mercer Mess," describing the snarl of traffic to and from the freeway at Mercer Street, immediately entered Seattle's lexicon.

Despite the focus on Interstate 5, there were several victories for rail transit proponents. Pressure from the Municipal League forced the state transportation department to study the inclusion of a rail transit component on the Mercer Island floating bridge—the bridge that would eventually become part of Interstate 90. This seed of a rail idea would eventually bear fruit—after 50 years.[35]

In January 1961, construction was underway on what would become Interstate 5 through Seattle. It would contain no rail component.

Meanwhile, Jim Ellis and the proponents of Metro had not given up on mass transit. In September 1962 they scheduled a public vote on this question: Should Metro "be authorized to perform the additional function of Metropolitan Public Transportation?" The Municipal League wholeheartedly backed the plan, but the usual suburban interests once again vehemently opposed it. These opponents were joined by the Automobile Club of Washington, better known as AAA, which charged that Metro wanted to deplete highway funds to pay for rail. Voters agreed, and the 1962 Metro transit proposal was easily shot down by about 59,000 to 39,000.

Ellis and Metro geared up for another try. In 1964, Seattle's Transit Commission, which still operated the Seattle Transit System, announced a new transit study, which was "to be coordinated with the regional highway plan, adequate to serve the Central Puget Sound region" for the next 20 years.[36] The plan was put together by the engineering firm of De Leuw, Cather and Company, and it included a significant rail component. However, there would soon be dueling transit plans. A new Puget Sound Regional Transportation Study was released in 1967, and once again, it rejected rail and endorsed local and express buses. These two studies differed in an even more fundamental way because—as we saw in the earliest trolley days—mass transit and urban growth go hand in hand. The De Leuw, Cather report essentially envisioned dense growth centered in Seattle, discouraging suburban sprawl. The Puget Sound Regional Transportation Study was considerably less Seattle-centric and anticipated growth scattered in emerging urban centers surrounding Seattle. This plan imagined a metropolitan area more similar to Los Angeles. If the more Seattle-centric theory was correct, rail mass transit would be more viable, since people would be commuting to a central hub. If the diffused-growth theory was correct, rail mass transit would have trouble attracting commuters. Complicating the debate was this consideration: The form of mass transit might *itself* determine how and where the region would grow.

The De Leuw, Cather report said that rapid rail transit would encourage the higher densities needed for rail. The Puget Sound Regional Transportation Study report concluded that transit would have little impact on land use and that the population would remain too dispersed to make rail succeed. For Seattle's political and business community, the choice was easy. They liked the Seattle-centric, rail-friendly plan. Mayor J.D. (Dorm) Braman appointed a Rapid Transit Advisory Committee and appointed Jim Ellis as its leader. Ellis and the committee heartily endorsed the De Leuw, Cather study with its significant rail component.

Ellis had already outlined an audacious plan for the city's future in a speech to the Seattle Rotary Club on November 3, 1965. He proposed ushering in a "golden age for Seattle," with new parks, a major league stadium and urban rede-velopment.[37] At the heart of the plan was an integrated rapid transit system that would preserve Seattle's Central Business District and protect open space outside the city. He wanted to use "electric" vehicles, presumably rail, because they were nonpolluting. Ellis pointed out that "the volume of move-ment needed to serve 120,000 jobs downtown cannot be met by existing freeway lanes" and if the city put "sole reliance" on freeways, "congestion will throttle growth." The Seattle Times editorial page immediately splashed cold water on Ellis's plan by asking, "But how badly do the property owners of Seattle and King County want to play Santa Claus for all of these proposed community assets? That is the unanswered question."[38] The paper did, however, admit that the ideas themselves had merit.

Ellis was appointed to chair a group grandly called the Committee of 200 (which would swell to 225). On June 1, 1967, the committee released its plan, giving it a name that reflected its audacity: Forward Thrust. It included an eye-popping menu of capital projects, including a domed stadium, parks, community buildings, arterials, and a huge new rapid transit system. The whole package came in at the eyebrow-raising price of $2 billion.

Over the next few months, Ellis and the Committee of 200 pared the Forward Thrust plan down to $819.2 million. It was divided into 12 separate bond issues. The biggest component by far was the $385 million bond issue for the rapid transit system. The domed stadium, by comparison, was only $40 million, and the new

De Leuw Cather & Co. put together an ambitious 1965 rapid transit plan (for completion in 1985), which included rail and subways. It was the germ of an idea that would grow into Forward Thrust.

RAPID TRANSIT
RECOMMENDED 1985 PLAN

parks (including an aquarium) were only $121 million. However, that $385 million transit price tag would actually buy a $1.15 billion transit system, because if the bond issue passed, the federal government had pledged to kick in the rest—about two-thirds of the total price. For local taxpayers, it was a spectacular bargain.

The full transit plan—developed by DeLeuw, Cather, based on its earlier plan—was unveiled in October 1967 and it was truly ambitious. It included 45 miles of rail, with lines converging on downtown from Renton, Bellevue, Greenwood/Ballard, and the University of Washington— a route map that bears a striking resemblance to what Sound Transit would propose decades later. Tunnels would take the lines underground into the central business district, directly under Third Avenue.[39] The trains themselves would be similar to San Francisco's BART trains—bigger and heavier than what would today be termed "light-rail." (Light-rail, which would later come into vogue, uses relatively smaller cars than standard railroad cars.) Express buses and local buses would funnel commuters into the outlying rail stations. In a concession to the American Automobile Association and the region's highway-loving motorists, the larger Forward Thrust proposal also included a separate bond issue to build new arterial highways, making it a "balanced-system" plan.[40]

Forward Thrust's message in this ad was clear—vote for the transit proposal or face ever-worsening traffic congestion. Voters were not swayed.

FORWARD THRUST ELECTION

750,000 more people are coming to King County!

Will we just move over? Or will we move ahead?...

The Municipal League and other good-government groups (nicknamed the "go-gos" by some people, and, less charitably, "the goo-goos" by others) mobilized 3,500 volunteers to go door-to-door for Forward Thrust. A strong push was essential, since state rules required that bond issues pass with a 60 percent yes vote, not a mere 50 percent majority. Endorsements began to roll in from organizations across the region and across the political spectrum. The *Seattle Times* editorial page strongly supported a yes vote on every Forward Thrust issue. The Forward Thrust theme, said the editors, was "Let us begin now to do those things we know we will have to do eventually—but later will cost much more."[41]

The *Seattle Post-Intelligencer* backed it as well. Still, there were a few ominous holdouts. The first big blow came when the King County Democrats endorsed all Forward Thrust bond issues, except the transportation issues. "We feel rapid transit should service the entire county," said county Democratic chair Jeanette Williams. "The areas of greatest growth in King County today—Kent, Auburn, and north and south suburbia—will not be serviced under the proposal as it appears on the ballot."[42]

This was followed by a far bigger blow from the King County Democrats, who, in their newsletter, called it "Forward Lust" and implied that Ellis would profit from the bond sales. A Teamster newspaper chimed in, calling it "Forward Bust."

Profile: Jim Ellis

James Reed "Jim" Ellis (b. 1921) was neither a politician nor a head of a municipal agency nor a Seattle business titan. Yet in the words of Seattle historian Cassandra Tate, he "left a bigger footprint on Seattle and King County than perhaps any other single individual."

Ellis, a lawyer and civic activist, was the driving force behind the Municipality of Metropolitan Seattle (Metro), which cleaned up Lake Washington. He was the architect of Forward Thrust, the 1968 initiative which resulted in the Seattle Aquarium, the Kingdome, new parks, and swimming pools. He led a successful effort to preserve farmlands in the county and to create the Mountain to Sounds Greenway. He spearheaded the creation and expansion of the Washington State Convention and Trade Center. He was, in short, the leader of many of the visionary causes in King County for the entire last half of the 20th century.

Ellis graduated from Franklin High School, Yale University, and the University of Washington Law School. He worked as a bond-counsel lawyer in a Seattle law firm and immediately became a key member of Seattle's "good government" Municipal League.

"He believes people live on by the things they do for others," said his wife, Mary Lou, in 1968. "He has to do something public-spirited or he'd burn up inside."

Ellis' biggest disappointment, by far, was in mass transit. A complete rail transit system—which looked a lot like today's Sound Transit plan—was the largest component of his 1968 and 1970 Forward Thrust bond issues. Both were defeated by the voters. Ellis correctly predicted that history would see this as another lost—and particularly costly—opportunity for the Seattle region.

Discouraged, he announced that someone else would have to carry on the transit fight. Yet only two years after the second Forward Thrust defeat, Ellis helped create Metro Transit, the first countywide transit system in King County. Decades later when Sound Transit was born, Ellis served as a valuable adviser and consultant. In 2008 when Sound Transit conducted its initial test runs of Link light-rail, Jim Ellis was honored as one of the first passengers.[43]

Jim Ellis, the driving force behind Forward Thrust and Metro, was haunted by the failure of the 1968 and 1970 rail transit votes. He finally achieved redemption decades later through his constant support of Sound Transit.

An opposition group called Citizens for Sensible Transit, led by Bellevue real estate developer Vick Gould, took out a newspaper ad right before the election, blaring "Don't Be Railroaded" and claiming the bond issue would "paralyze traffic" and "force you to ride the rails."[44] This was, of course, ridiculous. There would be no mandatory rail riding. Nevertheless, the central argument against Forward Thrust was based on fact. The entire package would cost taxpayers money—as much as $21 a year for a typical Seattle homeowner.[45]

This was no small potatoes in the 1960s. But viewed in perspective from a distance of 50 years, the transit bond alone was absurdly cheap. It would purchase 45 miles of rail for only $385 million in local money. The federal government was poised to kick in the rest, between $700 million and $800 million. A half-century later, costs for comparable plans would be measured in the tens of billions.

This is why the election on February 13, 1968, represented *the* most crucial turning point in the long history of Puget Sound transit. If the transit plan received more than a 60 percent yes vote, Seattle would build a complete rail-based transit system by, at the latest, 1985. If it received less than 60 percent, it would set back regional transit by decades—or, as it turned out, nearly half a century.

The result was not even close. The Forward Thrust transit proposal failed by nine percentage points, receiving a 51 percent yes vote. Ellis blamed "charges, claims, and distortions" by opponents for the defeat.[46] Transit was one of only five of the 12 Forward Thrust issues to go down to defeat, the others being: funding new community centers, low-income housing, storm water drainage, and maintenance shops. The stadium issue passed with 62 percent of the vote and would

An artist's conception of a future Metro rail station. Because voters twice rejected Forward Thrust's rail transit proposals, this station would remain strictly theoretical.

"We need a solution to traffic congestion"

Whoops . . . looks like a bit of a traffic problem here. Even the youngsters are finding out that you have to plan ahead to stay ahead in this bumper-to-bumper world.

Seattle Transit engineers have their problems, too, because our main thoroughfares are being choked by traffic. Day by day, it's becoming more difficult to maintain rapid, on-time service for you and your neighbors.

Right now, we're studying entirely new forms of public

transportation that will skirt around or above traffic strangle-holds. These new inventions, like Transit express lanes on our new freeways, are vitally needed to provide a safe, swift, comfortable ride to your destination.

All this takes monumental planning and a sizeable investment in the future. You can be certain, however, that Seattle Transit is investigating every possible solution to remain dependably *at your service*.

SEATTLE TRANSIT
at your service

Ad. No. TC-288 -- 5 col. x 9½"
Seattle Post Intelligencer -- April 29, 1959

Seattle Transit was already raising the alarm—although whimsically—about traffic congestion in 1959.

result in the Kingdome. Funding for new arterial highways passed easily, indicating that voters chose highways over the far more expensive rail. But Ellis was heartened by the fact that rail transit received more than 50 percent of the vote, indicating that at least a majority backed it.

Ellis and other transit backers picked themselves up off the mat and vowed to get a new rail transit proposal on the ballot as soon as possible. It would take another two years. Those were two critical years, since in that time Boeing's troubles—known as the Boeing Bust—put the entire Puget Sound economy into a tailspin. The region's unemployment rate soared.

Even so, Ellis forged ahead, revising the 1968 transit plan only slightly and placing a $440 million transit issue on the ballot in 1970. Once again, the federal government was poised to pick up the rest of the tab for what was now a $1.3 billion transit system. Washington's powerful U.S. senator, Warren Magnuson, personally guaranteed the federal match if local voters approved the plan. The new plan added a few miles to the rail system, for a total of 49, and threw in some expanded bus routes and an exclusive "busway" to West Seattle, a community that had voted strongly against the previous issue.[47]

Opposition groups mostly ignored the details of the plan and concentrated on the main issue that resonated with voters skittish about their jobs: higher property taxes. The chief opposition group named itself Overtaxed, Inc. And the Citizens for Sensible Transit once again charged that the entire project was too expensive and "infeasible."[48]

Heavy winds were blowing against the 1970 Forward Thrust issues—and the hurricane arrived on election day, May 19, 1970. All four Forward Thrust proposals went down to defeat, with the transit measure blasted hardest of all. It received only 46 percent of the vote—a deficit of 14 points. A dejected Ellis admitted that "we have rowed against a tide that was simply impossible." He ominously predicted that the region's transit needs would have to be met someday and "will cost more in the future."[49] Even he could never have guessed how much more.

Seattle Mayor J.D. "Dorm" Braman was a tireless advocate for mass transit.

Former Seattle Mayor J.D. Braman, who had worked tirelessly for transit and had become the Assistant U.S. Secretary for Transportation, said he was deeply disappointed that his city had lost such a "golden opportunity." He added glumly, "I think we must reconcile ourselves to the fact that we will continue to operate in a deteriorating traffic mess that has almost consumed older American cities. ... Seattle has committed itself to the same course."[50] Harley Hoppe, the head of Overtaxed, Inc., crowed that people were "fed up" with the downtown business establishment in general and Forward Thrust in particular.[51]

Hoppe had actually hit upon one of the main reasons that voters defeated rail transit in both 1968 and 1970. Seattle had what Crowley called a "long history of public hostility to grand schemes" hatched over lunch in the Rainier Club—or at least, that's where they were hatched in voters' minds.[52] Hoppe was probably wrong in thinking this was the predominant reason. Three other factors were probably more important.

First, most middle-class and suburban voters in the '60s and '70s did not consider public transit to be a part of their lives. They drove cars. Transit was what "other people"—mostly those who were poorer—used. In other words, mass transit by this time was barely considered "mass."

Second, rail transit was not particularly well-suited to Seattle, as that 1966 Puget Sound Region Transportation Study had pointed out. "Seattle and its environs were distinguished by extremely low densities, which made fixed-route rail transit a dubious proposition, unless and until residential patterns changed," said Crowley.[53] Rail itself would have likely changed those patterns; yet at the time, this was merely speculative.

The most telling line on this Seattle Transit System graph is the one labeled "passengers," showing a steady downward trend from 1945 to 1970.

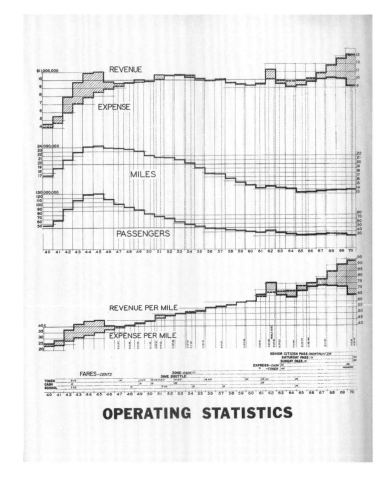

OPERATING STATISTICS

The final and indisputable reason was that the Washington State Constitution had insisted since 1944 on a 60 percent voter majority for major property tax increases. Without that high hurdle, the 1968 Forward Thrust transit issue would have sprinted to victory. This hurdle was not going away. The 60 percent rule was imbedded in the 17th Amendment to the state constitution and was, in Crowley's words, a "sacred cow" of Washington politics.[54]

The failed transit proposals of 1968 and 1970 shaped the region's transit story for the next 40 years, mostly for the worse. Ellis summed it up in a 2006 interview, when he lamented that it "would have saved us $6 to 8 billion; it would have been in place in 1985; it would have built more track than Sound Transit is doing, the last bonds would have been retired in 2006."[55]

The stinging, postscript to the Forward Thrust transit saga came in 1971, when the federal government took the $800 million earmarked for Seattle and handed it to Atlanta, a city which had managed to do what King County could not: pass a transit proposal. The result was the Metro Atlanta Transit Authority (MARTA), a rail system which opened in 1979. For the next few decades, visiting Seattleites could only ride it and weep.

Millions in federal funds earmarked for Seattle went instead to the Metro Atlanta Rapid Transit Authority (MARTA), which Atlanta used to launch its rail system in 1979.

CHAPTER FIVE

The Metro Mini-miracle

· · · · · · · · · · · · · · ·

Even Jim Ellis admitted that Forward Thrust and rapid rail transit were politically dead. The Puget Sound region was stuck with its old bus systems, which were on the verge of collapse. The Seattle Transit System's ridership sank to 33 million by the start of the decade—nearly 100 million below what it had been in 1944. The system was in a "spiral of failure," in the words of transit journalist and historian Bob Lane.[1] It was continually forced to cut service, which bit into ridership even more. Mayor Wes Uhlman and the Seattle City Council managed to stop the spiral by passing a 50-cent per household transit tax in 1970. This time the tax survived a legal challenge.[2]

Uhlman then went after federal funds in an attempt to modernize the system and boost ridership. One 1970 innovation was an instant success: the Blue Streak, a system of freeway express buses that zipped commuters between Northgate and downtown via designated express lanes. This was the region's first use of two innovations that would characterize transit planning over the next decades: "park and ride" lots and "High Occupancy Vehicle (HOV)" freeway express lanes. Commuters parked in a big lot at Northgate boarded Blue Streak buses for downtown, and sped past traffic jams on Interstate 5 in open lanes. The 500-car lot at Northgate was routinely filled to capacity. But as popular as they were, the Blue Streak buses came nowhere near solving the system's overall troubles. Ridership continued to drop and the deficit continued to build.

Left: The Blue Streak bus, using designated freeway express lanes, was an unqualified success story for the Seattle Transit System beginning in 1970.

Seattle commuters jammed the new Blue Streak express buses at Northgate in 1970.

Mayor Uhlman had become impatient with the Seattle Transit System's longtime director, Lloyd Graber, a transit traditionalist. Uhlman went after not just Graber, but also the commission itself. He offered Seattle voters a plan to replace the Seattle Transit Commission with a new city department, answerable to the mayor. Voters overwhelmingly approved the change. Graber retired after 30 years of admirable service under difficult conditions, and Deputy Mayor Robert Lavoie took over the renamed Transit Department of the City of Seattle. In one victory for traditionalists, the trackless trolleys were given yet another reprieve, in part because Seattle's environmentalists—a new category of activists—sided with clean electricity over diesel and freeways. Moreover, Seattle still had 56 rubber-tired trolleys.[3]

In the King County suburbs, the transit situation was desperate. The private Metropolitan Transit Corporation (not to be confused with Metro) now owned all of the smaller mom-and-pop bus lines in the suburbs, but it was losing money at a rapid clip. By 1970 only about 4,000 people in the suburbs commuted by bus—a number that explains not only why Metropolitan Transit was losing money, but also why the county's freeways and highways were jammed. That year King County was forced to subsidize Metropolitan's "ragtag fleet" of coaches in order to keep them afloat.[4] Metropolitan Transit was operating on such a shoestring, many drivers had to park their buses at home every night and service them themselves.[5]

This was pathetically inadequate for what had become a giant metropolitan area. After a brief post-Forward Thrust hangover, attitudes were beginning to

The Metropolitan Transit Corporation— not to be confused with Metro Transit— was a private bus line, inadequately serving Seattle's suburbs.

change. Grassroots environmental groups were blasting grandiose plans to build more freeways through Seattle. The R.H. Thompson Expressway was proposed through the University District, Arboretum, and Central Area. The Bay Freeway was proposed to soar over the Mercer Mess. Interstate 90 was marching westward through Mercer Island and the Central Area. Several groups—and a new

environmentally minded breed of city politicians, including council member Phyllis Lamphere—were aware that they couldn't simply be against freeways. They had to propose an alternative, and that alternative was mass rapid transit.

This new attitude encouraged Ellis and the other "go-gos" to make one more attempt to put Metro in the mass transit business. Knowing that bucking the 60 percent supermajority rule was

hopeless, they began looking at another funding source, a local option sales tax. A sales tax might not raise enough money to build an entire rail system, but it could fund a modernized bus system for all of King County. Plus it would require only a simple 50 percent majority for voter approval.

A bipartisan team of state legislators, led by Republican State Senator Joel Pritchard and Democratic State Representative David Sprague, began working in 1971 on a package of bills to prepare the groundwork for a vote. They proposed bills that extended Metro's limits to all of King County (rural areas had been previously excluded) and allowed Metro to ask for a three-tenths-of-one-percent sales tax for transit. The latter bill went through an agonizing near-death experience when the State Senate voted to prohibit Metro from getting necessary state funding, but a compromise bill finally passed on the last day of the session in 1971. The Metro Council was expanded to 36 members from the entire county, and the transit sales tax could now be taken to the voters.[6]

Even its backers weren't exactly confident. They remembered only too well that they had received only 46 percent of the vote in 1970. Some were convinced legislators passed the package only because they believed voters would reject the tax anyway. The backers—which included Metro's planning staff, the Puget Sound Governmental Conference, and the usual good-government groups—came up with a new strategy. They emphasized a more populist approach and recruited neighborhood opinion leaders to help plan the new system and to advocate for a yes vote.[7]

The Metropolitan Transit Corporation's fleet was in poor repair by 1970. This company would be acquired under the Metro banner two years later.

They held more than 50 meetings in which citizens could make suggestions about schedules. Thousands did. "People drew their own bus routes," said Aubrey Davis, the Mercer Island mayor who chaired the Metro Council's Transit Committee.[8] This, naturally, appalled the professional transit planners, but it reduced the feeling among voters that a plan was being imposed upon them.

After all of these sessions, the "1980 Plan" emerged, intended to steer Metro through 1980. It was drafted by the firm of Daniel, Mann, Johnson and Mendenhall, or DMJM—De Leuw, Cather having been pointedly *not* invited. The most obvious difference between this and the failed 1968 and 1970 plans was a complete lack of rail. It also differed fundamentally in its urban planning vision, which was less downtown-centric. Instead, the plan envisioned a "multicenter" transit concept, in which downtown would not be the only hub. Smaller hubs would also be established in the University District, Bellevue, and the Duwamish district. The plan intended to build on Seattle Transit's one big success story: the Blue Streak buses. This multicenter plan had the further advantage of appealing to suburban voters.

The 1980 Plan also called for building 25 park-and-ride lots throughout the county. New buses called "Freeway Flyers" would use the two express lanes already planned for Interstate 90, as well as more HOV lanes proposed for other freeways in the county. It also included a controversial plan for downtown. It suggested "contra-flow" lanes on Second and Fourth avenues—bus lanes heading the opposite direction of the one-way auto traffic on those streets.

Metro's initial plans included more free-way express lanes for buses—similar to these envisioned several decades later under the Sound Move proposal.

Metro intended to buy out the buses and all other assets of both Seattle Transit and the private Metropolitan Transit, for around $8 million. However, it did not propose using many of the company's antiquated buses for long. It planned to purchase 550 new buses, "employing the best available propulsion source at the time of purchase," which would turn out to be diesel.[9] It also planned to build 1,200 bus shelters and 6,000 new bus-stop signs. Fares would be 20 cents, with another 10-cent charge after crossing a certain

— S. Schienker

Regional express buses using HOV lanes with direct on/off ramps would provide fast, rail-like service.

Regional express buses would provide direct connections between suburban and urban centers.

The red ink in the Net Income/Loss column had grown to alarming proportions by 1970.

INCOME BY YEARS—SEATTLE TRANSIT SYSTEM TO DECEMBER 31, 1970

	Operating Revenues	Operation & Maintenance Expenses	Taxes & General Fund Assessment	Deprecia-tion	Bond Interest	Non-Operating Income and Deductions—Net	Net Income or Loss	Surplus Adjustments	Transit System Equity
Deficit resulting from operations and liquidation of Fixed Assets—April 1, 1918 to August 25, 1939—Municipal Street Railway									$ 4,282,550.31
**1939...	$ 1,572,645.66	$1,345,597.07	$ 22,139.83	$ 37,774.57	$ 70,060.14	$ 9,253.68	$ 87,820.37	†	4,194,729.94
1940...	4,627,194.10	3,750,758.86	173,945.13	352,884.79	321,693.12	16,120.07	11,792.13	†	4,182,937.81
1941...	5,530,747.75	4,033,067.49	175,592.04	586,278.74	458,690.62	119.45	276,999.41	†	3,905,938.40
1942...	7,985,328.90	4,906,750.17	236,867.89	617,147.71	474,750.00	9,798.68	1,740,014.45	†	2,165,923.95
1943...	9,768,908.37	6,194,413.17	359,802.43	682,848.74	355,800.00	171,235.86	2,004,808.17	3,000.67	164,116.45
1944...	10,901,267.09	7,001,902.00	392,423.34	697,606.78	269,500.00	10,000.00	2,529,834.97	625,331.68	1,740,386.84
1945...	11,085,377.48	7,617,447.16	422,614.56	665,766.40	104,708.40	71,709.48	2,203,131.48	675,002.15	4,618,520.47
1946...	9,809,087.42	7,799,720.86	412,140.77	624,515.62	64,198.75	41,544.00	950,055.42	66,674.57	5,635,250.46
1947...	9,622,673.07	7,998,956.13	425,188.49	760,886.21	50,925.00	62,149.80	448,867.04	54,398.11	6,138,515.61
1948...	9,711,911.40	8,329,925.30	428,077.15	950,653.88	42,175.00	100,281.00	61,361.07	55,492.81	6,255,369.49
1949...	10,072,601.88	8,679,026.38	424,979.75	564,494.39	33,425.00	43,776.98	414,453.34	341.65	6,670,164.48
1950...	9,910,834.65	8,806,953.18	429,013.86	553,736.11	24,675.00	36,838.87	133,295.37	8,380.14	6,811,839.99
1951...	10,688,787.03	9,025,369.79	437,599.78	560,493.32	12,337.50	37,639.81	690,626.45	52,434.34	7,554,900.78
1952...	10,649,921.95	9,406,981.44	550,875.18	526,306.71	....	51,474.33	217,232.95	33,089.50	7,739,044.23
1953...	10,717,952.61	9,484,974.42	549,900.91	478,098.25	....	83,434.24	288,413.27	3,751.44	8,023,706.06
1954...	10,270,010.19	9,695,020.33	554,149.19	423,238.70	....	74,867.53	327,530.50	31,164.00	7,727,339.56
1955...	10,267,649.29	9,123,620.71	564,195.51	238,090.66	....	81,580.51	423,322.92	13,950.20	8,136,712.28
1956...	10,021,010.57	8,862,757.45	634,454.00	399,474.07	....	38,390.21	162,715.26	64,630.01	8,364,057.55
1957...	9,928,298.71	9,346,175.32	437,411.94	390,207.15	....	69,659.43	175,836.27	217,874.75	8,406,096.03
1958...	9,539,349.45	8,924,844.72	383,277.24	385,526.33	....	105,741.98	48,556.86	92,121.12	8,449,660.29
1959...	9,353,995.26	8,718,528.52	410,870.45	386,858.29	....	125,092.87	37,169.13	105,362.26	8,517,853.42
1960...	9,208,591.84	8,651,887.76	309,179.09	387,342.74	....	129,534.90	10,282.85	83,419.88	8,590,990.45
1961...	9,431,454.23	8,632,175.35	308,912.93	387,174.32	....	125,063.50	228,255.13	77,927.16	8,897,172.74
1962...	11,015,300.05	9,421,013.27	331,697.93	389,905.33	....	313,450.72	1,186,134.24	55,053.03	10,138,360.01
1963...	9,546,752.55	9,112,819.46	344,938.99	511,437.41	....	154,487.42	267,955.89	52,164.90	9,922,569.02
1964...	9,185,589.63	9,141,784.71	339,280.10	401,285.59	....	119,138.70	577,622.07	22,389.87	9,367,336.82
1965...	9,366,687.39	9,173,614.44	331,588.09	394,947.12	....	138,344.09	395,118.17	53,880.11	9,026,098.76
1966...	9,833,794.60	9,444,203.41	416,815.56	365,713.69	....	196,464.64	196,473.42	929,731.37*	9,759,356.71
1967...	10,163,624.26	10,100,839.18	450,322.54	344,985.03	....	257,352.26	475,170.23	455,517.60*	9,739,704.08
1968...	10,272,149.84	11,047,451.48	507,574.31	344,760.76	....	264,925.61	1,362,711.60	42,224.33	8,419,216.81
1969...	10,207,368.61	11,872,793.76	550,995.35	330,858.81	....	172,086.20	2,375,193.11	2,644,896.03*	8,688,919.73
1970...	9,301,987.34	12,431,748.26	493,492.53	365,586.70		126,231.49	3,862,608.66	2,702,334.10*	7,528,645.17

**August 25, 1939 marks closing of books at time of installation of Seattle Transportation Commission.
†Surplus Adjustment of Prior Periods Re-allocated.
*Includes subsidies and grants, as follows:

1966—Capital grant from City of Seattle General Fund		$ 800,000.00
1967—Capital grant from City of Seattle General Fund		$ 400,000.00
1969—Capital grant from Federal Urban Mass Transportation Administration	$1,668,540.77	
Operating subsidy from City of Seattle General Fund	1,000,000.00	$2,668,540.77
1970—Demonstration grant from Federal Urban Mass Transportation Administration	287,113.36	
City of Seattle Household and Business Transit Taxes	910,450.00	
Operating subsidy from City of Seattle General Fund	1,600,000.00	$2,797,563.36

zone line. This was cheaper than some current Seattle fares, and cheaper by half than most Metropolitan Transit fares.[10]

The entire plan was projected to cost $95.2 million through 1980. This would not come entirely from the sales tax; the plan also assumed that significant help would come from the state and federal governments. Plus the 1980 Plan included a ridership goal that seemed, frankly, unrealistic. It projected 54.3 million riders per year by 1980. Seattle Transit was currently at about 30 million riders per year, and that number was still headed downhill.

Backers began to notice some promising shifts in public sentiment. In February 1972 Seattle voters overwhelmingly rejected the Bay Freeway and the R.H. Thompson Expressway. While not explicitly a vote in favor of mass transit, it certainly signified Seattle residents' opposition to new freeways. In fact, as the September 1972 Metro election approached, supporters became, if anything, over-confident. "The idea of a countywide transit system seemed so logical to me that I was surprised to find anyone opposing it," said Harvey Poll, a Seattle attorney who chaired the Citizens Transit Committee. "Actually, I feared that [voter] apathy would be our greatest enemy."[11]

He was wrong. The anti-Metro forces came out in force, and from a dizzying array of directions. The usual anti-tax forces that defeated the 1970 plan were revived, now with new names like Citizens Against Metro Taxes and Women Enraged Over New Taxes (together known as CAME and WENT), and the Society for Prevention of Excessive Nuisance Taxes (SPENT). This time, however, there was also opposition from the left. A group called Unite believed that Metro was undemocratic. They dismissed it as a "sewer company" trying to run transit and charged that the transit plan was tied in with highway interests. They wanted to ban autos from downtown altogether and use "people movers." They also charged that Metro would "subsidize suburban commuters at Seattle's expense."[12] Of course this was the exact opposite of what taxpayers in the suburbs were complaining about—that Metro was another example of the suburbs having to pay to fix Seattle's problems.

Once again the pro-trackless-trolley group COMET appeared, this time with a proposal to ignore the Metro plan and instead mandate that Seattle City Light take over Seattle Transit and build an all-electric system. This was ironic, since Metro had already chosen to keep the trackless trolleys, even to expand and modernize them, against the advice of some transit planners. The COMET idea wasn't merely annoying to Metro backers; it was downright alarming. COMET managed to place an initiative for its plan on the same September ballot, inevitably complicating the issue and possibly splitting the Seattle pro-transit vote.

On the other hand, the Citizens Transit Committee and the go-gos—the Municipal League and the League of Women Voters—were exceptionally well-organized and disciplined, creating an army of volunteers who were quietly building support for the proposal. As the Metro vote approached on September 19, 1972, these volunteers converged on the precincts most likely to vote yes. However, the city still hadn't recovered from its economic slump and supporters were privately resigned to another defeat, since they were asking county voters to increase their sales tax from 5 percent to 5.3 percent. Just before the vote, King County Executive John Spellman met with Jim Ellis to come up with a Plan B, on the assumption that defeat was inevitable. The two men privately agreed that King County would have to take over the transit system.

Then to the surprise of nearly everyone, King County voters gave a resounding "yes" to Metro, by a vote of 115,398 to 80,171. The win was credited to hard work, but Harvey Poll said the main reason was "we had a good product."[13]

An immensely relieved Jim Ellis called it a "historic go signal for transit."[14] The *Seattle Times* editorial page called the vote a "comeback for Metro transit" and said that "stripping down its rapid-rail transit plan … to a more modest all-bus model helped achieve the comeback win."[15] The COMET trolley proposal turned out to be a trolley crash, losing 68,562 to 27,442.

The startled (but happy) Metro officials had exactly 103 days to take over the entire county's transit system. "The ant woke up one day and discovered it had swallowed an elephant," said Chuck Collins, a Spellman aide who would eventually become the Metro Transit director.[16] Metro had only 248 employees and was preparing to take over a Seattle Transit system with more than 1,000 workers. The agency immediately put together a "100 Days" plan and began a nationwide search for a new transit director. One of the first things on the to-do list was settling on a name for the new system. Several awkward acronyms were suggested, such as KART for King Area Rapid Transit and SMART for Seattle Metropolitan Area Rapid Transit. A few silly names were also thrown around, such as Komet, Kismet, and Rainwater Highball. Eventually Metro settled, probably wisely, on the most mundane yet logical choice: Metro Transit.

A more difficult problem soon came to light: settling on a purchase price for all of the assets of Seattle Transit and the Metropolitan Transit Corporation. Nobody wanted a repeat of 1918, when the city vastly overpaid for the assets of the old Puget Sound Traction, Power & Light. One suggestion was to bring in an out-of-town expert to determine the price. This was immediately rejected. Instead, Metro and city officials negotiated all through the fall and winter, and eventually settled on a compromise price of $6.5 million for the Seattle Transit system. The price for the old Metropolitan Transit's suburban system was set at $1.2 million. These prices were well within what Metro had projected before the vote. There would be no repeat of 1918.

Seattle's city buses were rebranded as Metro Transit after the 1972 vote.

The Seattle Times recognized the 1972 vote as a "thumping victory" for Metro Transit, achieved in part because of Metro's "modest all-bus proposal."

Metro was now the proud owner of what Crowley called a "motley fleet of buses and trolleys."[17] Many of these buses were destined for the junk-yard within the next few years. Metro had applied for, and received, a federal Urban Mass Transit grant of $4.5 million, partly to purchase a new fleet of modern buses. At the same time, Metro was nego-tiating new contracts with both Seattle Transit and Metropolitan Transit employees. They were all guaranteed their jobs—or at least "comparable positions"—with Metro Transit. Not only did the company need these experienced drivers, they were bound by law to keep them.

The Seattle Transit System ceased to exist on the first day of 1973, when it was absorbed into Metro Transit.

The merger of the two organizations did not always go smoothly. Bus drivers had legitimate concerns about whether an organization with experience mostly in sewage and pollution control could understand their problems. "It was a shot-gun marriage," said Aubrey Davis, who would become a tireless proponent of regional mass transit and later the regional administrator of the federal Urban Mass Transportation Administration.[18] Yet Metro had the confidence that comes from innocence. Staff members learned as they went. "We were so naïve that it never occurred to us that we couldn't make it happen," said Metro's media director Penny Peabody.[19] The bus drivers began to realize that working for Metro had one main practical advantage: The new company had a steady stream of tax revenue to keep the system afloat. The Seattle transit system had been chronically needy since the day of its founding, so this was a pleasant new feeling.

Metro and its new employees worked together on making new routes and schedules. As the date for the changeover approached—January 1, 1973—drivers were issued new Metro uniforms. Metro Transit stickers were slapped on the old

Metro Transit buses were parading through downtown Seattle in 1975.

buses. Metro Director C.V. "Tom" Gibbs was apprehensive when he and his wife went out to the bus barns early on New Year's Day to see the drivers off. Fortunately, buses pulled out on time, the system ran well, and Gibbs breathed a sigh of relief because "we had climbed the mountain."[20]

A special committee immediately went to work on what we would today call branding. Kent Mayor Isabel Hogan, a stalwart transit supporter, headed the committee and asked bus riders to vote for two color schemes—blue-green-purple and brown-and-ocher. Since this was the era of earth tones, the brown-and-ocher "sunrise" livery won the vote.

Carle H. Salley, a Pittsburgh bus driver turned Allegheny County transit administrator, was chosen after a nationwide search to become Metro's first transit director. Salley had dreams beyond establishing a modern Metro fleet. He wanted to create a model bus—"a world bus" for the industry—to custom specifications.[21] This grand idea would cost far more than purchasing buses off the shelf. Metro applied for a federal Urban Mass Transit Administration grant of $86.3 million—"the largest sum ever requested for rubber-wheeled transit."[22] This grant would pay not only for park-and-ride lots and other system components, it would also fund buses that featured lower floors, bigger windows, more power, and, most importantly, the ability to bend in the middle. These "articulated" buses, which would allow 72 seats instead of 45, were familiar in Europe, but mostly unknown in the U.S.

Other new ideas continued to be encouraged. One idealistic young city worker proposed a startling idea: making the buses free. While that would never pencil out, other city officials began to warm to a modified plan: creating a free-ride zone in downtown Seattle. This might relieve downtown traffic congestion and help the retail core businesses. Mayor Uhlman liked the idea and pitched it to Metro, which liked it as well—as long as the city compensated Metro for it. Two obstacles still had to be overcome. The first—how to handle fares—was solved by having outbound riders pay when they left the buses, as opposed to the standard pay-when-you-enter rule. The second—a fair compensation price—was thornier. No one had any idea what the amount should be, leading the city negotiator to muse out loud, "That's the $64,000 question." As it turned out, that number

'WE PROBABLY COULD MAKE BETTER TIME IF IT WASN'T FOR THAT BUS UP AHEAD ～～ BUT THAT'S US !'
—THE SEATTLE TIMES

The Seattle Times *made fun of Metro's new articulated buses.*

Metro's articulated buses could seat 72 and accommodate a ridership spike in the mid-1970s.

was about the total cost of the old Dime Shuttle system, so Salley agreed on a $64,000 price for a one-year experiment. The "Magic Carpet" free downtown zone, as it was called, turned out to be a huge success. It remained a staple of Metro's system for decades until it finally ended in 2012, by which time Seattle's transit picture had been utterly transformed by light-rail.

The fare-free "Magic Carpet" zone in Seattle's central business district was a wildly popular innovation in the 1970s. It lasted until 2012.

A dedicated HOV lane made its debut in fall 1973 on State Route 520 in Redmond. Although this played a small role in easing East Side congestion, it had symbolic significance. Highways and transit, in Crowley's words, "had finally made peace with each other."[23] In 1973 the Arab oil embargo created an instant demand for more transit, as people scrambled to find enough gas for their cars. Total Metro ridership took an 8 percent leap, and the surge continued into the first part of 1974. Even though Metro had added new trips and new routes, it was still stuck with its old bus fleet, and director Salley was still writing the specifications for his revolutionary "world bus." One Metro board member quipped that Salley "preferred designing buses to operating them."[24] Another joked that Salley didn't want to put handrails on his buses "because nobody was going to have to stand" with his system.[25] The director finally came up with a plan to buy 605 new vehicles, including 200 articulated trolleys and buses, at a cost of $40 million. These huge articulated buses would allow fewer buses to carry more people. It would also cut labor costs.

This did not sit well with the Amalgamated Transit Union, which was also asking for higher wages and an eight-hour day, with two consecutive days off each week. The drivers walked out for two weeks in November 1974, and the impasse was finally broken through mediation. The drivers won their demands, but the Metro management also won new and stricter work rules, which it believed were vital for running a modern system. Ridership increased by another 2.7 million passengers in 1974, despite the strike. Metro moved ahead on its 1980 Plan by opening the first Freeway Flyer express bus station in Montlake. Meantime, the Metro Transit staff moved into its first permanent offices in the Pioneer Building at First Avenue and Yesler Street, a move that carried historical echoes. It was the same building that once housed Stone & Webster's Seattle Electric Company in the days when it ran the old trolley system.

On January 20, 1975, Metro scheduled what it expected to be a triumphant press conference. Officials were planning to open the bids for Salley's new $40 million "world bus" fleet. Reporters sat poised with their notebooks. TV lights flooded the room. An overflow audience watched as Aubrey Davis opened the first envelope. It was from General Motors, one of the companies that had been cooperating with Salley—or so he thought. The letter was read aloud: "We regret to inform you that we will be unable to submit a responsible bid because of our inability to comply with your specifications."[26] The company was unable or unwilling to build the kind of revolutionary buses Salley had envisioned. More envelopes were opened. More regrets were offered. Not one company offered a bid.

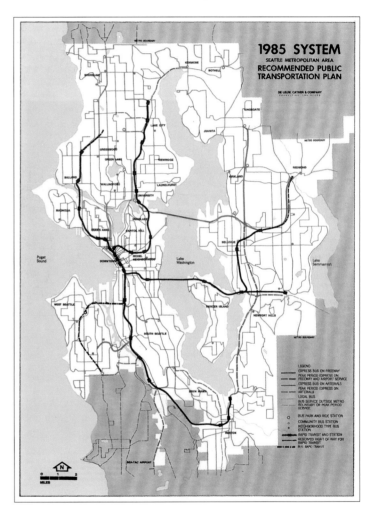

"There were moments of silence after the last envelope was opened," wrote Lane. "And then Aubrey Davis, chairman of the Metro Council Transit Committee said, 'I can only offer my deepest regret. … We have had conversations with manufacturers we thought would bid; we thought we would get responsive bids.'"[27] It was the most embarrassing moment in Metro's short history.

When the dust settled and the red drained from their faces, Davis said the council realized they would be unable "to shape the industry" the way they had dreamed.[28] Metro quickly drew up a new plan. They ordered 145 General Motors diesel coaches in 1975 and another 70 in 1976. They were standard coaches in most ways—but they were articulated. Their 72 seats were necessary to keep up with booming ridership.

The Metro Council soon asked for and accepted Salley's resignation. The bid fiasco was embarrassing, but by most other measures, Salley's tenure had been a rousing success. Ridership had gone up 23 percent over three years, and Metro Transit had become firmly established as a popular and efficient public service.

This De Leuw Cather plan, created in 1970, would have been up and running by 1985—if voters had approved the 1970 Forward Thrust proposal.

It was, by most measures, one of the most successful periods in the region's transit history. Salley was replaced in April 1976 by Chuck Collins, who had been instrumental in the transition to Metro Transit.

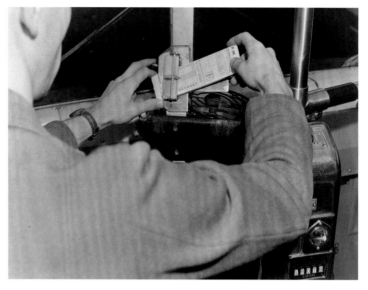

One of the first actions of Collins' tenure was a fare overhaul, promised in the 1972 vote and approved by the Metro Council in 1976. Instead of a baffling 30 zones, there would now be only two zones, inside and outside the Seattle city limits. Fares were 30 cents for the first zone, 20 cents for the other. Senior citizens and disabled riders had to pay only a dime. Transfers were good for any bus, any direction, within an hour. It was simpler for everyone—riders and drivers.

Funds that might have gone to a Seattle light-rail system instead went to Portland's MAX system, which opened in 1986.

A bus driver with Seattle Transit's transit slips.

One development would have huge implications decades later. The state finally agreed on a configuration for Interstate 90 that included what the Municipal League had negotiated years ago: two lanes reserved for transit in the middle of the freeway as it crossed Lake Washington. These middle lanes would be used initially as reversible traffic lanes to handle the morning and evening rush hours—yet were guaranteed for rail transit when needed in the future. At about the same time, a new Metro plan titled MetroTRANSITions, looking ahead to 1990, sought federal funds for rail transit planning through the Urban Mass Transit Act. Metro was shocked to learn in 1976 that the federal agency had awarded those rail-planning funds to Portland, Oregon, instead. When Davis asked why, the agency told him that they did not want to "lose the example" of what a city could do with a rubber-tired system. In other words, Metro was being punished for doing bus service too well.

The federal agency did, however, come through with money for new bus shelters, new buses, and new park-and-ride lots. When Metro Transit opened its Federal Way Park & Ride in 1979, it was filled to its 800-space capacity by the next day. Metro also committed to having a fully wheelchair-accessible fleet, the first in the nation to do so.[29]

Metro was also discovering the same thing Frank Osgood discovered back in the horse-drawn streetcar days: Stubborn downtown merchants had their own ideas about transit. Merchants had unstintingly resisted the idea of "contraflow" bus lanes—going in the opposite direction of the one-way auto traffic on Second and Fourth Avenues. They argued, with some justification, that this would deprive them of their loading zones, create a "wall of buses," and cause confusing headaches for downtown drivers. In other words, they thought it would be mess. Eventually, Metro backed down and settled for peak-hour transit lanes that went *with* the flow on those two streets.

In 1977 another contentious labor issue arose when Metro proposed an innovative way to increase service: part-time drivers. Metro was serious about meeting its goal of 54.3 million riders by the end of the 1970s, and its research showed that it could do so only if 40 percent of its drivers were part-time. The concept of part-time drivers was logical for an industry in which most of the customers were clustered in the morning and evening commutes. Few, if any, transit systems in the U.S. used part-time drivers. This proposal alarmed the union and a strike appeared imminent. However, at the beginning of 1978, Metro agreed to a 6 percent raise for drivers in exchange for the right to have 50 percent of them be part-time. It meant that Metro could now fill the HOV lanes during rush hours with large articulated buses drivon by part-time drivers.

Metro Transit touted a series of bus-service improvements in 1978 to keep up with increased demand.

Even Seattle's trackless trolleys were enjoying a resurgence. In 1977 Metro began modernizing and expanding its entire trolley system. It scrapped the old fleet, bought 109 new rubber-tired trolleys, and built 23 miles of new trolley routes over the next few years. Seattle was one of the few cities to keep trackless trolleys, largely because they were cleaner and quieter than diesel. They were also superior at climbing Seattle's steep hills. Today, trackless trolleys remain a prominent part of Metro's transit fleet—and a visible reminder of Seattle's trolley legacy.

The seemingly unattainable goal of 54.3 million riders by 1980 was exceeded a year early, as ridership hit 58.3 million in 1979. Then it rocketed to 66 million in 1980, partly because gasoline prices had once again spiked during the Iran hostage crisis, and partly because of Metro's innovations. Seattle's traffic was still bad—no question about that—but it would have been worse with those 66 million people in cars instead of buses. Metro had more than doubled ridership in its seven years of existence. "We built a transit system out of what had become dust," said Davis, looking back on those years.[30]

Despite success unprecedented in Seattle transit's previously troubled history, Metro was still in political and financial peril. In 1979 the King County Council put an initiative on the ballot to merge the King County government and Metro, which would spell the end of Metro as an independent agency. Metro supporters came up with an obvious and effective slogan—"If It Ain't Broke, Don't Fix It."[31] Voters evidently saw no need to "fix" the only agency in Seattle's history that had made transit work. They voted the initiative down by a nearly three-to-one margin. Even so, the merger idea was not quite dead.

In Snohomish and Pierce counties, the publicly owned transit systems had also expanded and come into the modern age. The Puget Sound region had grown into one giant Seattle-Tacoma-Everett megalopolis. Just as Seattle had discovered, a transit system limited to the city limits was insufficient for a sprawling population. In 1974 Everett voters twice turned down a proposal to create a countywide bus system. But in 1976 Snohomish County voters in Brier, Edmonds, Lynnwood, Marysville, Mountlake Terrace, Snohomish, and Woodway voted to create their own transit system, Community Transit. It still thrives today, alongside Everett Transit inside the city limits.[32]

In 1979 Pierce County voters approved the creation of Pierce Transit, a countywide system governed by its own municipal corporation, separate from the City of Tacoma. It served Tacoma and most of the surrounding area, and continues to do so to this day.[33]

This collection of logos encompasses more than eight decades of King County's transit history.

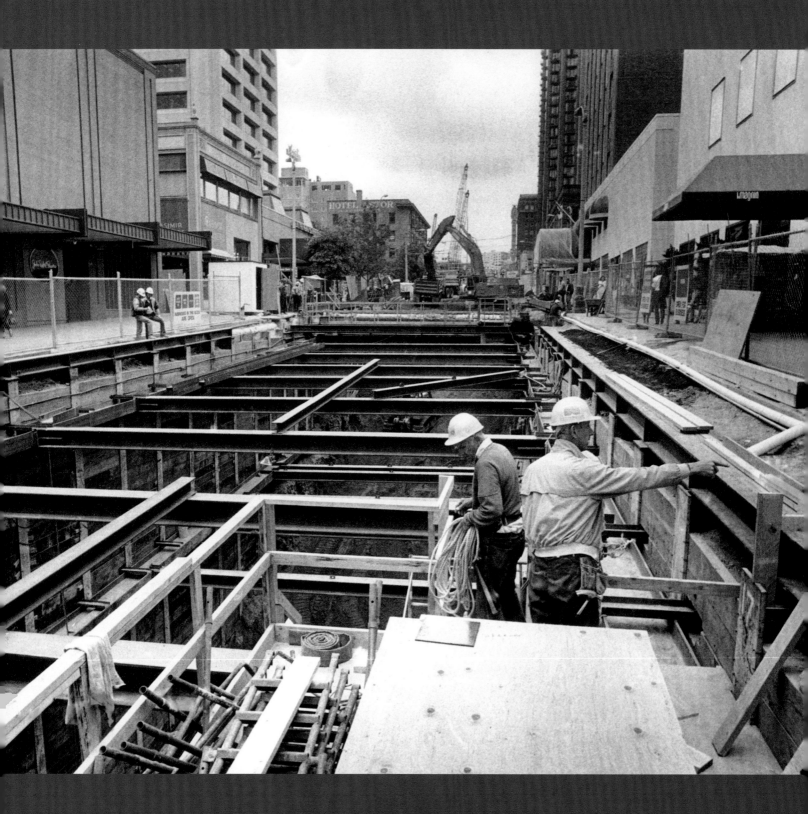

CHAPTER SIX

The Buses Go Underground

The 1970s had been, without question, the most successful decade in Seattle's transit history. In fact, it was too good to last. Another funding crisis was already brewing by 1980. More ridership did not equate to stronger financial health, because less than one-third of Metro's income came from bus fares.[1] The federal government was also moving away from support of mass transit, removing one of the region's funding props for capital projects. In May 1980 Metro tried to rebalance the books by raising fares to 50 cents (and 75 cents for multiple zones). This was not exactly popular, nor was it adequate. So in September 1980, Metro asked King County voters to raise their sales tax by another three-tenths of 1 percent. Voters rejected it by 53 percent to 47 percent. Metro immediately put the proposal back on the ballot in November 1980, and it finally passed by the thinnest of margins.[2] This tax increase would allow Metro to build a number of capital improvement projects over the decade—including what would become its signature project: a downtown bus tunnel.[3]

The funding crisis was averted, but equally thorny problems had no easy fix. Seattle's traffic—and that of the entire Puget Sound region—had become, put simply, a godawful mess. As impressive as Metro's ridership gains were, the system transported only a shocking 12 percent of the county's commuters.[4] Everyone else traveled by car.

Buses were stuck, all too often, in the same traffic jams as autos. The HOV lanes and the dedicated bus access ramps made a difference in a few places, but by the 1980s the entire suburban sprawl seemed to be tangled in tie-ups.

Left: Pine Street— and other downtown streets—were torn up during Seattle Bus Tunnel construction in 1987.

The phrases "Renton S-curves" and "Kennydale Hill" (on Interstate 405) were uttered on almost every radio traffic report—and never in a happy context. Farther afield, Everett had its "County Line" backups and "Dagmar Landing" slowdowns, while Pierce County had its Fife and Fort Lewis jams. The population was booming and most of the growth was in low-density suburbs like Auburn, which soon developed its own famous backups, and Bellevue-Redmond, where commuters into Seattle had a choice of only two bridges, both notorious choke points.

Heavy traffic on the 520 Bridge, circa 1989.

The MetroTRANSITions planners recommitted Metro to an all-bus strategy. They also announced a new goal of 120 million passengers by 1990. This did not seem totally fanciful. If ridership had shot up in the 1970s, why wouldn't it do the same in the 1980s? As it turned out, there were a couple of excellent reasons why it wouldn't. For one thing, the 1970s gains were driven partly by gasoline crises, which had subsided. For another, suburban commuters were no longer heading exclusively into downtown. They were heading from suburb to suburb—say, from Kent to jobs in Redmond. Designing bus routes to serve a vast, shifting host of "inter-suburban" commuters was complex and often impossible. Because of this, ridership actually dropped in 1981, for the first time in Metro's history. It dropped again in 1982, to 63.5 million. This was caused in part by yet another fare increase in 1982, which added a dime to fares for peak-hour riders. It was also because Metro desperately needed to solve two separate and equally difficult problems. The first was a suburban issue, which boiled down to this: It is nearly impossible to supply bus routes to every house if many of those houses are spread out over quarter-acre lots. The second problem was a familiar one dating back to 1884: the downtown Seattle dilemma.

In downtown, too many buses were crammed onto too few streets, with little sidewalk space to load and unload them. Second and Fourth avenues hosted a rolling parade of buses, which made about 420 trips through downtown every day during peak hours. This nose-to-tail line of Metro buses was now perceived, in Crowley's words, "to be part of the downtown congestion problem, not its solution."[5]

But what to do about it? That question sparked a three-year debate fiercer than any of the previous debates about downtown transit. At the beginning various factions proposed a number of solutions. Some suggested a buses-only trench, running below grade through downtown. This was derided as a "diesel ditch."[6] Others proposed the opposite of a trench— a raised "transit spine." Eventually, these ideas fell by the wayside leaving two viable concepts, each with its ardent advocates.

The first was to build two bus terminals north and south of downtown, where all of the buses would converge and unload passengers. Those passengers would then hop on circulating shuttles to get to their downtown destinations. Third Avenue would be made into an attractive transit mall. This was the concept supported by new Seattle Mayor Charles Royer. "I thought we could get more transit miles for the buck with a circulator system," he said.[7]

A Forward Thrust rail system would have been up and running by the mid-1980s, yet Seattle's transit system remained completely bus-centric.

These drawings convey two downtown Seattle bus mall concepts, circa 1980.

A New Waterfront Streetcar

While planning and design began on the Seattle Bus Tunnel, another project, which hearkened back to the earliest Seattle trolley days, was taking shape on the Seattle waterfront. In 1974 Seattle City Council member George Benson proposed install-ing a vintage electric streetcar line along the Seattle waterfront.

Why? Because it would provide a quick and easy way to get from one end of the long central waterfront to the other—and be a nostalgic tourist attraction. Benson was a self-pro-fessed transit history nut, who had never, his wife said, "gone to bed one night without a transit magazine in his hand."[8]

George Benson, left, and Seattle Mayor Charles Royer take the podium at the opening of the Waterfront Streetcar, 1982.

The concept was modest in the beginning. Benson wanted to use the old railway right-of-ways underneath the Alaskan Way Viaduct to build a 1.4-mile route. He found vintage 1927 streetcars in Australia at a bargain price: $5,000, plus $13,000 for shipping. Although Benson convinced Metro to go along with the idea, he soon discovered that his simple concept of buying a couple of vintage streetcars and putting them on existing tracks was naïve, to say the least. The railroad right-of-ways were enmeshed in legal issues. Five boarding stations had to be built, and they had to be wheel-chair accessible. The budget ballooned from just a few hundred thousand dollars to $3 million, and people began calling it "Benson's Folly."[9]

Benson persevered and walked the waterfront, drumming up support. He convinced merchants to embrace the idea, and they eventually agreed to create a local improvement district to fund the line. One downtown merchant

A crowd gathers for the official opening of the Waterfront Streetcar in May of 1982.

called it "the catalyst that will bring the whole waterfront together."[10] After years of complex planning and construction, the new trolley line opened on May 29, 1982, and was an immediate hit, carrying 277,000 passengers in its first year. Some riders were simply resting their tired feet as they toured the waterfront. Others, no doubt, were indulging in a nostalgic trip back to the days when the clang of the trolley pervaded Seattle. Washington Governor John Spellman said, "As someone who grew up with streetcars and cable cars in Seattle, it's good to see some of that coming back."[11]

In 1990 the line was extended east on Main Street directly into Pioneer Square, where it ended at the new bus tunnel portal. In a 1992 speech, Benson described the success of the project and the lessons he learned: "Do not assume that recreating or simulating an older system is as simple as it may sound. … Be especially alert to the layers of legal and regulatory arrangements in which older commercial rail lines may be entangled."[12] He had no way of knowing it at the time, but one more sad lesson was yet to be learned, 13 years down the tracks.

In 2005, after several years of waning ridership, the George Benson Waterfront Streetcar was shut down temporarily when its maintenance barn was demolished to make way for the Olympic Sculpture Park. By the time the park was finished, a massive waterfront redesign was in the works and there was no appetite within the city to fund the waterfront streetcar. The line's founder could no longer champion its cause—George Benson had died in 2004. As a result, the line never reopened.

Seattle's retro Waterfront Streetcar provided tourists and residents with a nostalgic feel for Seattle's streetcar legacy from 1982 to 2005.

The Metro Council was initially open to this idea. However, after studying both proposals, the council identified some major flaws. One was that all suburban bus riders would have to transfer at least once, and often twice, to get where they wanted to go. Metro's new executive director, Neil Peterson, hated the idea of making people transfer. "We felt strongly that those transfers were the *last* thing [people wanted]," said Peterson.[13] The Metro Transit chair at the time, Bob Neir, went even further, saying, "Nobody in King County should have to transfer more than once."[14] The Metro Council eventually leaned hard toward a second, and totally different, concept.

It was a transit tunnel, an idea that had been floated (halfheartedly) by Mayor Dore in the 1930s; again (fruitlessly) by County Engineer Evans in 1953; and again (presciently) by Forward Thrust in 1967. A tunnel under Third Avenue or Fourth Avenue would, of course, solve the problem of bus-clogged streets. One of the main arguments against it was a relatively simple one: Gasoline and conventional diesel buses create too many dangerous fumes to run in a tunnel, at least in large numbers. By the beginning of the 1980s, Metro believed the problem had finally been solved by technology, in the form of dual-propulsion buses. These buses were hybrids of diesel and electric power—and could operate like conventional diesel buses until they got to the tunnel. The buses could then hook up to a trolley pole and switch to electricity. Nobody in the U.S. had yet used these hybrids, but they were already operating successfully in Europe.

Mayor Royer was not to be swayed, declaring at one point to the Metro Council, "If you vote for a bus tunnel and we don't want one, there won't be one."[15] Peterson later recalled, "We got into a real tug of war. It was pretty brutal."[16] The Seattle City Council voted down the idea on October 6, 1983. But they had killed it only for a few weeks.

Within a month, several developments caused the City Council to change its mind. First, Metro offered to fund major improvements on Third Avenue. Royer was out campaigning for U.S. Senate following the death of Senator Henry "Scoop" Jackson, and he began rethinking his position. "I was against it; ambivalent; then for it," he later said.[17] The federal government, which would supply a large part of the funding for *any* transit plan, had also expressed its impatience with the city's vacillation over a bus tunnel. On October 31, 1983, the City Council reversed itself and voted unanimously for the bus tunnel. Metro Council formally endorsed it three days later and applied to the federal Urban Mass Transit authorities for funding.

Metro ridership continued to slip in the mid-1980s, hitting a low of 61.4 million in 1987. But thanks to a reinvigorated marketing campaign and a booming regional economy, it began creeping up again, reaching 73.4 million passengers by 1990. Still, this was not even remotely close to the 120 million riders projected by the Metro TRANSITions plan. It was, in fact, nowhere near the old Seattle Transit System's ridership in 1944. The reasons were legion: low gas prices, more dispersal of jobs to hard-to-serve industrial parks, inadequate HOV lanes, and the proliferation of far-flung housing developments. All of those non-bus commuters were driving their cars in an increasingly gridlocked metro area. A traffic congestion survey in 1990 gave Seattle the unhappy distinction of having the fourth-worst "commuter stress index" in the U.S.[18]

For the entire last half of the 1980s, the construction of the Seattle Bus Tunnel consumed Metro. It became mired in controversy, bickering, and narrow escapes. In other words, it was perfectly in keeping with Seattle's previous transit history.

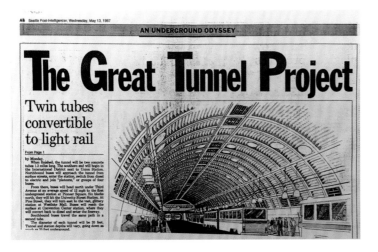

An artist's early vision of how a bus tunnel might look, circa 1983.

Money, of course, was one of the biggest problems. The estimated cost of the project (including some above-ground improvements) rose from $320 million to $416 million. About half of that would have to come from the federal government's Urban Mass Transit Act funds, but Seattle suddenly found itself with a lot less clout in Washington, D.C. By 1985 longtime Senators Scoop Jackson and Warren ("Maggie") Magnuson were gone, and the Urban Mass Transit administrator declared, "The tunnel is dead."[19]

As the Seattle Post-Intelligencer *noted in 1987, the Seattle Bus Tunnel was built with more than buses in mind. It also had light-rail potential.*

Luckily, the successors to Scoop and Maggie proved to have clout of their own. Senators Dan Evans and Slade Gorton went to work—along with U.S. representatives Mike Lowry and Norm Dicks—and the Urban Mass Transit director reversed course. The tunnel was not dead, after all. In fact, eventually Urban Mass Transit would declare it to be the "most cost-effective transit project" in the nation.[20] But there were more U-turns to come. The UMTA at one point complained that the project had "a ton of fat."[21] The cost eventually ballooned to $444 million and beyond, and downtown property owners had to approve a $40 million improvement district assessment. Yet the UMTA eventually came through with the necessary funds.

The tunnel's route and design still had to be hashed out. Should it go underneath Third Avenue or Fourth Avenue? There were advocates for both, but engineers ended the debate when they determined that Third Avenue would be $4 million cheaper. Should the underground loading platforms be high or low? Low was considered to be cheaper and friendlier to passengers, especially those in wheelchairs.

One early design decision proved to have repercussions years later. The tunnel was designed to accommodate rail, assuming that rail transit would be resurrected someday. George Benson, always a fan of rail, had pushed hard for this, and so did Mayor Royer, who had come around to endorsing the tunnel idea in part *because* of its future compatibility with rail. "I was persuaded by Jim Ellis, who said we would need the tunnel for rail service," said Royer. "He said downtown would be the most expensive mile of rail, and why not do it now?"[22]

Detractors staged last-ditch attempts in 1986 and 1987 to stop the project—citing high costs and dropping bus ridership—but the giant boring machines began their slow, laborious work in March 1987. Two parallel tubes were created from Union Station on the south end to Westlake Mall (being newly renovated as part of the overall plan) and Convention Place (beneath the Washington State Convention and Trade Center) on the north. In the process, workers uncovered one fascinating piece of Seattle's transit past deep beneath the Pioneer Square station: the giant iron cable wheel from the old Lake Washington Cable Railway. It is now on display in Pioneer Square Station, reminding commuters of Seattle's deep transit roots.

The so-called Mighty Mole gnawed its way beneath downtown Seattle.

A tunnel worker later made news when he attached a hose to a wrong connection, causing every toilet in the King County Courthouse to erupt like Old Faithful. This caused a lot of mess, not to mention mirth, but no lasting damage. The Seattle Bus Tunnel's more serious scandal came in 1989 from a completely unexpected direction—South Africa. At the time South Africa was still ruled by an apartheid government, and some U.S. institutions—including Metro—had enacted

Workers prepare the boring machine for its underground journey in 1987.

a prohibition of goods "manufactured or fabricated" there. When a local African-American activist discovered that Metro had purchased $480,000 worth of granite quarried in South Africa for Westlake Station, people were shocked. Ron Sims, a King County Council member, later to become King County Executive, said at the time, "Buying products from South Africa is like buying products from Nazi Germany."[23]

The Metro Council, which had initiated the ban, was not pleased. This "Granitegate" scandal would only get worse, after it turned out that some Metro staffers had known the granite was from South Africa all along, but had split hairs by arguing that the granite had been dressed and polished in Italy—making it, somehow, Italian. Sims later said that this was a prime example of a "certain arrogance" that Metro demonstrated in those days. He called it "one of the more deeply stupid and offensive things that I've ever seen done." Metro canceled the order and specified replacement granite. Metro Director Alan Gibbs, who did not know about the granite's origin, apologized in writing to an infuriated Metro Council. The situation was further inflamed when, three days after the apology, a worker noticed that some of the new dual-propulsion buses had replacement windows with stickers saying, "Made in South Africa." The entire incident was an embarrassment for Metro and led, indirectly, to the exit of Gibbs in 1989. He was certainly not entirely to blame for Granitegate, but his exit served to quiet the agency's many critics.

The Seattle Bus Tunnel opened for regular service on September 15, 1990—on time and within 5 percent of its original budget. This prompted the construction manager to boast that "this is absolutely unprecedented for a transit project in the United States."[24] Unfortunately, two big problems arose after the grand opening. First, the tunnel leaked. The leaks did not prove to be serious—they just made the

benches damp—but it prompted *Seattle Times* columnist Rick Anderson to crack, "You'd think that after paying $459 million for something, it shouldn't leak."[25]

The larger problem: The fancy new dual-propulsion buses were, more or less, lemons. This was a relatively new technology and Metro had received bids from only two companies. One was from Neoplan, a firm that had built a number of dual-propulsion buses that were successfully operating in Essen, Germany. The other was from Breda, an Italian company with no prior experience building these kinds of buses.[26] Unfortunately, Neoplan dropped out of the running because it

The specialized Breda buses were intended to be the solution to the "buses-in-a-tunnel" problem, but they ended up contributing to it.

The 1980s were dominated by one overriding transit debate: whether and how to build the Seattle Bus Tunnel, which opened in 1990.

was unable to provide the necessary performance bond. So Metro accepted the Breda bid. One Metro transit planner later described the ensuing process to be "like designing an elephant by committee."[27]

As soon as the 236 Breda buses were delivered, the problems were obvious. They weighed too much, even when empty. Their engines and transmissions were unreliable. During the first year, they averaged a service call every 1,000 miles. Parts had to be imported from Italy. Metro technicians and welders were able to keep these $450,000 buses operating, but before the decade was out, a quarter of the Breda buses were averaging one rebuilt engine *each year*.[28] Metro wisely canceled the second batch of 236s. Fortunately, by the time Metro needed more buses, technology had advanced so much that it was able to buy battery-powered hybrids that did not need wires or trolley poles at all. They could switch instantly from diesel to electricity.

Overall, the tunnel worked mostly as intended, removing more than 500 buses per day from the downtown streets. However, it never really swept all of the buses out of downtown. The tunnel simply didn't have that kind of capacity, said Greg Nickels, who was on the King County Council and Metro Council at the time. Buses had to be platooned in the correct running order on both ends of the tunnel, which meant they often had to wait to enter the tunnel, while impatient riders could do nothing but fidget. A number of buses still ran up above, on the downtown streets, but no longer was the wall of buses impenetrable. "The logistics of it were never

A Metro bus makes a test run in the Seattle Bus Tunnel in 1989.

perfect, but it certainly did improve the capacity and scheduling of the buses through that area," said Nickels. By opening up another huge transit conduit through downtown, the tunnel vastly increased overall transit capacity and gave riders a more "predictable ride," in Nickels' words. In the long run, however, the tunnel's enduring contribution had nothing to do with buses. It had to do with a point Jim Ellis had once made to Charles Royer: The tunnel provided a pre-built corridor for the next development coming down the tracks. That is, tracks.

Before the region reentered the rail era, Metro would have to go through a fundamental and wrenching change. In the early 1990s, Metro remained highly regarded by its peers—it was named several times as the best major transit system in the U.S. by the American Public Transportation Association. It was also well regarded by commuters, at least by Seattle historical standards. But the tunnel snafus had roughed up Metro's image, and at the beginning of the decade, doubts were even being raised about whether Metro was a truly democratic institution. The Metro Council, which had started with 15 members, had grown to an unwieldy 45, as more King County towns and cities were incorporated. What's more, the Metro Council was a federated system, with smaller towns having the same voting power as the bigger cities. A recent U.S. Supreme Court decision in a New York case had raised the possibility that such federated councils did not represent every taxpayer equally.

Nickels agreed. "A couple of colleagues and I thought that the federated system violated the one-person, one-vote principle, and so we went to the American Civil Liberties Union and we got them to file suit, based on the similar case in New York," recalled Nickels, who was a Metro Council representative from the county. The ACLU asserted that the Metro Council gave Auburn and Kent, for instance, one representative per 26,000 voters, while giving Seattle, Bellevue, and unincorporated areas one representative per 144,000 voters.[29] Federal Judge William Dwyer ruled in September 1990 that the Metro Council did, indeed, dilute the votes of some of its citizens. He ordered it fixed by April 1992.

County and city officials hastily convened a committee to come up with a new plan. Their recommendation: Metro and King County should be merged under an expanded King County Council. Under this plan, Metro Transit and Metro's water quality division would be transferred intact to the county and maintained as "discrete departments of King County government."[30] This plan required voter approval, with some unusual conditions. It needed at least a 50 percent yes vote both inside and *outside* the Seattle city limits. The plan went to the ballot on November 5, 1991, and Seattle approved it with a 56 percent yes vote. But the rest of the county voted it down, with only 47 percent approval. This killed the entire merger proposal. Metro was still alive, yet it clearly could not linger indefinitely.

The court's April 1992 deadline came and went while officials floated new ideas, and Dwyer issued a new deadline of April 1993. Another merger plan was proposed. This one called for a 13-member King County Council, which would assume all of Metro's functions. It went to voters on November 3, 1992, and that's when Metro's fate was sealed. This time the merger passed relatively easily in both the city and the county, probably because voters figured it was better than a court-imposed solution. The official Metro-King County union was consummated on January 1, 1994, and since that day, the transit system's official name has been King County Metro Transit—even though most commuters still refer to it as Metro Transit, or simply, Metro. It became a department of King County, reporting to the county executive.

While the buses of King County Metro kept rolling, impetus was inexorably building toward a regional transit idea that was both new, in the sense

A Seattle Times cartoonist captured Seattle's seemingly endless loop of transit debate in 1993, while the Monorail whooshes overhead.

that it did not currently exist, and old, in the sense that it hearkened back to the early clang-clang-clang days. Rail was a concept that had ridden in the back of the bus in Puget Sound since the Forward Thrust crash. "After the 1970 defeat, mass transit and light-rail were political road kill," recalled Nickels. "People wouldn't use those words in the same sentence." Yet the idea had never truly died among transportation planners for one exceptionally good reason: capacity. Rail was "really the only solution to get the capacity we were talking about, … over 100,000 riders a day," said Jared Smith, who would become the Regional Transit Manager for the City of Seattle. String a few light-rail cars together and you can carry hundreds of passengers at once, with one operator. A bus simply can't match that, even an articulated one.

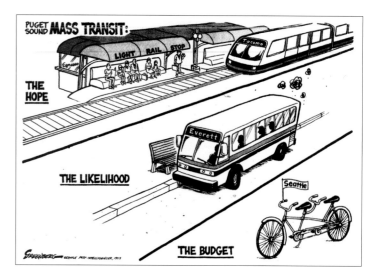

A Seattle PI cartoon *provided an astute reality check in 1993.*

A revival of rail had been foreshadowed in 1988, when King County Councilmembers Greg Nickels, Ron Sims, and Cynthia Sullivan put an advisory vote on the ballot asking this question: "Should public funding and development of a rail transit system to serve the residents of King County be accelerated so that service in King County can begin before the year 2000?" A 68 percent majority voted a resounding yes. A yes vote was easy when it did not include an actual tax hike or even a cost estimate. Still, it showed that King County loved rail—at least the idea of rail. "I think the people were well ahead of the politicians in saying, 'You know, we've got to have transit, and it's got to be *mass* transit,'" recalled Nickels.

This vote also encouraged the Puget Sound Council of Governments to push rail transit to the forefront of its Regional Transit Plan—a key change for a group that had formerly been lukewarm at best on rail. Metro planners, too, had long realized that Seattle's transportation system would require higher capacities in the long run, and that rail was an obvious option. In 1989 the Metro Council had approved a $15 million study of a 101-mile light-rail proposal.[31]

This triggered an anti-rail outcry almost immediately, with the same familiar arguments from decades past: rail is too expensive, not enough people will ride it, and it hasn't worked in other cities. These arguments had some merit. It *was* expensive, and even the most ardent rail advocates were aware that the Puget Sound area had more than the usual number of rail obstacles.

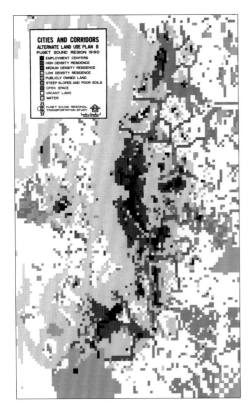

CITIES AND CORRIDORS
ALTERNATE LAND USE PLAN B
PUGET SOUND REGION 1990
- EMPLOYMENT CENTERS
- HIGH DENSITY RESIDENCE
- MEDIUM DENSITY RESIDENCE
- LOW DENSITY RESIDENCE
- PUBLICLY OWNED LAND
- STEEP SLOPES AND POOR SOILS
- OPEN SPACE
- VACANT LAND
- WATER

PUGET SOUND REGIONAL
TRANSPORTATION STUDY

Mass transit is about more than buses and trains, it is about fundamental issues of land-use and population density. From the beginning, transit has determined how the Puget Sound region has grown.

"The glaciers of 15,000 years ago left us with a blessing and a curse," said Smith. "Blessing us with magnificent bodies of water and hills and mountains nearby, and the same glaciers left us the hills that are impassable by rail. The only alternative is to tunnel underneath and that's a great expense. And so that's why Seattle was one of the few major metropolitan areas that hadn't implemented a regional rail mass transit system yet. We knew it wasn't ever going to be easy, and it was never going to be inexpensive relative to Portland and San Diego and other areas."

People were increasingly fed up, and *Seattle Times* columnist Peyton Whitely channeled their anger in a cry from the heart on October 28, 1990. "Don't tell me about cost-effectiveness," wrote Whitely. "It's not important. Anything's more cost-effective than what we have. ... In the next 10 years, we're going to spend about $100 billion on our car-based system. ... That money will accomplish nothing. There will be virtually no new roads in this area. Our commuting times will be longer. The invisible erosion of our freedoms will continue. ... Nearly invisibly, your freedom, your mobility has been taken away, a few minutes at a time, year by year. We can continue to waste that money. Or we can take part of it and risk building something permanent, something that has a chance of making a significant difference. Too big a risk? Too bad. Courage counts."[32]

Walt Crowley, wrapping up his history of Seattle transit in 1993, expressed a similar frustration when it appeared that the same old Seattle gridlock was growing worse on both highways and in local politics. "The story of public transportation in metropolitan Seattle is far from over. Something will be done to solve today's problems, maybe not tomorrow, or the day after, but eventually. It will probably be too little and come too late, and the citizens of the future will look back on our era and say, 'Why didn't they see this coming?' The answer is, we did."[33]

With this kind of public sentiment, support was building not just for a rail system but for a truly regional rail system. The megalopolis had grown so large that the traffic problems engulfed three counties—King, Pierce, and Snohomish—and spurred a demand for regional planning. One of the most strongest proponents of a light-rail solution was State Representative Ruth Fisher from Pierce County, the chair of the House Transportation Committee. "She was the one who understood that we as a region were going to have to go beyond the things we've done in the past," recalled King County Executive Dow Constantine, who served with her in the state legislature. She spearheaded the High Capacity Transit Act in 1990, followed that same year by the Growth Management Act and in 1992 by the Regional Transit Authority Act. All three bills would play a central role in the creation of what would later be called Sound Transit—and why Sound Transit's boardroom would later be named the Ruth Fisher Boardroom. "Simply put, she was the Mother of Sound Transit," said Sound Transit Board Chair John Ladenburg. "Her legacy and her memory is in every mile of track we build and every mile our trains and buses travel."[34]

Fisher's Regional Transit Authority Act, signed into law in 1992 as RCW 81.112, was the act that truly gave birth to the agency. It authorized elected officials from two or more counties to form a Joint Regional Policy Committee. This committee could, theoretically, do the following: create a Regional Transit Plan; create a Regional Transit Authority taxing district; and finally, ask voters to approve that plan and pay for a brand spanking new regional mass transit system.[35]

This is exactly what would eventually happen—but, this being mass transit in Puget Sound, it wasn't easy and it wasn't quick.

By 1995, Puget Sound area commuters were becoming more and more convinced that the train had left without them.

CHAPTER SEVEN

The Birth of Sound Transit

· · · · · · · · · · · · · · ·

For the first time in history, the transit agencies of King, Snohomish, and Pierce counties—Metro, Community Transit, Everett Transit, and Pierce Transit—came together, signed agreements with each other, and began working toward a common transit solution. They formed a Joint Regional Policy Committee, as allowed under the Regional Transit Authority Act. This was a historic first, said Nickels, if only because the three counties had "never done anything together— everything stopped at the county lines." The committee then authorized the creation of a Regional Transit Plan, which would map out the future of the entire region's transit system. This would be the master document for all of Puget Sound's transit future. Even Metro folded all of its long-range planning into the Regional Transit Plan.

The Joint Regional Policy Committee laid down four basic goals for a transit system—with only one that seemed to be directly related to transit: ensure the ability to move around the region. The other three goals addressed issues that reflected transit's inevitable role as a driver of urban and suburban development. They include preserving communities and open spaces, improving the region's economic vitality, and safeguarding environmental quality.[1]

The key questions were rail or buses? Tracks or freeways? The latest studies by the Puget Sound Council of Government had come to an eye opening conclusion. Even with 18 new highway lanes, congestion would *still* be five times worse by 2020.[2] With that in mind, the Regional Transit Plan planners identified three options. The first was a more-buses option, along with more ride-share services, and more HOV lanes. The second was also bus-centric, but kicked it up a notch with more elaborate HOV lanes and more dedicated freeway ramps for buses.

Left: Union Station in Seattle began as a railroad hub in 1911 and was reborn in 1999 as the Sound Transit headquarters. It is pictured here in 2001.

111

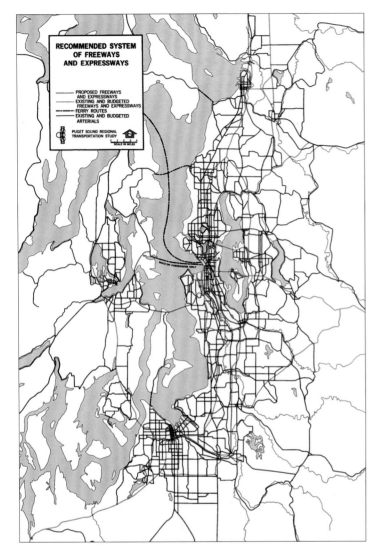

A 1990 Puget Sound Regional Transportation Study mapped out current highway routes and proposed many more.

The third option was rail: a 126-mile light-rail system from Tacoma to Everett, on both sides of Lake Washington, along with heavy "commuter rail" on existing railroad tracks from Seattle to Tacoma. Planners concluded it was the only option that had the massive capacity to give Puget Sound commuters the ability to actually bypass freeway gridlock.

Despite its logic, this option was the most contentious. It would be the most expensive, estimated at $11.5 billion (and that would prove low). It was also considered an almost radical idea for a generation that had grown up in the auto/freeway era. There was some irony in this, considering that the proposed rail option was essentially a throwback to 1900.

The Regional Transit Project plan, prepared by a consultant team led by Parsons Brinckerhoff and finalized in 1992, was a compromise. The light-rail system was scaled back to 88 miles. And $1.2 billion was allocated for traditional bus-based improvements, such as HOV lanes and transit ramps. The full price tag was around $13.2 billion. The reaction was predictable. The scaled-back rail map skipped some suburban cities, such as Renton and Bothell. People there wondered why they should pay for a system that didn't serve them. Meanwhile, erstwhile transit planners came out of the woodwork with their own, sometimes fanciful, plans, including one that envisioned the return of the classic Stone & Webster-era streetcars. This was never going to happen. The old-fashioned trolley had been left behind by smoother, faster light-rail cars.

A vocal and influential anti-rail group, led by Bellevue mall developer Kemper Freeman Jr., issued a 56-page blast titled, "Heading Down the Wrong Track." The Freeman family had long been the most influential anti-rail force in the region. Freeman's father, Kemper Freeman Sr., had helped defeat the Forward Thrust bonds in 1968 and 1970. His son was just as determined to stop the Regional

Transit Project's rail plan. Freeman Jr. believed that, when it came to the public's transportation preferences, "the automobile has won."[3] For evidence he could gaze over his Bellevue Square shopping mall and its 5,500 parking spaces. The *Seattle Times* also emerged as an editorial opponent of rail transit. On April 25, 1993, the editorial page urged the Joint Regional Policy Committee to "scratch its ambitious rail plan." "Quit stewing about pricey rail," said the editors. "… Rail might be exciting or sophisticated, but the region cannot afford that gilded piece of the Regional Transit Project."[4]

Despite these ominous signs, support from local governments remained strong. Leaders were acutely aware that the region had to do something, and quickly. Their constituents wanted forceful action on an issue that profoundly affected their lives, every single day. "They were very, very frustrated at how slow the political system was working to address what they saw as a core need," said Nickels. In mid-1993, all three county councils approved the Central Puget Sound Regional Transit Authority. The vote was unanimous in the Pierce and Snohomish county councils, but was a squeaker in King, by a one-vote margin.

Some of the supporters on the King County Council, such as Bruce Laing, had been preaching the gospel of mass transit for years. Others, like Ron Sims, had required years of persuasion. Sims, a Democrat, began his tenure on the council as a believer in the auto. He drove to work and assumed everyone else wanted to drive, too. He credits his conversion to Laing, a Bellevue Republican and an "honest and decent visionary," in Sims' estimation. One day, Laing took Sims aside and said, "I know you feel strongly about education."

So he asked Sims to take a look at the Metro ridership statistics for the bus route from Sims' home in the Rainier Valley to the University of Washington. "I was sold after that, because I didn't realize so many people from southeast Seattle were taking the bus out to the University of Washington," said Sims.

"That was how they got there. ... I locked in on that. I just went boom. I had no idea. I saw the bus was packed." From that point on, Sims realized that mass transit was not just about transportation—it was also about "something as fundamental as access to a major educational institution"—and helping make college affordable to people in his own Rainier Valley community. The Regional Transit Authority (RTA) was born.

Before it could evolve into Sound Transit, it had some painful growing up to do. Laing, who became RTA's first chair, said that the authority's first challenge was to answer two questions: "What should the initial plan be, and how much should we bite off?" Some of the elected officials were naturally wary about a tax issue reaching into the billions. "There were a lot of people who, having been involved in the Forward Thrust mass transit elections, said, 'It's too late. We've lost it.' And I just found that very frustrating, because the same arguments could have been made in 1911 with the Bogue Plan," said Nickels. Young leaders like Nickels believed that the failures of the past made it even more imperative that the plan be aggressively pursued today. "Now I tell people that I wish it had been passed in 1968 or 1970—but my life would have been *so* much less interesting," said Nickels.

The RTA board tried to overcome some of the opposition by splitting the Regional Transit Plan into two phases. The first phase, to be presented to voters in 1995, would be a $6.7 billion plan that included a smaller light-rail system that would run from Tacoma to Lynnwood, but not all the way to Everett, a fact which spawned vigorous opposition from the Everett mayor and city council—and even a lawsuit. Over on King County's Eastside, opposition was just as vociferous. Kemper Freeman Jr. was, in Nickels' words, "upholding the family tradition and opposing mass transit and other things that are progressive."

The Seattle Times skewered the region's modest ambitions for light-rail in 1991.

The opposition, however, had its own problems. The only idea they had to offer in exchange was more highways and more buses. "But largely, they didn't have an alternative, which was to our advantage, in that we had this specific alternative to present," said Nickels. Even the *Seattle Times*, clearly no fan of light-rail, urged a yes vote on the grounds that an imperfect plan was better than none at all. And, unlike those Forward Thrust votes, this was a sales tax increase, requiring only 50 percent approval.

Unfortunately, the RTA would squander any advantage it had by making what appears, in retrospect, to be a fundamentally flawed political decision. It put the vote on a March 1995 special-election ballot. "That was stupid," said Nickels, with the benefit of 20-plus years of hindsight. "We should have been on a general election ballot, and in fact we should *always* be on a presidential ballot." Young people, he said, vote in presidential elections, and young people are the voters who will live long enough to see the benefits of such a giant, long-term capital project. For all of those reasons, the RTA's 1995 plan was destined for the same depressing fate as Forward Thrust.

Voters trounced it on March 14, 1995, with a 53 percent no vote. A *Seattle Times* poll showed that voters generally liked the plan but did not like the high price tag. "It was more than the electorate could swallow," said Laing. Analysis of the precincts showed that the measure won in Seattle, was close in King County overall, and was "just killed in Snohomish and Pierce," according to Nickels. "We were less popular [in Snohomish County] than Prohibition, and in Everett, that's pretty bad," he said. Nickels and other backers weren't sure they could come up with a plan that would ever satisfy voters from every county. Light-rail immediately became anathema in the State Legislature and among many Republicans.

Snohomish County executive Bob Drewel refused to let the rapid transit dream fade away after the 1995 defeat. He helped lead the drive for a vote on a new plan in 1996: Sound Move.

The Highline Times *in South King County had a premonition that the 1995 Regional Transit Authority vote would be an uphill battle.*

Before long, however, a new champion emerged from an unlikely quarter. Snohomish County executive Bob Drewel took over as chair of the RTA board, and he was determined to come up with a new plan and try again. He understood why Everett had been so vehement in its opposition, yet he had become convinced that it was high time that his county faced up to its regional responsibilities. Commuters poured into his county to jobs at Boeing and the Port of Everett. They also poured out of his county to jobs in Seattle and the Eastside. The idea that Snohomish County residents "could enjoy everything we had and it would go on forever, without some [transit] investment," was simply not true, said Drewel. Politically, he faced a tough sell, but in the end, he believed he could persuade leaders and voters in his county to step up to their responsibilities.

Drewel and other influential leaders, including Seattle City Council Member Martha Choe, went out and asked the hard questions: "What didn't you like about the plan? What can we do to come up with a plan you'd be willing to vote for?" Laing retired after the 1995 vote, but he looked on with admiration as his former colleagues simply refused to let the idea die. "It took a lot of guts and a lot of foresight to just say, 'We're not going to let the steam go out of this,'" he said.

It was not easy. "We worked this *hard*, and I will emphasize that point," said Drewel. "More than that, we had to bust some myths." For instance, opponents were fond of saying that it would be more expensive to build a light-rail system than to put every commuter in a Cadillac and feed them breakfast. Yet Drewel began to notice a "maturation" process taking hold in public opinion—"a coming of age," he said, both in his county and throughout the region.

When this Interstate 5 interchange was being built in 1964, new freeway construction was the preferred transportation solution. By the 1990s, people increasingly questioned this.

Dave Earling, an original RTA board member who would become Edmonds mayor and an influential Sound Transit board chair, had to go through a version of that maturation process himself. When he first arrived on the board, he said, he was "a real skeptic about the value of rail transit." He was a bus guy, a member of the Community Transit Board in Snohomish County. But over time he came to understand the region's geographic challenges. "We didn't have the land mass, the flat areas, to simply add more lanes," he said. The people, Earling concluded, "wanted sensible transportation options and that includes light-rail."[5]

"It was an educational process," said Nickels. "People weren't willing to say yes until they understood more about what it was, what it would do, and what it would cost them." Meanwhile, the RTA was dangling by a thread. It had no revenue, "not a dime," said Nickels, who was then the finance chair. The agency had to borrow money from King County to stay afloat. It reduced its staff to a bare-bones 22. "I started every one of my finance committee reports with, 'We have no money,'" said Nickels.

The board was hanging on for one last try: another vote in November 1996, on the presidential election ballot. Mike Vaska, a Seattle civic leader, issued a warning: "They know this is their last shot, so they better make it a good one."[6] Bob White, the RTA's executive director, unveiled a new, much smaller plan in January 1996, and it was refined and debated until May 1996, when the final package was announced. Drewel, Nickels, and the rest of the board were desperately trying to apply the lessons of the 1995 vote and realized they had to make some compromises. The board shortened the plan from 20 years to 10. They reduced the light-rail part of the package to 22 miles, so that it started near SeaTac Airport, not

Tacoma, and ended near the University of Washington (or possibly Northgate, depending on cost), but not all the way to Lynnwood. They added much more bus and HOV infrastructure. Crucially, they dropped the price tag to $3.9 billion.[7] They even added some marketing savvy, giving the proposal a catchy name: Sound Move.

The Sound Move proposal also addressed a serious concern among some voters: that their particular region was not getting enough out of the project. The solution was called "sub-area equity" and, according to Nickels, it proposed that "all of the money would go back into the different regions in proportion to what came in." Nickels believed that subarea equity was a mistake as a policy matter, but politically necessary. Each area would get something in the new package roughly equivalent to its tax contribution. The subareas were defined as Snohomish County, Pierce County, Seattle, South King County, and East King County. Since Snohomish and East King County, for instance, were not on the light-rail route, they would get more regional express buses, more park-and-rides, and more HOV entrance and exit ramps. Subarea equity would cause complicated issues down the road—it has been "cussed and discussed" ever since, said Drewel—but it succeeded in disarming one of the main arguments against the plan: There's nothing in it for us.

The bottom line, said Drewel, was that subarea equity "got us to the vote." On November 5, 1996, the "last shot" chance for light-rail had arrived. The Sound Move election was every bit as momentous as the Forward Thrust votes of 1968 and 1970—and backers were acutely aware of how those votes turned out.

In 1996, voters were asked to approve this $3.9 billion transit plan, dubbed Sound Move. The measure passed, reversing a long losing streak and paving the way for Sound Transit.

Still, they felt optimistic heading into the vote for several reasons. Snohomish County officials—led by Drewel—not only backed the proposal, but had campaigned feverishly for it. Also, the Kemper Freeman Jr. arguments seemed to be falling on deaf ears this time, even on the Eastside. The *Seattle Times* editors urged a yes vote and said, "opponents are running out of ideas and credibility."[8]

Another historic turning point had arrived, this time, without the bitter aftertaste. After decades of frustration, light-rail supporters had an election to celebrate. Sound Move not only passed; it won by a landslide. The bill had 60 percent approval in King County, as well as a solid majority in Snohomish County, and a

slim one in Pierce County. It even won handily in Bellevue. "I think we got it right," said a vastly relieved White. Even Rob McKenna, the most vocal opponent on the King County Council, admitted that the voters were saying, "Let's get on with it."[9] Looking back on that momentous night, Drewel said, "I think it was the right issue at the right time—and if we had failed there, I don't think we would have the stars lined up for a number of years."

It was the birth of Sound Transit, even though it would not acquire that name quite yet. The *Seattle Times* editorial page provided a word of foreboding when it said, "Ugly tales of cost overruns will doom any dreams to move RTA beyond a starter system."[10] However, the general mood, after so many Seattle transit failures, was buoyant. Nickels remembered his elation on election night. "It was great, it was just

A year after the Sound Move victory, Sound Transit was beginning—slowly— to get the wheels rolling. Nobody knew how bumpy the ride would turn out to be.

wonderful," he said. "We felt like we had really accomplished something, … something big. And, of course, the realization came pretty quickly: Oh my God, now we've got to actually build this thing!"

Jared Smith was one of the people who went to work right away. He was a Seattle native (whose parents had been involved in the Forward Thrust efforts), a civil engineer, and was working as a manager for Parsons Brinckerhoff, Quade & Douglas Inc., a key consulting group for the RTA. In fact, some of his colleagues were immediately hired by the RTA to augment its meager staff. Smith took an alternate track and was appointed by Mayor Norm Rice as the City of Seattle's first Regional Transit manager—or "transit czar." The city—actually *all* of the cities in the region—would have to work hand-in-glove with the RTA in designing and building the system. "Seattle leaders wanted to organize the city to mirror, or complement, how Sound Transit was being organized," said Smith. "… We decided to create a new office as an extension of the mayor's office, and we would hand pick staff from [other] departments." Their task was nothing less than implementing the light-rail and commuter rail programs inside Seattle. It involved, among other things, major alignment decisions and land use changes at each of the 14 light-rail stations from southeast Seattle to Northgate.[11]

At the time, the city was known for having the "process" be the "product," as Smith delicately puts it. For such a massive project, that would not be sufficient. "Getting things done" had to be the product, said Smith. "The charge that I had from the city council and the mayor was to help expedite

Seattle prepares for regional transit system

By CLAIR ENLOW
Journal A/E editor

Seattle is right in the middle of the new regional transit map. But the completion of Phase 1 of the system — the "Sound Move" plan approved by voters last fall — is still 10 years away.

Getting the City of Seattle from here to there is the special responsibility of transportation planner and engineer Jared Smith, who was appointed to the newly created position of regional transit manager in July.

While the Regional Transit Authority (RTA) sets about implementing the entire $3.9 billion system, Smith is asking the question for Seattle: "What does it do for our citizens?"

The city's stake in the RTA's planning process is very high, by any measure. Portions of the system within city limits account for $1.6 billion of the $3.9 billion budget. Mayor Norm Rice and City Council member Richard McIver

sit on the RTA board.

From an office on the third floor of City Hall, Smith will work with nearly every department of city government — from neighborhoods to transportation to utilities to land use and budget. City Light will power the system and the city will be involved in every aspect of life safety. Thus Smith will be dealing with issues ranging from tunneling under Capitol Hill to providing emergency services once the system is in operation.

But for now, an important part of Smith's job is attending meetings and keeping people up-to-date on what has been decided and what hasn't.

For instance, "We know that light rail will go down the Rainier corridor," said Smith. "But we don't yet know if it will be laid at grade, above the ground or parallel to Rainier Avenue as much as a block away."

One issue left unsettled is whether a tunnel under Capitol Hill should be part of the light rail link between downtown Seattle and the University District.

About the time Smith took his

this, so that we could say to Sound Transit, 'You won't be able to attribute delay to the infamous Seattle Process,'" said Smith. The City of Seattle teamed with Sound Transit, the Seattle Housing Authority, and community leaders to develop a plan that would promote increased density around the proposed stations.

In those early days, the RTA had several startup tasks to complete. It had to find a headquarters; establish its creditworthiness in the markets; issue bonds; and give itself a new name. Its official name was far too clunky: the Central Puget Sound Regional Transit Authority. In August 1997 the board rebranded the organization as Sound Transit, which was both a clever play on words and a logical extension of the Sound Move branding. The only other finalist was simply "Regional Transit." The board also established new names for its system components. Light-rail would be called Link; the commuter train from Lakewood to Everett would be called Sounder (because it skirted Puget Sound); and the 20 new regional express bus routes would be called "Regional Express," later renamed ST Express.[12]

The original Sound Transit headquarters were located in a temporary space in a Rainier Bank building downtown. Nickels took the lead on finding a permanent headquarters. Many of the places he looked at were standard downtown office spaces, but one intriguing option came with a vast amount of historic character:

Jared Smith was named Seattle's regional transit manager in 1997, with the daunting task of implementing the Sound Move plan within the city.

Union Station was a regional transportation center in 1912 and would be reborn as the Sound Transit headquarters.

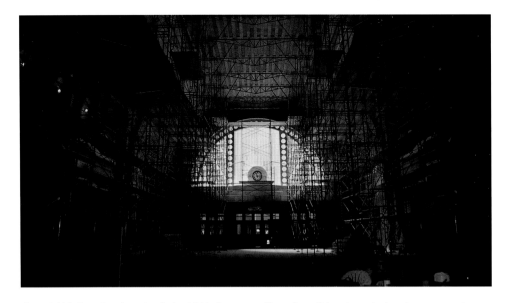

Union Station's Sound Transit make-over was underway in 1998.

the old Union Station, built in 1911. It was a Seattle rail landmark, having served as the Milwaukee Road/Union Pacific depot until 1971. It had been sitting empty and nearly derelict since then, so it qualified as a fixer-upper. It was a symbol, said Nickels, of the region's transportation heritage and had great potential for restoration.[13] "Union Station penciled out pretty well compared with a 'vanilla' office building," said Nickels. "And, it made a *statement*." That statement was: Rail is back.

Sound Transit entered into a deal in 1998 with the owners—Union Station Associates, a Paul Allen partnership—to purchase it for the cost of renovation, about $21 million. Once restored to its former architectural glory, Union Station Associates would sell it to Sound Transit for a token $1. After 14 months of renovation, Sound Transit moved in on November 1, 1999. Just before the official opening, Sound Transit Board Chair Paul Miller said, "I believe that at the end of the next century, Union Station will stand as a tribute to a generation that stopped talking about the transportation problems that threaten our region and acted upon them."[14]

Link, the light rail component, would require many years to complete, since it would have to be built from scratch. The two other major components, Sounder and Regional Express, would come together more quickly. "The first services that we put on the street were buses," said Nickels. "We decided not to hire bus drivers; we decided that we would contract with Metro, Pierce Transit, and Community Transit, and we would pay

Bob White, Sound Transit executive director (right), and Paul Miller, Sound Transit board chair.

them to run our buses. So from that standpoint, we were very popular with Metro and the other transit agencies, because we were a customer of theirs." This symbolized a new kind of partnership in Puget Sound area transit, with the county transit agencies continuing to run their own local bus systems while cooperating with Sound Transit on the larger intercity and inter-county routes. Sound Transit's Regional Express buses did not compete with the old vehicles; they were strictly high-capacity buses using dedicated freeway access ramps and HOV lanes. The first Regional Express buses rolled out in 1997, and more routes were added two years later.

This 1996 Regional Transit Authority graphic illustrated the difference between light-rail and commuter (heavy) rail.

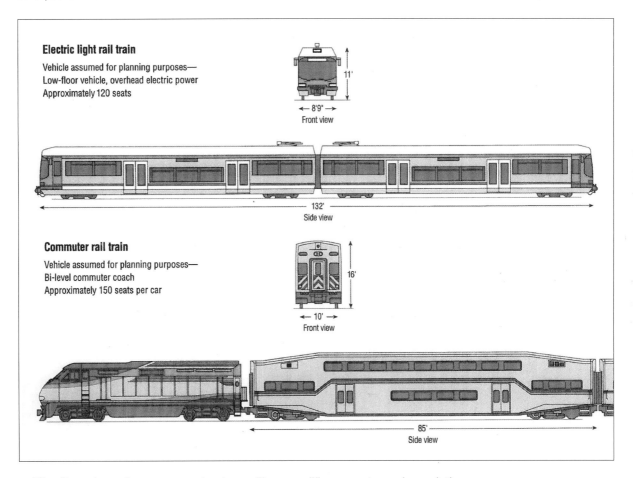

Electric light rail train

Vehicle assumed for planning purposes—
Low-floor vehicle, overhead electric power
Approximately 120 seats

11'
← 8'9" →
Front view

132'
Side view

Commuter rail train

Vehicle assumed for planning purposes—
Bi-level commuter coach
Approximately 150 seats per car

16'
← 10' →
Front view

85'
Side view

The Sounder train was conceived as a "heavy rail" commuter, using existing Burlington Northern Santa Fe railroad tracks from Lakewood straight through to Seattle and eventually on to Everett. "We did have to invest in some new track, a small stretch, so that we could avoid some of the freight traffic," said Nickels. "There were some sidings and some signals we had to build. The negotiation at the end was pretty tough—railroads are a tough partner to work with."

Tough is an understatement. "One of my fun stories about that was [Senator] Patty Murray called me and the CEO of Burlington Northern Santa Fe to her office in D.C.," said Joni Earl, who became the Sound Transit executive director. "And she took us down to her hidey-hole office and said, 'OK, here's the deal. I'm prepared to bring in sleeping bags until you guys cut a deal.' We got a deal—we got it done that day." Sound Transit would soon order 38 passenger cars and six clean-diesel locomotives.

The first public Sounder test ride took place on February 29, 2000. Regular service from Tacoma to Seattle began in September 2000, and the Seattle–Everett leg would

Mayor Norm Rice, Washington Secretary of Transportation Sid Morrison, U.S. Secretary of Transportation Rodney Slater, King County Councilmember Maggie Fimia, and King County Metro Director Paul Tolliver at a Metro event, 1995.

come three years later. Unlike light-rail, Sounder used full-size rail passenger cars, seating 140 people on high-backed upholstered seats with work tables, surge-protected outlets, and restrooms.[15] Just like the old interurban trains, the cars were fancier than trolley cars or light-rail cars. "It's comfortable because it's a train car … so people love it," said Nickels. The *Seattle Times* quoted two happy Sounder commuters on that inaugural ride who rated it far superior to their old bus ride from Tacoma. "We've been on that thing [the bus] for three hours at a time. You're cramped, there's no bathroom, you're not moving anywhere. It's awful."[16]

Sounder was conceived as a longer-distance option to light-rail, which means it had stops only about every five miles, instead of every mile. Sound Transit contracted with Burlington Northern Santa Fe to run the trains and with Amtrak to maintain the fleet. Sounder's capacity, said Nickels, was not particularly high because Sounder had to compete with freight trains and couldn't run as frequently as it would with its own tracks. As a result, Sounder was mostly a rush-hour service. Yet like the old interurban trains, Sounder was fast, zipping from the Tacoma Dome to downtown Seattle in about an hour. It proved popular from the beginning, and not just with commuters. The first Sounder "Homerun" train to a Seattle Mariners game in May 2000 sold out almost immediately. After just two weeks of regular commuter service, Sounder had already exceeded its goal of 1,000 passengers per day and was up to 1,290.

Progress was slower on Link light-rail, although Sound Transit had a head start in one important area: system planning and routing. A great deal of planning had already been accomplished in presenting the Sound Move plan. For instance, the planners and board had already grappled with a momentous question: Should Link go up the Duwamish Valley or the Rainier Valley? The Duwamish industrial route was the earliest recommendation, because it made sense from a strictly geographical standpoint. It was the shortest route from SeaTac International Airport to downtown. Some observers and critics considered a Rainier Valley route, via Martin Luther King Jr. Way, to be too "circuitous," said Regional Transit Manager Jared Smith. However, rail transit has, from the very beginning, been tied to larger issues of urban development. The Duwamish industrial corridor was relatively light on population, while the Rainier Valley was one of Seattle's lowest-income districts, full of people who needed—and would use—mass transit.

Early in the process, Seattle officials preferred the Rainier Valley alignment because it "was a way of connecting jobs to the community that needed help," said Smith. Nickels later recalled that "Mayor Norm Rice and the Seattle City Council said, 'Let's go where the people are, and we can use that as an economic driver.'" Exact details on the alignment—whether it should be surface, tunnel, or elevated—were still up in the air. But the decision to go up the Rainier Valley was settled. Seemingly.

It should come as no surprise to anyone familiar with the long, wild history of Seattle transit, that city politics almost immediately threatened to derail this plan.

Sound Transit ad featuring the Sounder train, 2000.

During the fall of 1997, Paul Schell won the race for Seattle mayor after Norm Rice decided not to seek reelection. Schell, a lawyer, developer, and former dean of the University of Washington's department of architecture and urban planning, had his own thoughts about the Link route. "He had this idea that it would be better to run it down the industrial area [the Duwamish route] and possibly up I-5, and miss Capitol Hill, because it would cost less and reach farther north and south," said Smith.

Soon after the election, Mayor Schell and some associates came to Smith's office "with drawings under their arms," on which they had mapped out their ideas for a Duwamish Link route. Smith and his staff were taken aback. They tried to explain to the mayor that "there was a lot of water already under that bridge." Schell was not to be swayed. Eventually, the Sound Transit board had to delicately explain to Schell that the alignment's pros and cons had already been thoroughly debated, a decision had been made, the alignment was set, and it was too late to change it. In Smith's telling, Schell eventually conceded, "OK, I get it." But the issue was far from settled.

In 1997, Sound Transit published this map and timetable in its Wheels in Motion newsletter. The light-rail projections proved to be hopelessly optimistic.

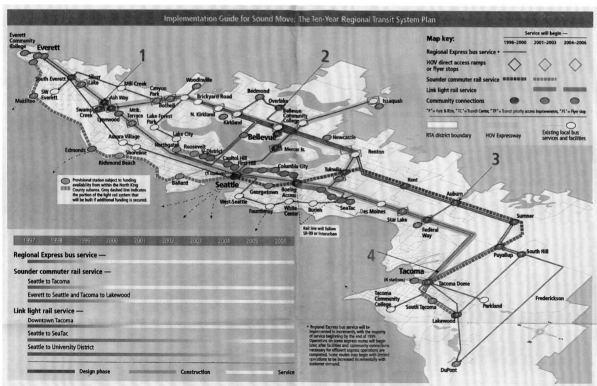

THE FIRST STEP
The blueprint for Sound Transit is *Sound Move*, a ten-year financing and construction plan for providing major transit improvements throughout our region. One of the first steps the agency took following the November 1996 election was to develop a ten-year implementation guide for scheduling design, construction and operation of the many projects that make up *Sound Move*.

Putting the regional bus and rail systems in place and coordinating implementation of the other transit projects and facilities in the plan is a challenging and complex task. The implementation guide is essential to balance cash flow and the hundreds of schedules, budgets, and partnerships with other jurisdictions and agencies needed to deliver the Sound Transit system as promised.

Profile: Greg Nickels

Early in his career, Gregory James "Greg" Nickels (b. 1955) made mass transit his signature political issue—and "early," in his case, means at a remarkably young age. By the time he turned 20, Nickels had already interned for U.S. Senator Warren Magnuson, been elected president of the Washington State Young Democrats, and gone to work as a purchasing trainee for the City of Seattle.

In 1978 at age 23, he managed Norm Rice's victorious campaign for Seattle City Council. Nickels then joined Rice's staff as his legislative assistant and remained there for the next eight years. "I was just trying to find a path where I could make a difference," he later said.

Nickels threw his own hat in the ring in 1987, in an attempt to become, at age 32, the youngest King County Council member in history. He "decided to make transportation and mass transit one of the keystones of my platform" partly because he wanted to differentiate himself from his mentor, Rice, but mainly because he felt it was just plain "nuts" that King County had no true high-capacity mass transit system.

Upon winning the election, Nickels immediately dove into transit issues. He and fellow council member Cynthia Sullivan decided that "we needed to kick-start the mass transit debate" by putting an advisory question on the 1988 ballot, asking voters whether the county should start planning a light-rail system. The voters answered a resounding yes. This advisory vote became the tiny spark that would grow, over the next decades, into the Sound Transit light-rail system.

Nickels would later become the first finance chairman of the fledgling Sound Transit and later chair of the Sound Transit board. He was, in many ways, the public face of Sound Transit. This was not exactly the ideal image for a politician, especially during some of the agency's difficult times. During his successful campaign for Seattle mayor, an editorial cartoon depicted him yoked to a light-rail car. He always believed that his 2001 mayoral victory was achieved despite, not because of, his association with Sound Transit. Four years later, with Sound Transit's reputation on the rise, he won reelection in a landslide.

He was also a key driver of Sound Transit's first two ballot measures, Sound Move and Sound Transit 2. He later called getting the $17 billion Sound Transit 2 to the ballot "the most fun that I ever had in public life"—mostly because he had to personally wrangle every vote from a dubious board. Voters eventually approved the measure in 2008, and Nickels would later say, "I was very proud of the people of Puget Sound on that day." After four decades, they had finally reversed the Forward Thrust failure.[17]

Greg Nickels became the youngest King County Council member in history at age 32, and then became Seattle's mayor from 2002 through 2009. His wholehearted support of Sound Transit was at times a political liability, yet it never wavered.

CHAPTER EIGHT

The Dark Days

The first forebodings of serious trouble for Sound Transit came in mid-1999. A *Seattle Times* editorial columnist, O. Casey Corr, wrote that "a quiet crisis builds" for "a not-so-sound transit plan." He spelled out a daunting list of problems. One of those was, once again, the Link route through Rainier Valley. "Schell wants to revisit an idea he raised, studied, and dropped shortly after taking office last year," wrote Corr. "He's interested in a high-capacity system to run down Seattle's spine, in the south through the Duwamish, not down the Rainier Valley as is now planned."[1] Sound Transit Executive Director Bob White told Corr that some of his staff members were distressed at being asked to revisit plans already vetted with city officials and settled, but White agreed that "asking the questions isn't harmful." Corr wondered if anyone had "the guts to say the package needs to be reworked."

Another problem was nothing new in Seattle transit history: Downtown property owners were unhappy. They threatened to withhold their support because it seemed that the net result of the Seattle Bus Tunnel might be more, not fewer, buses on the downtown streets. Sound Transit was, in fact, deep in talks to acquire the bus tunnel, in preparation for its eventual conversion to a light-rail tunnel, which would be Link's route through downtown. The Sound Transit board announced earlier in 1999 that it planned to convert the Seattle Bus Tunnel to rail-only. This seemed especially galling to downtown merchants, since the whole idea of the original Seattle Bus Tunnel was to get buses *off* the downtown streets. This issue was volatile at the time, but in the long run it would prove relatively easy to defuse. Sound Transit changed its stance and agreed that the tunnel could handle both buses and trains, at least during a long transition period.

Left: Seattle Mayor Greg Nickels was greeted by a host of problems when he took office in 2001, and Sound Transit was one of the biggest.

Other issues were not so easy to resolve. Corr noted that "the University of Washington fears that rattling trains will disrupt delicate equipment." The university, after initially supporting the idea of light-rail access to campus, had raised serious concerns that an underground light-rail tunnel would compromise the university's sensitive physics and medical experiments because of vibrations and

In 1999, Sound Transit was picking up bad vibrations regarding its tunnel route beneath the University of Washington.

electromagnetic interference. Sound Transit was already negotiating this touchy—and potentially very expensive—issue with the university. It was, in Sims' words, "our ugliest fight ... I mean, God, we went on and on forever."

Another problem was much more vital to Sound Transit's mission—and potentially more damaging for public opinion. "Trains will go nearly empty to Sea-Tac Airport, but stop short of Northgate, forcing riders to take buses or use cars," wrote Corr. Indeed, Sound Transit had cut down its plan so much following the 1995 defeat that it showed a dashed line between the university and Northgate, which meant that section would be built only if budget savings were realized— and budget savings had become a fantasy. Because of subarea equity, Sound Transit had been forced to pour more money than expected into the Eastside Regional Express buses and other non-Link projects. That meant Sound Transit no longer had anywhere near the budget to build the Link line all the way to Northgate. That was considered a "Phase II" project. Corr was surely speaking for thousands of Northside commuters when he wrote, "The already marginal plan voters approved in 1996 is diminishing to the point of unacceptability."

The most damaging allegation was this: Sound Transit was seriously in the red. Corr charged that the agency was "$216 million over budget and looking for stations to delay or eliminate." Sound Transit continued to insist that finances were on track, but in fact, staffers within the agency were privately worried that Link was going to cost more—far, far more—than originally projected. If there was one thing that could truly kill the most ambitious mass transit project in the region's history, it was, as the *Times* had said three years earlier, "tales of ugly cost overruns."

Opponents formed a group named Sane Transit, led by Rob McKenna and Emory Bundy. Bundy was a former KING-TV broadcaster who believed that an improved bus system could solve the region's transit problems more cheaply and efficiently than light-rail. These and other critics demanded an independent audit to evaluate charges that Sound Transit was way over budget. This demand was rejected by Dave Earling, then the Sound Transit board chairman. The board still believed what staff members were telling them, which was, essentially, everything's fine. But federal and state funding were beginning to look shaky. The feds were dragging their feet and the state had just passed a ballot measure, Initiative 695, which threatened to drastically reduce state motor vehicle excise tax revenue. This, in the words of Seattle transit journalist Josh Cohen, "blew a hole in Sound Transit's funding plan," although the state would eventually figure out a detour around it.[2]

Sound Transit forged doggedly ahead, designing numerous Link stations and breaking ground on Sounder stations, park-and-ride lots, and HOV projects. Meanwhile, the lingering question of the Link route was coming to a head. In February 1999 the Sound Transit board had formally confirmed the Rainier Valley alignment, along with a tunnel under Capitol Hill to the University of Washington. Another pivotal issue had also been worked out: where to put the Link maintenance base. This was one of the most important considerations for any light-rail plan. At first, the planners thought they would have to put it in the Dearborn Street

Sound Transit found an ideal site for its maintenance base right across the street from the big red R: the old Rainier Brewery.

area near Interstate 90, which required 11 acres and would entail "significant eminent domain issues," to quote Smith. It also meant Sound Transit might have to cobble together a parcel among a group of unwilling sellers. Soon word arrived that the Stroh Brewery, which owned the old Rainier Brewery complex near Forest Street and Interstate 5, was interested in selling the bottling plant immediately west of the old brewery.

The advantages were many. It was one large parcel, with a willing seller and fewer eminent domain issues. But there was one significant drawback. It wasn't exactly on the planned Link route. For this to work, the Link route would have to be altered. It would have to tunnel all the way under Beacon Hill, from Martin Luther King Jr. Way to Forest Street. Tunnels are expensive. The planners and the Sound Transit board conducted a pro-con analysis, and determined that, all things considered, the Stroh site "made a lot of sense," said Smith.

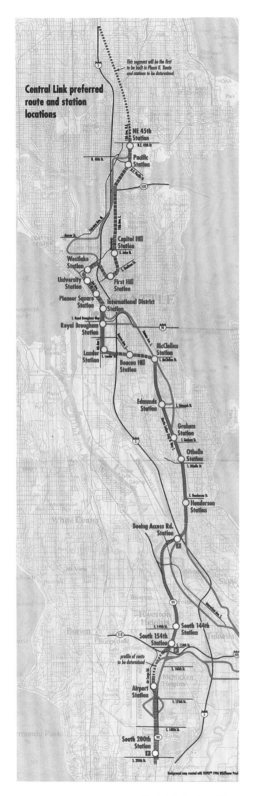

Central Link preferred route and station locations

This segment will be the first to be built in Phase II. Route and stations to be determined.

NE 45th Station
Pacific Station
Capitol Hill Station
Westlake Station
University Station
First Hill Station
Pioneer Square Station
International District Station
Royal Brougham Station
Lander Station
Beacon Hill Station
McClellan Station
Edmunds Station
Graham Station
Othello Station
Henderson Station
Boeing Access Rd. Station
South 144th Station
South 154th Station
profile of route to be determined
Airport Station
South 200th Station

Background map created with TOPO!™ 1996 Wildflower Prod.

The question was: What was simpler? A tunnel or a complicated land-acquisition process? The tunnel won.

On November 18, 1999, the Sound Transit board announced its final decision on the Link route. It would, in fact, be routed at street level down Martin Luther King Jr. Way, then tunnel under Beacon Hill to the Forest Street maintenance base, connect to the Seattle Bus Tunnel, and then continue in a new tunnel under Capitol Hill and Portage Bay to the University of Washington. And that's where it would end in the north—although the board did "commit" to look for additional funding to extend it another three miles to Northgate. This was magical thinking, as subsequent events would prove.

The southern part of the route—from Sea-Tac Airport— was set to go north on Pacific Highway South (Highway 99) into Tukwila before crossing Interstate 5. But the board hedged its bets by passing a separate resolution at the same meeting, in which it agreed "to have further analysis done on a new route proposed by the city of Tukwila."[3] In other words, the final route was *still* not the final route. Tukwila was balking.

In fact, the Tukwila portion would be altered later, much to the chagrin of Nickels, because of overwhelming Tukwila opposition. "I was chairing the public hearing down at the Tukwila Community Center," said Nickels. "We called that hearing the Thrilla in Tukwila. There was not one single person who supported that train going down Highway 99." About 250 people jammed the room, and they wanted the route moved farther east. Tukwila had just embarked on an ambitious plan to revitalize Highway 99 (today's International Boulevard) and did not want to disrupt it by putting tracks down the middle of the highway.

Link light-rail director Paul Bay told the crowd that the Highway 99 route was quicker and cheaper by about $125 million.[4] Ultimately, however, Sound Transit had to give in and move the route down SR 518 and Interstate 5, a decision that Nickels still regretted almost 20 years later. "Highway 99 is a nice, wide right-of-way and it would have been the right place," said Nickels. "We could have

Sound Transit identified this "preferred alternative" for the Link route in 1999, but the eventual route would look far different in several stretches.

served lots of people. But instead we have to go along the freeway, because there was zero support. You fight the fights you can fight."

Another battle soon arose, this one laden with irony. A Rainier Valley group called Save Our Valley had formed with the goal of getting Link off Martin Luther King Jr. Way and putting it in a tunnel instead. Residents were worried about noise, traffic hazards, and obstacles presented by a track running down the center of the street. They also asked why affluent North Seattle was getting a tunnel, but they were not. This eventually resulted in a federal civil rights lawsuit in which Save Our Valley alleged that Sound Transit's surface track plan amounted to discrimination against Rainier Valley's largely minority population.

The irony was that planners had gone out on a limb to keep the Link route through the Rainier Valley, believing it to be a potent economic driver for a community in need. Would an underground route, preventing commuters from seeing the businesses and shops, be as effective? Several other Rainier Valley community groups argued that it would not. They said "if you want economic development, you have to encourage at-grade rail—you have to have eyes on the street to see what's happening."[5] It turned out to be a moot point. A Rainier Valley tunnel would have cost another $400 to $500 million, which Sound Transit manifestly did not have. Meanwhile, the federal courts dismissed the Save Our Valley lawsuit in 2001 and denied a 2003 appeal. The Rainier Valley route would stay on the surface.

A "Save Our Valley" movement sprang up, with the goal of putting the Link route underground through the Rainier Valley. Ultimately, the route would remain on the surface.

However, to address the Rainier Valley's valid concerns, Smith pitched an idea to then Mayor Paul Schell that eventually resulted in the creation of a $50 million community development fund to provide small business loans and many other forms of assistance to those affected by the Rainier Valley Link project. This plan was adopted by the Sound Transit Board and mitigated many of the impacts on southeast Seattle residents and business owners.

Many of these problems were in the category of learning experiences, inevitable in any massive new transit project. But there were early signs of a more significant crisis in September 2000, when a citizen oversight panel said, "We're concerned that they have agreed to spend more money than they have."[6] More rumblings came in October 2000, when the *Seattle Times'* Lance Dickie, usually a light-rail advocate, wrote that costs were up and "caution flags were waving."[7] Emory Bundy warned that "there is growing public concern that the value of Sound Transit's Link light-rail has been exaggerated and its cost understated."[8]

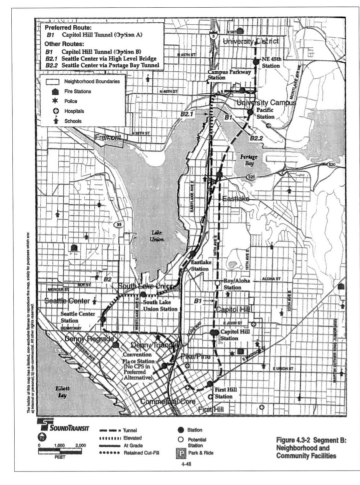

Figure 4.3-2 Segment B: Neighborhood and Community Facilities

4-48

This 2000 map showed several early Link route options— including the original and highly problematic tunnel route (B1), beneath Portage Bay. Eventually, the tunnel would take none of these routes, but shift farther east, avoiding Portage Bay altogether.

Then in November 2000 the full magnitude of the disaster was revealed. When the new bids were opened for the proposed University District tunnel, only one contender submitted an estimate. (Two others had dropped out, in an echo of the painful 1975 Metro bid-opening fiasco.) That bid was jaw-dropping. Modern Transit Constructors submitted an estimate of $728 million, a whopping $171 million over the $557 million budget. Even worse, this was the contractor's *pared-down* number. The company's original estimate had been $844 million. A shocked Sound Transit had already quietly begged the contractor to come up with a cheaper alternative. The best the contractor could do was shave it down to $728 million—not remotely low enough.

The board emerged glumly from a November 16, 2000, meeting and was forced to admit disaster. Mayor Schell summed up the situation by saying, "We can't support a project we can't afford." A clearly shaken Nickels, who was then the board's vice-chair, said there was nothing to be done except begin searching for a solution. "The time is now for us to step up," he said, after the climactic board meeting. "Failure is not an option."[9]

Nobody was blaming the contractor. The higher costs were for a variety of reasons, ranging from "tricky soils" to a scarcity of qualified tunnel builders. More blame would eventually be found within Sound Transit itself. But this bombshell development set off a series of repercussions. The board:

- Immediately put the Link tunnel plan on hold
- Accepted the resignation of Link Director Paul Bay
- Received a new cost estimate for the entire Link project, which jumped from $2.5 billion (adjusted for inflation) to $3.6 billion
- Pushed the Link completion date back three years to 2009
- Announced the creation of the Central Link Project Review Committee, chaired by former mayor Charles Royer

The fiasco also seemed to confirm the criticism that had been building for more than a year and raised the specter of bigger revelations to come. Light-rail critic Bundy told reporters, "My belief is that every component is over budget."[10] The *Seattle Times* editorial page said, "With the tunnel estimate so massively wrong, it's clear Sound Transit's estimates of other items need scrutiny."[11] That scrutiny, from both friends and foes, would now begin in earnest. It was the darkest day of a period known forever after at Sound Transit as the Dark Days.

How did the cost estimates go so massively wrong? In the final analysis, it was a fatal combination of early initial compromises, poor internal communication, and wishful thinking. Smith, an insider during this period, believes that the light-rail portion of the plan had been pared down so much between the failed 1995 vote

In the spring of 1999, Sound Transit's newsletter was full of optimism for the Tacoma Link project —but storm clouds were gathering for the rest of Link.

and the successful 1996 vote that "it was a shoe-horned budget right from the get-go." When problems inevitably arose—such as the issue of "tricky soils" under Portage Bay—there were no adequate contingency funds. "Senior staff were pretty aware of this … and everyone was struggling with it," said Smith, "But the hope was that, if they could get a good design-build team, they [could] find innovative ways of saving money. It was based on a hope and prayer—that the initial contract would not come in as high as people thought it might."

According to Smith, some people in Sound Transit management ascribed to the Robert Moses philosophy of public works (named for the legendary New York public works czar): Dig a hole and the money will follow. They dug a hole, all right, but "unfortunately the money didn't follow," said Smith. Board member Sims said that some people on the Sound Transit staff "were not listeners, and in our business that's really important. … To me it bordered on elitism."

Tacoma Link finds roots in Pierce County

In February, the Sound Transit Board defined most of the Tacoma Link light rail route and station locations.

Tacoma Link will begin operating 1.6 miles of electric light rail in 2002. The line will connect the Tacoma Dome Station with key destinations in the downtown core.

"The Tacoma Link route will provide many opportunities, not only for transit riders, but local businesses as well. We are very excited about this achievement with Link light rail," Paul Miller, board chair and Tacoma councilmember, said.

In January, the final environmental impact statement for the light rail line was released. For study purposes, the line was divided into east-west and north-south portions, creating an L-

From the start, citizens and businesses have been involved in Tacoma Link's progress.

shaped route. Three east-west and two north-south route and station location options were studied.

A final decision for the east-west and most of the north-south portion of the line was made. Two alternatives for the remainder of the north-south line will be studied further. One option would run on Pacific Avenue and the other would run on Pacific Avenue and Commerce Street, as shown on the map. Further studies will be undertaken so Sound Transit can coordinate with the City of Tacoma's development plans for the area during the same time period.

Tacoma Link will have the convenience of five stations. The South 13th Station and Theater District Station locations will be determined by a final decision on the northern section of the Tacoma Link line.

In the meantime, engineers, artists and community members will continue working on Link's station designs. Each station will be unique and reflect the character of the community it serves.

Look for meetings in the Tacoma area where citizens can view and comment on station designs and concepts.

Above: Tacoma Link will connect major destinations between the Tacoma Dome Station and the downtown core. Below: Link trains will get the power to move from overhead electric lines. Doors will open at platform level for easy boarding.

PugetPass available this fall

You can get there with just one pass this fall in Central Puget Sound.

Sound Transit, in partnership with Pierce Transit, Everett Transit, Community Transit and King County Metro, announced an agreement to coordinate the price of bus fares in Central Puget Sound.

The agreement led to a regional fare payment system that created a series of of passes, called "Puget-Pass" that can be used on all public transit agencies in Snohomish, King and Pierce counties. The goal is to make it easier than ever to transfer and ride transit around Puget Sound. Riders will be able to ride on all transit services in the region

up to the value printed on the pass. If a rider wants to take a service or trip that costs more, the rider pays the difference between the fares.

There are a variety of PugetPass values available depending on the rider's needs and are designed with themes found around Puget Sound.

"Our whole purpose is to improve mobility around most of the Central Puget Sound region. Integrating fares brings us one step closer to that goal. And as our transit services are regional,

we thought the design of the transit passes ought to reflect that," Dave Earling, boardmember and Edmonds councilmember, says.

The regional passes are being printed now so there will be plenty to distribute in September.

One pass is all you need! PugetPass will be accepted by all transit agencies in the Central Puget Sound region.

Upcoming events

Sounder trains running together

Link environmental studies continue

ST Express buses arrive and go to work

Tacoma Link line finalized

Citizen Oversight Panel reports on Sound Transit's progress

Compounding the problem was the fact that staff knew about the budget shortfalls long before the board knew, then failed to warn them. This is disastrous in most organizations—especially in public agencies. "There was, I think, a lack of communication, a lack of trust, between the staff and the board," said Nickels, almost 20 years later. "… Ultimately, the board realized that we were being pushed toward something that likely was going to be a failure. … The board stepped up and said, 'Time out.'"

The board's goal through the ensuing Dark Days was daunting in scope, yet simple in essence: Find a way to save Link in particular and Sound Transit in general. Executive Director Bob White presented the new $3.6 billion Link plan to the board in December 2000 and continued to insist that "this new project is affordable with reasonable adjustments to our financial plan."[12] This continued unwarranted optimism would cost White his job within a month. Nickels remembers a "very painful" board meeting in January 2001, at which "we had to tell our executive director, who we were very fond of [goodbye] because the staff was not being completely forthright with us about the level of risk."[13] White issued a resignation statement in which he conceded that "new leadership, unencumbered by past issues and decisions," was needed in order to "restore public confidence."[14]

By 2003, Joni Earl was being celebrated for doing the seemingly impossible: rescuing Sound Transit from the edge of disaster.

Earling, the board chair, said he accepted his resignation "with some regret, and yet he was doing what was right for the agency."

Joni Earl, the former deputy county executive in Snohomish County, would become the figure who would, more than anyone, restore that public confidence. Earl had been hired in August 2000 to serve under Bob White as Sound Transit's chief operating officer, responsible for the agency's overall administration and day-to-day operations. She had worked closely on Sound Move with Bob Drewel while at Snohomish County, so she was well-versed on transit matters. However, no amount of experience could prepare her for what happened after she started her Sound Transit job. Shortly after she arrived, "all hell broke loose," she said.

"I'd been there about six weeks and they asked me to look at the light-rail project from top to bottom, because the bids were coming in high on the tunnel portion," said Earl, 18 years later. "I took it to the staff and we worked night and day and went through every cost estimate. I came out of that process announcing we were $1.1 billion over budget and three years behind schedule." Even the staff was thunderstruck. "They knew there were problems in the budget, but they didn't know what they were," she said.

Nor had they been willing to admit to the board that there were problems at all. "In fact, I sat in on one meeting with Bob White and Paul Bay, and Paul Bay said, 'If the board would just say no, we wouldn't have cost problems.' And I said, 'What does that mean, if the board would just say no?' And he said, 'Well they keep saying yes.' And I said, 'Has anybody told them they can't afford it?' And he said, 'Well no.' … Every time the board would add scope to the project, staff needed to say either we can afford it or we can't afford it. And they weren't doing that."

On December 12, 2000, Earl stood before the cameras at a press conference and laid out the full extent of the problems—not just with the Capitol Hill–University tunnel, but with all of the Link overruns. The public learned, for the first time, that the entire Link project would cost $1.1 billion more than originally planned. Some of that extra cost would be because of the new 2009 completion date. She told reporters, "We need to make sure we're candid and honest and make sure we don't repeat the errors with too much optimism. We hope the public stays with us, because we believe the public still wants this project."[15] Sound Transit became front page news for weeks. Some of its opponents filed suits and "tried to put the nails in the coffin," said Earl.

On January 25, 2001, two days after Bob White was let go, the board named Earl the acting executive director. Many years later, when asked how she felt about this promotion, Earl replied, "Overwhelmed and fearful." Yet the board had confidence in her, since she had diagnosed the problems so completely and created a realistic new budget. Board chair Dave Earling said this had "earned her a great deal of respect from board members."[16] She later said she felt bad, mostly, for the elected officials, because they were the ones "hanging out there," with their reputations and careers on the line. "I just felt a lot of pressure to figure this thing out, so it didn't end up sticking to any of the board members," she said.

Over the next few months, Earl had two giant tasks. The first was to create a new culture at Sound Transit. "Joni said the only way we're going to climb out of this hole is to be totally transparent," said Smith. She laid out her expectations right away. "One of the big ones was, if there is a problem I need to know," said Earl. "Because I

The PI *was already calling Link "the train to nowhere" in 2002—with Greg Nickels at the wheel.*

135

can't solve a problem I don't know about—like what had happened with that $1.1 billion." Nobody would be fired for flagging a problem, only for hiding it.[17] "My most notorious statement to staff was, 'Optimism is not our friend' —meaning optimism in cost estimates and revenue estimates," Earl later said. She also had to deal with a shell-shocked staff. "Joni said, 'If you don't have the energy to continue this battle, I need to know so we can bring people in,'" said Anne Fennessy, a communications consultant who helped deal with the avalanche of bad news.

Earl's other urgent task was to rebuild credibility with the federal government, which had been badly damaged by the budget fiasco. Earl had learned to her alarm that a memorandum was sitting on U.S. Secretary of Transportation Rodney Slater's desk, which recommended scuttling Sound Transit's $500 million federal grant. Without that money, Sound Transit was "seriously dead," said Sims. Slater phoned Sims, who was on vacation in the Philippines, and told Sims that he had a list of 23 conditions that Sound Transit must meet before he would approve the grant. Slater asked Sims to promise that all 23 conditions would be met. Sims said, "Secretary Slater, I promise. You have my word." It required staff changes, reorganization, and major overhauls, all changes with which Sims concurred. Besides, it was either that or no funding at all. Slater, satisfied, signed off on the grant agreement on January 20, 2001—the last day in office for both Slater and his boss, President Bill Clinton. Incoming Transportation Secretary Norm Mineta went along with Slater's recommendation.

However, by March 2001, the House Appropriations Subcommittee warned that "red flags are still flying" about Sound Transit.[18] All federal funding remained in doubt. "I had to go back and testify in front of Congress," said Earl. "I was under oath and I had to testify about all of the problems, and that was pretty frightening." One congress member described Sound Transit's plans as not "completely baked."[19] The alarmed feds ordered an audit by the department's Inspector General, which put the grant on hold. At best, the grant would be delayed a year or two. At worst, it could be canceled altogether.

Light rail hurt but alive, says top critic

By David Quigg
THE NEWS TRIBUNE

Sound Transit took such a drubbing from Washington, D.C., this week that the can-do talk emanating from the agency seems downright delusional.

Until you speak with Emory Bundy.

Bundy, a well-connected critic of Sound Transit, would like nothing better than to dance on the grave of the agency's planned Seattle-to-Sea-Tac light rail project.

But the prominent Seattleite wasn't dancing at week's end. Despite Wednesday's release of a withering independent federal review. Despite Thursday's news that the Bush administration wants to deny both this year's and next year's federal funding – $125 million Sound Transit was counting on.

Bundy lamented that Sound Transit officials probably are right when

Gridlock Standstill Sounder

The train arrives this fall. SOUNDTRANSIT MOVING FORWARD

"That impacted our cash flow, so the project got delayed a little bit longer," said Earl. "And I had to tell the board that we couldn't afford the project as planned. So that wasn't a very fun year." The Dark Days of 2001 would become even less fun when the *Seattle Post-Intelligencer* published a story on May 4 that accused Sound Transit of "deception" and "concealing" the true cost of the Sound Move project from voters and bond investors.[20] It even raised the possibility of securities fraud. This outraged Earl and her staff. "A whole bunch of us spent the weekend going through all the documents and coming up with a three-ring binder that proved, paragraph by paragraph, that the story was wrong," she said. "We went to the *PI* and asked for a correction. We finally got a front-page correction—which is almost unheard of. But they had really messed up." The paper's managing editor wrote, "[The] story did not meet the Post-Intelligencer's standards for accuracy and fairness. We regret that and want to set the record straight."[21]

The Sound Transit staff had been demoralized all year, to the point where some of them were covering up their ID badges while riding the bus to work, said Earl. Yet the *PI* incident had the ironic result of actually cheering up the staff for the first time in months. "It was a turning point for the agency," said Earl. "The employees saw we would fight for them; the board saw we would fight and win." Earl had also restored a level of trust with federal authorities in Washington, D.C., according to Peter Rogoff, who was on the staff of the Senate Appropriations transportation subcommittee (and would later become Earl's successor). He said that Earl "became identified as this extraordinarily trustworthy partner with all the players up and down the chain."

Sound Transit continued to build-out and promote the Sounder system, 2001.

Mountain-biking in the 'burbs   M's bruise Red Sox 10-5, tie series
GETAWAYS   SPORTS D1

THURSDAY, MAY 10, 2001

Seattle Post-Intelligencer

A HEARST NEWSPAPER | WWW.SEATTLEP-I.COM

KING, SNOHOMISH, PIERCE CO. & BAINBRIDGE
ISLAND, KITSAP, THURSTON CO. 50¢ | ELSEWHERE 75¢

25¢

Sound Transit costs story incorrect

Contingency was never set at higher, recommended level

P-I STAFF

A Seattle Post-Intelligencer story Friday asserting that Sound Transit concealed the true cost of building a light-rail line from voters and bond investors by leaving out hundreds of millions of dollars in contingency costs was incorrect.

Agency leaders on Tuesday provided a complete list of cost changes to the light-rail project between 1993, when the core segment's cost was estimated at $2 billion, and 1996, when the estimate submitted to voters was $1.4 billion. Those changes, which include shortening the rail line and changing its grade, fully account for the $600 million drop in costs.

"We believe the facts show and the documents prove that the Sound Transit board, staff and consultants acted openly in public and with integrity," Sound Transit Director Joni Earl said.

David McCumber, managing editor of the Post-Intelligencer, said: "Friday's Sound Transit story did not meet the Post-Intelligencer's standards for accuracy and fairness. We regret that, and we want to set the record straight."

The most significant savings between the 1993 and 1996 plans came from dropping 20 blocks of tunnel from the rail line's north end and changing the technology at the south end from grade-separated to at-grade. Those two changes accounted for $533 million of the drop in price, according to Sound Transit's newly prepared documents.

The P-I had incorrectly reported that those changes saved only about $200 million based on a cost comparison outlined in a 1999 environmental impact document. The agency's chief light-rail engi-

SEE TRANSIT, A11

The Seattle Post-Intelligencer *took the exceedingly rare step of publishing a front-page correction in 2001. Joni Earl and her staff had presented the* PI *editors with a three-ring binder, showing exactly how an earlier* PI *story about Sound Transit was wrong.*

In May 2001 the Sound Transit board launched a nationwide search for White's permanent replacement. Acting executive director Earl was not certain, at first, whether she wanted to apply. She considered herself by no means a transportation expert. She was frazzled from working every day until 3 or 4 a.m. and starting over again at 8 a.m. She had been in the hot seat for months. But she had come to love the employees and the challenge. She was, she said, "hooked on Sound Transit." So she applied for the job. "Some of our board members wanted some internationally known light-rail person to come in and take over the operation," said Earling, the board chair. "I knew, from my personal work with Joni at Snohomish County, of the credibility that she would bring automatically … at both the local level and the federal level." In June 2001 the Sound Transit board passed over several national candidates and formally offered Earl the position. The board told her they didn't need a transportation expert; they needed somebody who could solve problems and get the agency back on the rails.

Once again, regional transit teetered on the precipice. "It could have gone either way, if the board had not stood firm, and if Joni had turned out to be a bad hire, rather than a great hire," said Nickels. Earl didn't waste much time fretting over the agency's perilous position. "We just put our heads down and went to work," she said. Sound Transit continued to build Sounder stations and Regional Express routes. In the summer of 2001, work began on the Tacoma Link light project—a kind of mini-Link running 1.6 miles through downtown Tacoma from the theater district through the museum district to the Tacoma Dome. This was basically a short streetcar line.

The question remained: What to do about the big Link project? Earl huddled with her staff and made the critical decision to split the project into two segments: The North Link, running from downtown to the University of Washington, and the Central Link, running from Tukwila to downtown. She told the board that they had only enough cash flow to build one. Earl and the board had to make some wrenching decisions: Should they wait until they could afford both? Or build one now? And if so, which one, North or Central?

138

On September 27, 2001, the board chose to forge ahead on the Central Link from downtown to the airport. This route had the distinct advantage of *not* including the troublesome Capitol Hill-University tunnel. The engineering and construction would be easier to get done quickly, and Sound Transit had decided it was imperative to get wheels on rails as soon as possible.

"I kept telling staff, 'We can't just tell people we're good, we have to show we can deliver this stuff,'" said Earl. "That was my motto: We just gotta show 'em." Nickels and most of the board firmly backed the plan. This was an especially risky position for Nickels, because at this moment he was engaged in a brutal Seattle mayoral campaign. He had knocked Schell out in the primary and was now facing attorney Mark Sidran in November 2001.

The Tacoma Link line, echoing the old Tacoma streetcar routes, was Sound Transit's first light-rail line, and was finished in 2003.

In an echo of the bruising Seattle mayoral races of the 1910s and 1920s, the number one issue was transit. Sidran opposed the Sound Transit plan and, if elected, promised to scrap it. Nickels stood stalwartly behind the plan, as battered as it had been in 2001. "You know, there are times in your life when you need to look in the mirror and decide who you are and what you stand for," said Nickels. "And this is something that I had already worked on for 14 years. We'd overcome election defeat, we'd overcome a complete lack of revenue, and I was determined that we would get through [this]." This stance nearly cost him the election—but not quite. "I believed that if we had not had the Dark Days, I would have won that election going away," said Nickels. "As it was, I won by 3,158 votes."

Sound Transit had also won a staunch supporter at a crucial time, in a crucial position. "One of the first meetings I ever had, [I gathered] all of the staff in the mayor's office who were working on light-rail, and I said, 'Our job is to be a partner with Sound Transit and to make it successful,'" recalled Nickels. "And they all kind of gave an audible sigh of relief, because they knew what their marching orders were. Whereas they didn't under the previous mayor."

Sound Transit ad, 2001.

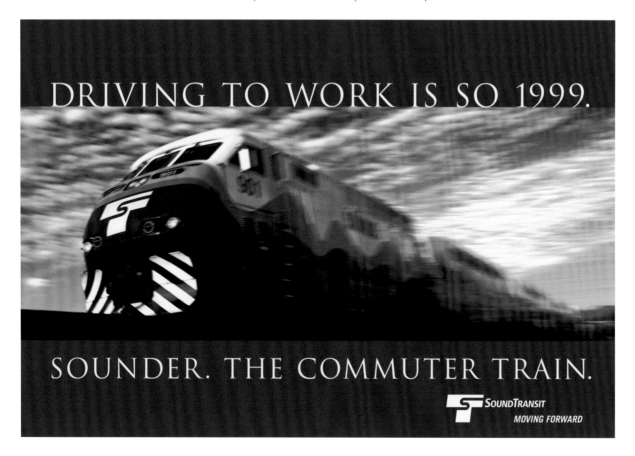

140

The mayor's race: a summation...

MEANIE!

WEENIE!

Seattle mayoral candidate Greg Nickels was depicted, in 2001, pulling his favorite toy: a light-rail train.

Over the next two years, Sound Transit tried to gradually rebuild its ragged reputation by getting as much non-Link work done as possible. By 2002 all 19 Regional Express bus routes were completed. The Overlake Transit Center and Bellevue Transit Center, serving both Sound Transit and Metro buses, were dedicated that year, making life a little easier for Eastside bus commuters. The Tacoma Link work was finished. On August 23, 2003, electric streetcars began rolling through the streets of Tacoma, as they first did in 1890. Ron Sims, then the King County executive and Sound Transit board chair, said it was "a shining example of what we can accomplish when we stop bickering and start building."[22]

There would be another such example in 2003. After complicated negotiations with Burlington Northern Santa Fe, an agreement was reached to extend Sounder service from Seattle to Everett. The first Sounder train rumbled into Everett on December 21, carrying a capacity crowd of 700. About 64 years after the demise of the beloved interurbans, commuter train service was back between Tacoma, Seattle, and Everett. Bob Drewel, who had fought so long to get rail back to his city, was overcome with emotion. "It's very hard to describe my feelings," Drewel said. "To have a 57-year-old man's eyes well up over the opportunity to ride a train ..."[23]

Sounder Commuter Train at Everett Station where service began in 2003.

Quietly, things had also been looking up for the Link project. In mid-2003 Sound Transit held two bid openings—events which, in previous years, had been fraught with terror. This time both bids—for track construction and for the maintenance base—came in *under* estimates by 15 percent. This was an indication that Sound Transit had recovered its competence when it came to cost estimating. Nevertheless, the pending Inspector General's report from the U.S. Department of Transportation was still hanging over Sound Transit's head. A negative report would probably kill off Sound Transit's $500 million federal grant. In July 2003 the best possible news arrived. The Inspector General issued its report and gave Sound Transit a clean bill of health, saying it had "substantially strengthened its proposal" since 2001.[24]

The $500 million wasn't quite in Sound Transit's pocket

Sound Transit found it quicker and easier to launch its ST Express bus services than to build a light-rail system from scratch. All 19 routes were finished by 2002. Here, buses line up at the Bellevue Transit Center in 2006.

yet. The money was scheduled to come in yearly installments, the first supposedly being $75 million. One House committee member knocked that number back to $15 million, and there were rumors around the nation's capital that the entire federal grant was "a long shot."[25] Washington's U.S. Senator Patty Murray entered the fray on the side of Sound Transit. She set up a meeting between Sims and Alabama's Republican Senator Richard Shelby, the Senate transportation chair. Shelby sternly told Sims that he would recommend the funding only if Sims would give his solemn promise that Sound Transit would meet strict conditions about

Sounder commuter train service to Tacoma and Everett rekindled memories of the old interurban lines to those two cities.

performance, professionalism, accuracy, and integrity. "I will meet all those [conditions], and this is my personal word," Sims replied. "And if this doesn't happen on my personal word, I will publicly resign."

Murray managed to get the $75 million reinstated as part of House-Senate conference committee negotiations. The entire $500 million grant was approved with the full $75 million first-year appropriation. In announcing the grant, Murray called Sound Transit "the little engine that could," while Sims called Murray a

Earl announces the approval of the federal light-rail grant in October, 2003, with (from left) Sound Transit Board Member Dwight Pelz, Board Chair Ron Sims, Senator Patty Murray, and Board Member Richard McIver.

"true hero."[26] Sims later came to believe that Murray and Shelby were unsung heroes in the rebirth of Sound Transit, and that Murray, especially, was one of Sound Transit's saviors. "Senator Murray rode us really hard," said Sims, 15 years later. "I can remember always saying, 'I hope one day she can just smile.' That's what I wanted on her face. But Sound Transit was not a smiling issue until we began to perform pretty ably."

Once again, light-rail had escaped a near-death experience. Earl breathed a massive sigh of relief, because without the federal grant, "we just didn't have enough money to do it." Earl and her staff wasted no time. On November 8, 2003, two weeks after the grant was announced, Sound Transit finally broke ground on Central Link light-rail. An earlier transit hero from Seattle's past, Jim Ellis, weighed in on that day, giving credit to Joni Earl. "She took something that was in a pit and pulled it out remarkably. That's hard to quarrel with," Ellis told reporters.[27] On the last day of 2003, bids were opened for the Rainier Valley light-rail construction, and they came in $30 million under budget. The Dark Days were over.

Greg Nickels, Joni Earl, Ron Sims, Richard McIver, and King County Councilmember Larry Phillips, (from left) at the Central Link ground breaking, 2003.

143

One Track Mind:
Seattle's Monorail Flirtation

Since 1962 Seattle has looked upon its 1.3-mile monorail line as a civic symbol, nearly as iconic as the Space Needle. Tourists flocked to it; Seattleites regarded it with a warm glow, as a quirky vestige of the World's Fair. This nostalgic affection may be the only explanation for why Seattle was sidetracked for eight years by the prospect of a vast 40-mile monorail system.

In 1997 a group of Seattle civic activists, led by a cab driver and a poet, envisioned four new extensions in the shape of a giant X, snaking into each corner of the city. They put Initiative 41 on the city ballot, calling for the creation of the Elevated Transportation Company, which would seek private capital to build the system. The initiative was vague on details like a price tag, but Seattle voters loved it. To the shock of civic authorities, it passed with a 53 percent yes vote—with no funding for implementation.

The Seattle Center Monorail was built as a futuristic people mover for Seattle's 1962 World's Fair. It has been gliding over its 1.3 mile route ever since.

After considerable wrangling, the City of Seattle appointed an Elevated Transportation Company board and allocated $200,000 for initial planning work. The plan soon became bogged down in politics and in the sheer engineering challenges of creating a vast one-track elevated system. In 2000 the Seattle City Council came within a whisker of killing the idea and repealing Initiative 41 but retreated after a public backlash. Instead a new ballot measure, Initiative 53 went to voters later that year, authorizing $6 million to create a more realistic, scaled-down monorail plan. People remained enthusiastic about the idea and approved it by a 56 percent margin.

Two years later the Elevated Transportation Company released its plan, which called for a single 14-mile north–south route, from Ballard to West Seattle, with a price tag of $1.75 billion. To pay for it, Seattle voters were asked to

The 2002 preliminary monorail plan produced by the Elevated Transportation Company.

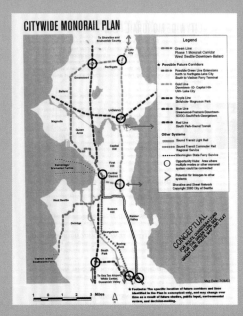

approve a 1.4 percent increase in motor-vehicle excise taxes. The entire concept was viewed with alarm by those who were trying to create a city transit strategy to integrate with Sound Transit. "Monorail proponents did not acknowledge that the proposal would integrate poorly with other parts of the planned regional system," said Jared Smith, who raised these concerns during early planning. "The technology could only operate elevated on a concrete beam, whereas light rail could operate either elevated, at grade, or in tunnels with easily connected tracks. Monorail also relied on the use of proprietary, lower capacity vehicles seldom used anywhere in the world, except in a few locations." Yet Seattle voters remained enamored of the idea and narrowly approved the tax increase.

The Seattle Monorail extension plan was considered an unwanted guest by transit planners who had their hands full with light-rail. Yet, Seattle voters kept approving measure after measure, before finally killing it in 2005.

Unfortunately, the excise tax increase turned out to be woefully insufficient and the plan had to be scaled back again. Opponents were becoming fed up with this long-running monorail saga and placed a "Monorail Recall" initiative on the November 2004 ballot. But Seattle's love affair with the monorail was not over yet. Voters rejected the "recall" measure by a 63.5 percent majority.

In 2005 Seattle finally began to lose its enthusiasm for this increasingly problematic plan. Cost estimates kept shooting up. Negotiations with the sole construction bidder were going poorly. A revised plan was drawn up with an alarming $11 billion price tag. "You've got to be kidding me," said State Treasurer Mike Murphy, as quoted by Jane Hadley of the *Seattle PI*. "That's ludicrous." Mayor Greg Nickels finally lost patience and withdrew all city support. Proponents tried once more to keep the idea alive with yet another voter initiative in November 2005, proposing an even smaller route of 10 miles. It was the fifth monorail initiative in eight years.

It was also the last. Voters rejected it by a 64 percent margin, rendering the monorail plan stone dead. After spending over $200 million on initial planning, design and right of way purchases, not one foot of the 40-mile monorail plan was ever built.[28]

The Return of Rail

Joni Earl's strategy of getting wheels rolling as soon as possible was proving effective. By the end of 2004, the Tacoma Link line had carried its millionth passenger. The newly expanded Sounder line was carrying about 3,000 passengers every day, and the number of daily trains was increasing. New federal funds had freed Sound Transit to begin working feverishly along the Central Link route. By mid-2004 construction was underway in Rainier Valley, the stadium district, downtown Seattle, and underneath Beacon Hill.

A few storm clouds from the Dark Days remained. Several lawsuits were still pending against Sound Transit, one of which threatened to kill its motor vehicle excise tax—20 percent of the agency's revenue. Another suit asked for Sound Transit to actually issue refunds to taxpayers. Yet the most potentially disastrous lawsuit was filed by Sane Transit in 2002, demanding light-rail work be halted because it wasn't the same project that voters had approved in 1996. It was, of course, a considerably scaled-back version. Sound Transit board chair and Pierce County Executive John Ladenburg called Sane Transit's argument "silly," since "any agency has to have some latitude on how things turn out."[1] Despite that, the Sane Transit lawsuit went all the way to the State Supreme Court. If Sound Transit lost, light-rail construction would have been delayed for at least two years—or stopped altogether. In March 2004, the court majority ruled in favor of Sound Transit, saying that voters had approved a resolution that allowed for changes if money ran short. Sound Transit General Counsel Desmond Brown would eventually prevail in the other cases as well.

Left: Sound Transit Link car testing I-90 track bridge prototype in Pueblo, Colorado in 2013.

Work was well underway on the Beacon Hill tunnel in 2005.

Another nagging criticism still dogged Sound Transit. Negotiations over a Sea-Tac Airport station had stalled, partly because the airport had been forced to revise its terminal-construction plans in the wake of the 9/11 attacks. Sims, however, believed that airport officials dragged their heels for another reason: They were afraid Link would cut into their parking garage revenue. Regardless, no agreement had been reached with the airport by the middle of 2004. This left Sound Transit in an embarrassing position. The southern end of the Central Link route ended, essentially, in a parking lot in Tukwila. This led critics to deride Link as the "train to nowhere."[2] Passengers would have to disembark at Tukwila Station and take a bus to the airport. Finally, at the end of 2004, Sound Transit and Sea-Tac Airport/Port of Seattle came to an agreement to run the Link extension into the fourth level of the airport parking garage. Sims said he was never happy with this compromise—he wanted the Link station in the terminal itself, or at least closer to the check-in counters—but at least Link now had an airport station on its map. Because of the delay, completion of the airport track lagged about six months behind the rest of the Link route. Still, Ladenburg was happy to announce that Link would soon be "the train to somewhere."[3]

The Central Link route was sometimes on the surface, sometimes underground, and sometimes elevated, as in this under-construction stretch in Tukwila.

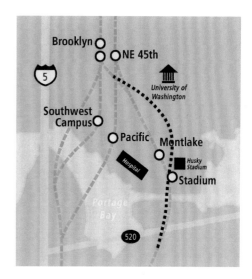

Plans were progressing swiftly, even for the still-theoretical segments of the overall Link plan—those yet to be funded. In April 2004 the board gave final approval for the future North Link route from downtown to the University of Washington. The problematic tunnel had, in the interim, become less problematic. The route had been shifted to the east, so that it went under the Lake Washington Ship Canal near the Montlake Bridge, instead of under Portage Bay. This avoided the "tricky" soils that engineers had discovered under the Bay. The new alignment also shifted the route to the east side of the campus, so there would now be a station near Husky Stadium. Additionally, the university and Sound Transit had come to an understanding on the thorny problem of underground vibrations and electromagnetic interference. Sound Transit agreed to an elaborate and costly system of mitigation: putting the underground tracks on "floating slabs." Eventually, the route would continue mostly straight north underground to Northgate, although this leg would have to come much later, as it turned out.

In 2004, Sound Transit settled on a North Link tunnel route (black dotted line) that was farther east than the earlier alternatives (blue dotted lines).

Work began in 2005 on the most critical stretch of the entire Link route: the downtown bus tunnel. In May 2000 King County and Metro officially transferred ownership of the tunnel to Sound Transit for about $195.6 million. Now Sound Transit was preparing to shut down the renamed Downtown Seattle Transit Tunnel for two years beginning in September 2005 to prepare it for light-rail.

Prepare it for light-rail? Wasn't it built with light-rail in mind? Yes, but as everyone soon discovered, the tunnel was far from Link-ready. The old rails had to be ripped out, the track bed lowered, and new, insulated rails had to be installed. The original rails had been installed without the insulation necessary for an electric rail system. Headlines in the *Seattle Times* screamed "Bus Tunnel Error is Costly in Shutdown Today," which was true, but not exactly that simple.[4] Jared Smith, whose consulting firm was involved in the original tunnel design, said that late in the tunnel design process, engineers had been told to put in rails, since that was a key political selling point. However, since Metro had been running short on budget, it chose to put the rails in without insulation, on the theory that by the time the tunnel was converted, light-rail technology would have undoubtedly changed so much that it would make little difference. This, according to Smith, is more or less what happened. Sound Transit had long ago decided to go with new low-platform train cars for easier passenger and wheelchair access, which meant the old rails were too high. The agency would either have to raise the tunnel's curb and platform height, which would involve ripping out all of the granite that had caused so much heartache during Granitegate—not to mention modifying all of the elevators and escalators—or it would have to lower the track bed by six inches. It was easier and cheaper to lower the track bed. In fact, because the non-insulated rails had been imbedded in the concrete base, there was less reinforcing steel to remove, so lowering the track bed was easier. "It turned out to be a bit of blessing," said Smith.

The Beacon Hill Tunnel boring machine was dubbed the Emerald Mole in a grade-school naming contest.

The project required closing the tunnel for two years and dumping all of those buses back on to the streets. About 140 more buses *every hour* would be lumbering down Second, Third, and Fourth avenues.[5] Third Avenue would become almost exclusively a bus thoroughfare during rush hours. (Autos would be allowed to drive only one or two blocks before turning off.) After some initial consternation, downtown merchants, represented by the Downtown Seattle Association, broke precedent and actually applauded the closure. "This puts hundreds of potential new customers right in front of [our businesses]," said the association president. "Isn't this a tough problem to have? Too many pedestrians up on the street. A lot of downtowns across the country would do anything to have this problem."[6]

Although George Benson's Waterfront Streetcar line was permanently closed in 2005, other streetcar projects were in the works. In 2005 the city approved construction of the South Lake Union Streetcar line, running from the Westin Hotel downtown to the Fred Hutchinson Cancer Research Center on the rapidly developing south shore of Lake Union. Like the streetcar lines of old, it was intended to boost development and residential construction—and maybe even transform Lake Union Park into a popular destination. It cost $52 million—a big number for a 1.3-mile line—with half of its construction funding coming from a Local Improvement District tax on adjacent property owners. However, the project defied the typical transit stereotype by taking only two years to complete. The South Lake Union Streetcar opened in December 2007 and gained humorous national notoriety when local entrepreneurs printed up T-shirts that said, "Ride the S.L.U.T.—South Lake Union Trolley." On opening day, Mayor Nickels told the crowd, "I don't care what you call it, as long as you ride it."[7]

Along the Central Link route, the first new rails were finally being hammered into place. Construction continued at a furious pace in 2006, with the "Emerald Mole" beginning its journey underneath Beacon Hill. (Emerald Mole was the name that Sean Davidson, age 7, gave to the Beacon Hill Tunnel boring machine in a kids-only naming contest.) The work continued on budget and on schedule but was the scene of a tragedy when tunnel worker Michael Bruce Merryman, 49, died on February 7, 2007, when he was thrown from a supply train.[8] Today, a plaque in the Beacon Hill Tunnel is dedicated to him.

The Federal Way Transit Center opened in 2006. Plans called for it to eventually serve Link trains as well as buses.

The Sound Transit board was well aware that Central Link was essentially a starter route. It didn't serve the Eastside and didn't even go north of downtown. To truly move people around the freeway congestion—which continued to get worse—the agency would need to extend Link not only north, but also south and east. In 2004 and 2005 they began planning for another major ballot issue, which would eventually result in Sound Transit 2, aka ST2. In July 2006 the board came up with three options. The first and cheapest, which would increase the sales tax three cents on a $10 purchase, called for extending Link north to Northgate, east to Bellevue, and south to Kent. The second option, costing four cents per $10, extended Link north to Mountlake Terrace, east to Bellevue, and south to Federal Way. The third option, costing five cents per $10, extended Link north to Lynnwood, east to Redmond, and south to Tacoma.[9]

The board eventually opted for the full package: the five-cent option to Lynnwood, Redmond and Tacoma.

Sound Transit had originally wanted to go on the ballot in late 2006, but the Washington State Legislature had other plans. In fact, it actually passed legislation barring Sound Transit from the 2006 ballot. "Almost the last day of the legislative session, we got a fax from the governor that said they were forbidding Sound Transit to go out for ST2 by themselves," recalled Earl. "… We were just stunned. … I called and chewed out the governor's chief of staff something bad. It didn't help. It just felt better."

The Legislature had its own gigantic ballot measure in mind, which went beyond transit. "They wanted to take transit and marry it with highways; they were planning on a ballot issue in 2007—which ended up being called Roads & Transit," said Nickels. "… The legislature in its wisdom thought the only way it could pass would be *with* transit." Nickels was skeptical—he called it a "shotgun marriage"—but he and the rest of the board went along with the idea since it seemed better than no ballot issue at all. The package was called Proposition 1, Roads & Transit. At $18 billion it was the largest tax package in Washington State history. It included Sound Transit's 20-year plan for 50 more miles of light-rail—the five-cent option—plus 186 miles of new highway and freeway lanes in the Puget Sound region. Its fatal flaw, aside from its price tag, was that backers had managed to craft a measure that voters on both sides of the issue could oppose. Transit supporters could reject it because it included roads, and highway supporters could reject it because it

Sound Transit workers signed the hull of the tunnel boring machine at a January, 2006 launch ceremony.

The Central Link line went straight down the middle of Martin Luther King Jr. Way through Rainier Valley. Here, it is shown under construction in Columbia City in 2007.

included rail. Dow Constantine, who had joined the Sound Transit Board in 2006 as a King County Council member, later said, "If you have the Sierra Club and the traditional anti-transit crowd on the same side of an election, you don't have much chance of success." Nickels put it even more starkly: "It never had a chance. … It died a slow, ugly death."

The defeat was total. When voters weighed in on November 2007, the measure barely mustered a 44 percent yes vote. Sound Transit board members were dejected. It looked like another, possibly final, chance had slipped away. But some saw a sliver of hope in a postelection poll, which indicated that a transit proposition, alone on the ballot, would have won by a 53 percent margin. Mayor Nickels was elected Sound Transit board chair in late 2007, and he was determined to get Sound Transit 2 on the ballot in November 2008—by itself this time. Few others shared his zeal. Nickels said there was almost "no political appetite" for Sound Transit 2 among leaders in Pierce and Snohomish counties, whose voters had massively rejected Roads & Transit. In fact, all three county executives were reluctant to reenter the fray. On the 18-member Sound Transit board, Nickels was certain of only three votes—Constantine's being one. Then Nickels went to work, attempting to convince the skeptics that a November 2008 ballot issue would be Sound Transit's best, and maybe final, chance. First, he argued, the measure would be on a presidential election ballot "and I had learned *that* lesson 12 years earlier." Second, he believed the legislature might take away Sound Transit's taxing authority entirely if it didn't act now. "We would have been squeezed by the state legislature out of any expansion," said Nickels. It was, in other words, another "last chance" proposition for transit.

Despite the long odds—or maybe because of them—Nickels relished the battle. "It was the most fun I had ever had in politics, putting the votes together to put it on the ballot and then putting the campaign together to get it passed," said Nickels. He said he personally negotiated with each member of the board—persuading, cajoling, and "arm-twisting"—and by July 2008, those three votes had turned into 16. The motion succeeded, 16–2, and it meant that a new ST2 package would face the voters on the same day that Barack Obama would face John McCain.

The staff of Sound Transit, including Joni Earl (center, behind the sign) gathered to celebrate the Sound Transit 2 victory in what would later be called the Joni Earl Great Hall at Union Station.

Joni Earl celebrates the Sound Transit 2 ballot victory with Sound Transit executives (from left) Ron Lewis, Bonnie Todd and Ahmad Fazel.

This new proposal was for a 15-year plan, extending light-rail to Lynnwood, Bellevue, Redmond, and Federal Way. It also included major Sound Transit Express bus expansions. The proposal had a total price tag of $17.9 billion— counting inflation, operations, maintenance, and reserves.[10] If it didn't pass, Sound Transit's future was bleak. "I'd [have to] start laying off staff," said Earl.

The subsequent Sound Transit 2 election campaign had its discouraging moments, especially when it came to fundraising. "The business community was really burned after the statewide fiasco of the year before," said Nickels. For instance, Microsoft spent "hundreds of thousands of dollars" backing Roads & Transit, but for Sound Transit 2, "they would barely return my calls." The entire campaign was conducted by Nickels' own political organization, "the people who got me elected," he said. Yet he sensed a swell of grassroots enthusiasm—"… there were people holding up signs at intersections all over." Another good omen: gas prices jumped briefly to over $4 per gallon, making voters even less enamored of cars and freeways. On a more dismal note, this was the autumn that the housing market collapsed and the Great Recession took hold. People everywhere were terrified about their financial future.

Seattle Deputy Mayor Tim Ceis (left) and Ric Ilgenfritz, who led the planning for Sound Transit, at the ST2 ballot victory party.

The usual opposition popped up, led once again by Kemper Freeman Jr. Sound Transit 2's record-breaking price tag seemed to be an insurmountable political problem. One group of opponents produced ads saying it "costs too much, does too

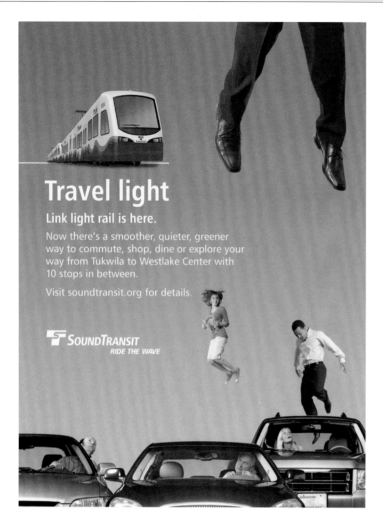

This Sound Transit ad focused on the Central Link's Tukwila to Westlake Center service.

little, and takes too long."[11] But Sound Transit had commissioned polls that showed something surprising: Voters were not *that* concerned about the money. They just wanted more service. So Nickels chose to embrace the issue, arguing that the proposal's size proved that this was no weak half-measure. "People threw at me that it was the largest tax increase in our region's history," said Nickels. "And I accepted that just fine." He countered that "we were a competent organization, building real stuff … and the public was absolutely wanting more."

During a debate at the University of Washington, Freeman and Nickels faced off. Freeman argued once again that light-rail would do nothing to reduce congestion and that "our leaders have led us on a wild goose chase on this issue."[12] Nickels replied that he envisioned a system "not shaped entirely, or even mostly, by the automobile," but one in which a commuter's biggest decision would be whether to walk to work or walk to transit. Ten years later, Nickels remembered the result of the debate. "I just hammered him on every point … I just cleaned his clock." Maybe so or maybe not, but the verdict on the plan's merits was about to be issued by the voters on November 4, 2008.

The suspense was over early that night. Sound Transit 2 cruised to a 57 percent to 43 percent victory. For the second time in 12 years, light-rail supporters were euphoric, and no one more so than Nickels. "This thing that I had put my passion into—and, really, my public life behind—was passing despite these horrible, horrible economic headlines," said Nickels. "It was really gratifying." The nation's first black president had also been elected on that historic night, but in the Puget Sound region, the election was historic in another way. It guaranteed the construction of a 55-mile rail transit system, roughly equivalent to what the region might have had 30 years earlier under Forward Thrust.

Sound Transit was already carrying 16 million passengers a year on buses and Sounder trains, but finally, work was nearing completion on the system's splashiest component, Central Link light-rail. New low-platform railcars were already making tests runs. Finishing touches were being put on Link stations, which were often more of an engineering challenge than the tracks themselves, especially the underground stations. The Downtown Seattle Transit Tunnel was ready for Link and had already reopened for buses in September 2007. Planning was underway on the next Link phase, the Sound Transit 2 extensions, but the nationwide financial crisis was already taking a toll in the form of decreased sales tax revenue forecasts. This was partially offset by good news arriving from Washington, D.C.

Jim Ellis and Senator Patty Murray (bottom right) on the VIP/ media ride with other Seattle dignitaries to celebrating the start of light rail, 2009.

The Federal Transit Administration awarded an $813 million grant for the University Link extension in January 2009. Federal stimulus grants began to arrive later in the year. Perhaps the best moments for the University Link project came in March and August of 2009, when bids were opened for the Capitol Hill/University District tunnels—and again, to everyone's relief, they came in well below estimates.

The first day of Link operations was on July 18, 2009, a day people had awaited since 1941, when the last streetcar had rattled through Seattle. A ribbon-cutting ceremony at the new Mount Baker station kicked off this new era. Seattle Mayor Nickels, who had been reelected to a second term in 2005, had for the past two years driven along the construction route on Martin Luther King Jr. Way, anxiously watching the progress. He admitted he was nervous even on the day before the opening. Then on July 18, 2009, all of that anxiety vanished as he cut the ribbon and took his first ride. "It felt like 22 years of filth was washed away," said Nickels. "And filth is the wrong word. But 22 years of political challenges and engineering challenges. It just felt like—this was worth it."

The lost opportunities of Forward Thrust were redeemed at the 2009 Link opening ceremony with a forward thrust of a giant pair of scissors.

It was among the most dramatic turning points in the long history of Puget Sound transit. An astonishing 45,000 people hopped aboard Link on that inaugural day; 92,000 on its opening weekend; and 6 million in its first year. One opening-day passenger told reporters, "It makes Seattle feel like a real city. … It's about time."[13] Ridership numbers were boosted significantly in December 2009, when the last leg to Sea-Tac Airport, aka "the train to somewhere," was opened. These ridership figures were solid, but not spectacular for a region with three million people. Link was still basically a 14-mile starter system, serving only one narrow commuting corridor, and by no means the busiest. The other corridors to the east and north were still on the drawing, but taxpayers no longer had to wonder if Sound Transit could deliver. It was racing through the city, jammed with commuters.

The momentum was slowed somewhat by the continuing Great Recession, which threatened to cut into the Link expansion plans. In late 2010 the Sound Transit board announced that its tax revenues were 25 percent lower than forecast at the time of the Sound Transit 2 vote. Sound Transit vowed to run leaner, and in mid-2011 also raised its fares. Tickets on Regional Express buses would now cost $2.50 within one county, and $3.50 on trips over county lines. Link tickets rose a quarter, to $2 and $2.75. Additionally, the Sound Transit board had to push a few project deadlines back toward the end of the 15-year plan. Link was now projected to reach Northgate by 2021 and Lynnwood by 2023. The Bellevue/Overlake route was also scheduled for completion in 2021. The Federal Way extension was pushed back, too. Only the University Link was still on track for 2016, with tunneling for the once-calamitous Capitol Hill tunnel beginning in May 2011.

Greg Nickels and Joni Earl devoted huge parts of their careers to this moment: riding on a Link train.

Route alignment again became a contentious issue, especially on the route to Bellevue. The first big decision was how to get over Lake Washington. Smith said a tunnel was considered in early planning stages, à la the 1911 Bogue Plan. However, Lake Washington is deep—too deep, it turned out, for a tunnel. Light-rail cars have the same traction issues as the old trolleys; they can handle only a certain degree of grade. Engineers considered a new, Link-only bridge, but soon realized that building a bridge would entail a nightmare of right-of-way issues.

Eventually, it became clear that the best solution was the most obvious one: use the existing Interstate 90 bridge, which had been built—thanks to the 1960s Municipal League—with enough width for two light-rail lanes down the middle. Those lanes had been used as reversible rush-hour and HOV lanes, but now Sound Transit was claiming them for their intended purpose. It seemed like a simple solution—but, of course, few Seattle mass transit solutions have ever been simple. Kemper Freeman Jr. sued, contending that the bridge could be used only as a highway because it was funded partially by gas taxes. The Washington State Supreme Court rejected the suit.

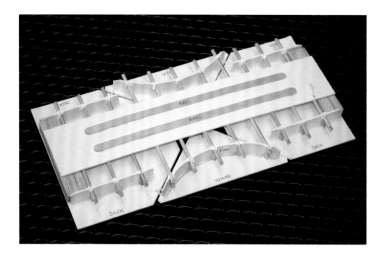

Putting light-rail tracks on the Interstate 90 floating bridge required engineering ingenuity. This is an early mockup of the design.

It turned out that putting light-rail tracks on a floating bridge was problematic for a more startling reason: It had never been attempted before, anywhere in the world. The engineers went to work and came up with a concept for a transition track that "floats and moves to the whims of the water and the wind."[14] Just to make certain it would work, they built a stretch of the track at the national railroad test site in Pueblo, Colorado, shipped two Link cars there, and tested it extensively. It was a success.

Other East Link issues were just as thorny. On the east side of Lake Washington, the route curved north and was originally conceived as a surface route through downtown Bellevue. However, neighborhoods near the route protested. The Bellevue City Council was split on the issue. Once again, Kemper Freeman Jr. weighed in, saying the neighborhoods were "being trampled to death by Sound Transit."[15] After urging from the Bellevue City Council, Sound Transit agreed to switch the downtown Bellevue route to a tunnel, with the costs to be shared between Bellevue and Sound Transit. With these problems finally settled, the East Link route was finalized in late 2011.

Link cars were shipped to Pueblo, Colorado, to test whether the floating bridge design would work. It did.

In the midst of those bigger plans, a smaller rail project was undertaken by the City of Seattle and Sound Transit. It was the First Hill Streetcar line, a 2.5-mile modern electric streetcar line connecting Pioneer Square and First Hill with the future Capitol Hill light-rail station. The First Hill Streetcar plan had been included in the Sound Transit 2 funding package as a compromise to a contentious issue: whether or not to have a First Hill Link station. Sound Transit had reluctantly abandoned the idea of a station in this population-dense part of the city because it would have been deep underground by necessity—and deep meant expensive. Sound Transit worked out a deal to build this surface streetcar line, paid for by Sound Transit, built and owned by the City of Seattle, and operated by Metro. This line, even more than Link, resembled a throwback to the trolley days. Ground was broken in 2012 and the line opened in 2016, joining the South Lake Union Streetcar in Seattle's mini-system of modern streetcars.

Just as Joni Earl and Greg Nickels had hoped, the opening of the Central Link line made a massive difference in the public perception of Sound Transit. Ridership hit 28 million in 2012 and 30 million in 2013, nearly double what it had been in 2008. People were voting, so to speak, with their ORCA—or "One Regional Card for All"—cards. These prepaid electronic fare cards were unveiled in 2009 by Sound Transit, Metro, Pierce Transit, Everett Transit, and Community Transit. Sound Transit's reputation was boosted by another announcement, in November 2013: The University Link line was going to open six months early, in March 2016, because it was under budget and ahead of schedule.

SOUND TRANSIT FUTURE SERVICE

This 2017 Sound Transit map projected future plans out to 2041.

ORCA (One Regional Card for All) provided a simple way for riders to pay fares on any of the region's bus or rail lines.

Just when everything seemed to be going the agency's way, it was shaken by an accident—not a transit accident, but a pedestrian-bicycle accident in April 2014. Joni Earl was on a walk near her Tacoma home when a little boy on a bicycle ran into her and knocked her to the pavement. Her head was gashed and her wrist broken. She went into surgery a few days later to repair her wrist. It seemed a minor setback, but while recovering from surgery the next day, she "woke up with this horrendous headache." She was rushed to the hospital, where doctors discovered she had suffered a brain bleed. After brain surgery, she emerged with serious stroke-like symptoms. "My right leg doesn't work right and my right arm doesn't work right," she would later say. She was in the hospital for nearly six months and was unable to work for most of the next two years.

In her absence, deputy CEO Mike Harbour was appointed Acting CEO in June 2014. The staff and board moved ahead, not only on the Sound Transit 2 projects, but on the germ of a new and vastly more ambitious idea: a gigantic Sound Transit 3 ballot proposal. Dow Constantine, now the King County Executive and Sound Transit board chair, knew that Sound Transit 2 had been, by necessity, "a bit of a half-measure." Constantine was a passionate advocate for high-capacity transit, and he and others had begun to say, "Gosh, we could have done more." As they talked to political leaders and the public, it dawned on them that what people really wanted was a complete system. When Constantine floated the idea of a Sound Transit 3 measure, he was simply "responding to strong support for continued expansion," as he said at the time. Clearly, Sound Transit was not finished by a long shot. The target date for a potential ballot measure was set for November 2016.

A year earlier, after it had become clear that Earl would not be able to fully resume her duties, the Sound Transit board hired a new CEO, Peter Rogoff, the former head of the Federal Transit Administration. He was the man who had signed the $813 million grant in 2009 and was aware that he was replacing a legend. "I am not the best candidate," he told the board. "The best candidate is a healthy Joni Earl."[16] Sadly, that was no longer in the cards. Earl officially retired in April 2016. She later said of her old job, "I miss it every day."

Just before Earl retired, the light appeared at the end of the tunnel—literally—for the University Link, a project that had first been promised nearly 20 years earlier. By the beginning of 2016, the twin-tunnels were bored, the tracks were laid, and the two stations beneath Capitol Hill and the university were finished. Both were

In the original Sound Move proposal, Link's Capitol Hill Station was projected to open around 2005. The confetti finally cascaded down in March 2016.

actually ahead of schedule (the Sound Transit 2 schedule, at least, not the original Sound Move schedule). On March 19, 2016, the University Link finally opened, and first-day riders were impressed by its efficiency and speed. It took only four minutes to get from the University of Washington to Capitol Hill. "We were absolutely flying," one rider said.[17] The University station, designed by LMN Architects, with art by Leo Saul Berk, had a spectacular 55-foot-high central chamber, which the architects described as "one of the highest interior volumes in the city." The opening of what was essentially a $1.8 billion subway "marked a new era in transit for the congested Seattle area," said the *Seattle Times*.[18]

Even Sound Transit planners were startled by the University Link demand. After the first week, they put longer trains into service to handle the crowds. Rogoff, who spent a few Saturdays at University Station as a volunteer guide during UW football games, said Husky fans used to sit in cars for hours getting in and out of parking lots. Now, they were astonished at getting "that many hours of their weekend back." By May 2016 overall Link weekday ridership was up 83 percent over the previous year, and most of that increase could be attributed to the University Link. Planners had long projected that Link's strongest ridership would come

At the University
of Washington,
an escalator and
elevator pass through
a 55-foot-high
central chamber,
one of the highest
interior volumes in
Seattle. Leo Saul

Berk's artwork,
Subterraneum, *inte-*
grates with the LMN
Architects design to
suggest underground
soil layers.

from the north, and these numbers confirmed it. These statistics also put to rest one longstanding criticism about light-rail. Naysayers had persistently predicted that ridership would be anemic. "They were wrong when they said it, and they're wrong now," said Sims.

Link had finally gone beyond a starter system. That fall the line would grow another 1.6 miles, as the stretch from Sea-Tac Airport south to Angle Lake opened. Almost exactly 20 years after Sound Move had passed, Seattle now had 19 miles of light-rail. "It was amazing," said communications consultant Anne Fennessy. "People loved, loved, loved the services and wanted more of them. Now the question was, 'Why are you taking so long?'"

The Sound Transit board, under chairman Constantine, had already tackled the most urgent question posed by a potential Sound Transit 3 measure: Where would the money come from? In 2015 the Washington State Legislature and Governor Jay Inslee gave Sound Transit additional funding authority, which included the now-standard five cents per $10 sales tax. It also included a property tax assessment of up to 25 cents for each $1,000 of assessed valuation and a Motor Vehicle Excise Tax levy of about $80 per year for a $10,000 vehicle.[19] Constantine did not think this was the ideal funding solution—or anything close to it—"but that was the hand we were dealt, and we needed to play it as well as possible." It would cost the average adult in the Sound Transit taxing district about $169 per year.[20]

The Capitol Hill Station, shown here, along with the entire University Link, proved immensely popular.

Sound Transit would eventually need that extra taxing authority, because the Sound Transit 3 plan was a whopper. It was a $50 billion plan that would add 62 more miles of light-rail. It was also the largest tax increase proposal in the state's history, by billions. Nickels, who led the previous record-setter at $17 billion, later said, "I feel like a piker now." For Sound Transit it was an audacious all in bet, but the board was confident. The agency's polling showed solid public support for a major expansion, even at a record-setting cost. In fact, when the board asked for public input on the original $50 billion draft plan, people had one consistent request: We want more and we want it sooner, please.

"As we went out and talked with people, it became clear that the public's interest had been piqued by the opening of light-rail," said Constantine. "… People recognized that the old way of doing things just was not going to work, because we could not possibly build enough roads, and enough city streets, and alleys and driveways and garages, to function based on this automobile-only model. We needed an alternative. We needed something different. And so everywhere we went—and not just in the cozy confines of downtown Seattle or near the cities—everywhere we went, people were asking for more." That's why, in the final plan, deadlines were moved up and the price tag went to $54 billion.

The final Sound Transit 3 ballot measure, adopted by the board in June 2016, went beyond even the 1911 dreams of Virgil Bogue or the 1968 dreams of Jim Ellis. It would fund light-rail all the way north to Everett and all the way south to Tacoma where it would hook up with the existing Tacoma Link line. Light-rail would also go all the way east to downtown Redmond and Issaquah. The measure would fund a new line from downtown Seattle to Ballard, and a spur line to West Seattle. It would add more Sounder trains and extend the route south all the way to Joint Base Lewis-McChord and Dupont. It would add more express buses throughout the east, north, and south sides of Seattle. And it would, said Rogoff, make Link one of the biggest rail transit systems in the country, comparable with California's Bay Area Rapid Transit (BART) and Washington, D.C.'s Metro.[21]

Constantine called the plan a "combination of Sound Transit 3 and Sound Transit 4," because it completed the system in one giant package. Even the folks at the farthest reaches of the system—Everett and Tacoma—had a vested interest in funding the system in one big measure. They were concerned, rightly or wrongly, that once the central part of the project was completed, the people in the center might lose enthusiasm for finishing it up. Constantine did not believe that was an issue—people in King County "wanted to see themselves as the center of a system that opened up the whole region to mass transit"—but he was certainly in favor of throwing the dice on one all-encompassing measure.

Opposition sprang up immediately from many of the usual quarters. The Seattle Times editorial board urged voters to reject Sound Transit 3, because the paper calculated that the issue would end up costing taxpayers far more than the official $169 per year figure. That number, said the Times, did not include the taxes people were still paying for the previous Sound Transit measures. The editors said it would actually cost the average King County household $20,000 over 25 years. Most alarming of all, the editors warned, the measure would give Sound Transit "permanent taxing authority," which would commit taxpayers to "a lifetime of taxation."[22]

Sound Transit leaders pushed back hard on these "permanent" and "lifetime" allegations, saying it was legally bound to roll back the taxes after the projects were built. They also strongly denied that the true costs were somehow hidden. Constantine would later say that he didn't think there "has ever been a tax measure with more transparency about what things would cost." Meanwhile, other critics cited long-familiar arguments: The plan was Seattle-centric, it pushed light-rail at the expense of buses, and it was a gigantic waste of tax money.[23]

Sound Transit 3 still had a remarkable array of influential supporters. Constantine, who led the campaign, lined up support from labor, business, environmental groups (including the Sierra Club), and advocates for social justice. "Freeing people to be able to reach opportunity is in itself a social justice investment," said Constantine. "In fact, the lack of mobility is a limiting factor in whether you can succeed in life." Constantine also helped raise a $3.7 million campaign chest, thanks to local corporate heavyweights, including many of the same businesses that sat on their hands during Sound Transit 2.

Dow Constantine (right) and Sound Transit CEO Peter Rogoff tour the Roosevelt site, 2016.

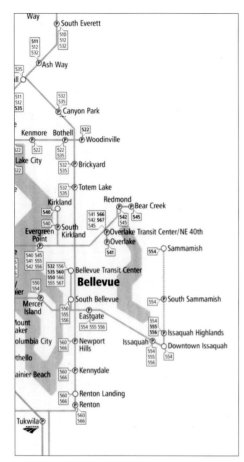

This 2016 map of ST Express bus routes illustrates how buses continue to play a crucial role for Eastside commuters —especially until Link finally makes it across Lake Washington.

Constantine recalled one critical moment when he received a call from a key Microsoft official. "I stepped out onto a little alcove in front of an abandoned store on the sidewalk in D.C. with my papers on the ground … and talked to him for probably 35–40 minutes about the need and the vision and what this meant to our community—and the fact that the moment had arrived," said Constantine. "And that we needed the business community to really embrace this as something not just for their individual business but for the good of this community. And I left it at that." Shortly afterward, Constantine received word that Microsoft had just made the campaign's largest contribution. "They did not do this grudgingly or as a matter of mere duty, they were enthusiastic about it," he said. "… The fact is, they were having more and more trouble getting their employees to work—not just Microsoft, but all businesses—and that [means] money to them, right? But having a globally significant business stand up and say, 'This is the thing we must do for our region now' and reaching out to their peers—that made a big, big difference. And others joined in."

On election night, November 8, 2016, Constantine said he was "very nervous"—more nervous than during most of his own elections. When the results rolled in, it was clear once again that Puget Sound voters were not particularly concerned about whether they were creating a "permanent taxing authority"—they just wanted to get to work on time. Sound Transit 3 sailed to victory with about 55 percent of the vote. A happy Constantine summed it up that night by telling reporters, "People have just plain had it with the traffic."[24] Looking back on it a year later, he said it was "the greatest victory, probably the greatest achievement in my life—the thing I'd been building towards for my nearly 20 years in office." A few days later, Seattle Times editorial columnist Mark Higgins put the vote in historic context by saying, "Tuesday's vote should finally put to rest 50 years of regional hand-wringing over mass transit."[25]

Actually, he had that slightly wrong. It was more like 130 years of hand-wringing. The region had approved one of the largest transit projects in American history.[26]

Tukwila Station was the end of the Link line until the route was finished to Sea-Tac Airport five months later.

Profile: Joni Earl

Joni Earl was Sound Transit's executive director from 2001 to 2016.

When Joni Earl joined Sound Transit in 2000, she had no idea that, in her words, "all hell" was about to break loose.

"I took a weekend off then didn't get a day off for five months," Earl told the *Seattle Post-Intelligencer* in 2003. "I worked every day for four or five months and had several 24-hour loads. I look back over those five months, and I don't know how I physically or emotionally did it. I think it was just fear."

There was, indeed, fear to spare during what came to be known in Sound Transit circles as the Dark Days. Fear may explain how Earl survived, but it doesn't explain how she eventually thrived. She was also exceptionally well prepared to take over a large public agency. She had demonstrated notable competence and command of local government right out of college.

Earl was born and raised in Bremerton, Washington, where her father, Morrie Dawkins, served as mayor. She attended Olympic Community College for two years then transferred to Washington State University and graduated in 1975 with a degree in accounting and would later earn an MBA at the University of Puget Sound. Within a year of leaving WSU, she tested for and won a job as assistant city treasurer of Bremerton. She was 22 years old and she had 17 people—all of them older—reporting to her.

At 32 she became city manager of Mill Creek—a Snohomish County suburb of nearly 10,000 people. She ran the Mill Creek government for five years and left in 1992 to become deputy county executive of Snohomish County. Her entire career had been in local government—but not necessarily in mass transit issues. Earl had worked closely with Snohomish County Executive Bob Drewel on the Sound Move ballot proposition, but that was the extent of her mass transit experience.

"Transportation was not on my horizon or in my thinking," she said. "I applied for the Sound Transit job (Chief Operating Officer) because I'd been at Snohomish County for eight and a half years and I was ready for a change."

And what a change it turned out to be. She had been there two and a half months when the Dark Days descended. The executive director departed and Earl was named acting executive director. Suddenly, the weight of the entire multi-billion-dollar project was on her shoulders. "I've never worked for an agency that's just flat out had a lousy reputation," she told the *PI*.

Yet her skills and talents were exactly what Sound Transit required. She was realistic, ethical, precise, collaborative, transparent and, in her words, "tough on the issues, but not hard on people." When the Sound Transit board chose a permanent executive director in 2001, they chose Earl over several nationally known transit experts because she had already demonstrated the ability to identify problems, fix them, and gradually heal the agency's self-inflicted wounds. If she had failed at any one of those tasks, Sound Transit's story might have been shorter and sadder.

Even after Earl's 2016 retirement following a health crisis, her name still echoed through Sound Transit headquarters. The Joni Earl Great Hall at Union Station was dedicated in 2017, reflecting her integral role in Sound Transit's history—and the larger history of Puget Sound mass transit.[27]

Joni Earl pulled Sound Transit out of the "Dark Days" and became, by nearly universal consensus, the most important figure in Sound Transit's history. She is shown here at the 2009 Link ribbon-cutting.

CHAPTER TEN

A Link to the Past, a Link to the Future

· · · · · · · · · · · · · ●

If the hand-wringing was finished over *whether* to build light-rail, the issue of *how* to build it had just started. In mid-2017 Peter Rogoff announced that the Link extension to Lynnwood was $500 million over budget and six months behind schedule. Sound Transit subsequently had to move Lynnwood's estimated opening date back from 2023 to 2024. In mid-2018, more bad news arrived. The projected cost of the Link extension from Angle Lake to Federal Way jumped from $2.09 billion to $2.55 billion. This caused considerable concern among Sound Transit's staff and board. Mike Lindblom of the *Seattle Times* summed up the problem: "You can't make tracks to Tacoma without reaching Federal Way first."[1]

This was no replay of the Dark Days. The faulty projections were not due to blind optimism, but to soaring land costs in Seattle's wild 2017–2018 real estate market, along with higher prices for steel and copper. Rogoff predicted in July 2018 that the Federal Way extension would finish on time in 2024. There was good news for other parts of Link as well. The extension from the University of Washington to Northgate was "trending under budget and a little bit ahead of schedule," said Rogoff in mid-2018. Then in December 2018, the Federal Transit Administration came through with a $1.17 billion grant for the Link extension to Lynnwood—the largest transit grant yet awarded by President Donald Trump's administration. Construction began in early 2019 and the mid-2024 opening date seemed assured.

If history has taught us anything, it's that more drama lies ahead. Problems will arise from unexpected directions. Rogoff likes to remind people of the sheer scope of the undertaking. Sound Transit 3, he said, is "the most ambitious transit expansion plan in the United States." Dow Constantine is also perfectly aware that problems are simply part of the job. "We're doing something that is inherently very,

Left and previous page: University Station was Link's northernmost terminus as of 2019

very difficult and that requires … long-term planning and an enormous amount of discipline," he said. "And, you know, politicians by their nature see things in terms of the next year, or the next election. But we have to nurture a culture, and an agency, that thinks in terms of decades and longer." In stark contrast to Seattle's transit tangle of 120 years ago, a plan is firmly in place and a funding strategy is laid out.

Here's the status of that Sound Transit plan, as of early 2019:

- Central Link: completed and running between Angle Lake and the University of Washington

- North Link: under construction and scheduled to open to Northgate by 2021, to Lynnwood by 2024, and to Everett by 2036

- East Link: under construction and scheduled for completion to Bellevue and the Redmond Technology Center by 2023, and to downtown Redmond by 2024

- Issaquah–Kirkland Link: in planning and scheduled to open in 2041

- South Link: under construction and scheduled to open to Federal Way in 2024 and to the Tacoma Dome in 2030

- Tacoma Link: extension to the Hilltop area scheduled to open in 2022 and to Tacoma Community College in 2039

- Ballard Link: in planning and scheduled to open between downtown Seattle and Ballard by 2035

- West Seattle Link: in planning and scheduled to open to Alaska Junction in 2030

- Bus Rapid Transit: in planning and scheduled to open from Lynnwood to Burien (via Interstate 405 and SR 518) in 2024, and from Woodinville to North Seattle (via SR 522) in 2024

- Sounder: completed and running from Everett to Lakewood, with 11 round-trips every weekday from Seattle to Tacoma, and four round-trips every weekday between Seattle and Everett; southern extension to DuPont is scheduled to open in 2036[2]

Sound Transit was the flashiest part of the transit scene, yet despite all of the rail drama, most mass transit was still handled by buses. In fact, transit was largely operated by the local agencies that had been getting people to work for decades: Metro, Pierce Transit, Community Transit, and Everett Transit. As of 2016 only about 17 percent of transit ridership was light-rail, and even by the time the entire Link system is scheduled for completion around 2041, light-rail is still projected

A Transit Tour, 2018:
ST Express Bus

What was it like riding the Sound Transit system, circa 2018? Here's the author's account of riding the ST Express Bus, Route 512 from Seattle to Everett:

On Fourth Avenue the ST Express 512 rolls to a stop on Pike Street. I climb on board and insert $3.75 into the fare box next to the driver. I am one of the few to do this—almost everyone else simply taps their ORCA card.

I take a seat and am startled to see someone climb up what appears to be a stairwell. It dawns on me that this is one of Sound Transit's double-decker buses. I climb up the narrow stairs and find an expanse of seats and even better view. Soon we're rolling out of downtown and pulling onto Interstate 5. The ST Express is posher than the average bus. The seats are well-cushioned and everyone has a reading light and ventilation controls—like an airline seat. At the front of the bus is an electronic message board scrolling the name of the next stop.

We are rolling along with the auto traffic in the regular lanes of Interstate 5 until we exit to a dedicated transit freeway stop at N.E. 45th Street. Before long, however, we merge over to the far left—the HOV lane. We exit left at the Mountlake Terrace Freeway Station, pick up some more passengers, and merge smoothly right back into the HOV lane. Not all of the stops are quite so seamless. At the Ash Way Park and Ride, we have to make a few turns on the surface streets to get to our stop. There are one or two stoplights, but it takes only a few minutes.

Most of my fellow passengers are students and many disembark here. We circle back to the freeway and, after just a few more quick stops, we pull off onto the surface streets of Everett. We drive into Everett Station, the route's terminus. People scatter to their cars or head for one of the waiting buses from Community Transit or Everett Transit. The entire trip has taken 54 minutes.

The Everett Station bus loop, 2014.

to handle under 50 percent of transit riders.[3] The local bus systems, increasingly interconnected with Sound Transit's trains and express buses, continued to be the backbone of the transit network, and riders weren't necessarily concerned with whose buses they were taking. "I don't think people distinguish between Pierce, Metro, Community, and Sound Transit," said Anne Fennessy, who has done research on local transit attitudes. "They just want a bus." Constantine said the goal of the entire interconnected system "is to present a seamless experience for the passenger."

In a way, the local bus routes, not light-rail, remained the 2018 equivalent of the old trolley routes, fanning out from downtown and reaching deep into neighborhoods. Even in the Sound Transit era, the buses and trackless trolleys remained vital and well-used. Sims liked to use an apt metaphor: Link was the spine, and the buses were the ribcage. Metro bus ridership hit 122.2 million by 2017, not far from the old Seattle Transit System's all-time high of 131.2 million in 1945. Pierce Transit's annual ridership was 9 million in 2017; Community Transit's was 10 million in 2016; and Everett Transit's was 1.9 million in 2016.

In 2010 Metro launched a new bus service called RapidRide that mimicked light-rail by running on fixed routes at least every ten minutes. "With the RapidRide buses, we're shifting from the era of a spiderweb of relatively low-capacity bus services to one where we have trunk lines of high-capacity, very frequent, don't-need-to-look-at-the-schedule service," said Constantine, who, as King County Executive, is also Metro's boss. Constantine wants Metro to evolve as the county's "mobility agency." Mobility is, after all, both the product and goal of transit. He envisions a Metro that asks and answers the question: What is it going to take for us to give you the most mobility, using all of the region's assets?

By 2017 more and more people were flocking to this growing, interconnected system. A study showed that 48.4 percent of the central Seattle workforce arrived at work via transit—during an era when transit use was generally stagnant in most other cities.[4]

The most startling growth was at Sound Transit. In 2017 its annual ridership soared to 45.3 million: 21.4 million on Link, 18.4 million on Sound Transit Express buses, 4.4 million on Sounder, and close to 1 million on Tacoma Link. Together with the local bus systems, the Seattle area had the highest total transit growth among all large U.S. cities in 2017, according to the National Transit Database.[5] Overall transit ridership throughout the region increased by 11 percent from 2012 to 2017, bringing the greater Seattle ridership to an all-time high of 218.6 million—easily eclipsing the old Seattle-only record. In fact, Seattle ranked number eight among

Metro's Annual Ridership

Sources: King County Metro Annual Performance Measures, King County General Manager's Quarterly Management Reports

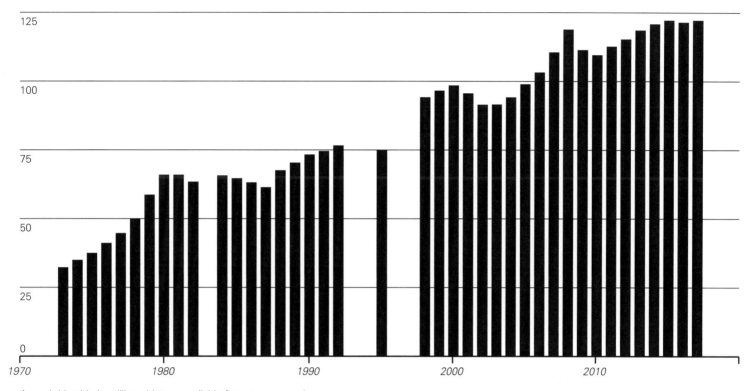

Annual ridership in millions (data unavailable from some years)

U.S. cities for transit riders as of 2017. The *Puget Sound Business Journal*, which analyzed transit use in late 2017, wrote, "The uptick in ridership is good news for the Puget Sound region, which is struggling with increasingly congested roads. ... Most of the newcomers—70 percent—take transit."[6]

What will it be like when the entire Sound Transit 3 project is completed in 2041? Constantine predicted that commutes will finally possess a rare quality— predictability. "A lot of people who currently sit in traffic on that University Bridge, trying to get down from Lynnwood or Everett, are going to just skip over, get on a train, and have absolute predictability about when they'll get to work," said Constantine. People will no longer have to face a trip across Lake Washington with dread. "You can hop on light-rail in Bellevue in 2024 and within a couple of stops be in downtown Seattle," said Rogoff. "It's going to kind of redefine what you will consider downtown." And finally, nearly a century after the death of the interurbans, Tacoma, Seattle, and Everett will be tied together with frequent, fast rail service.

A Transit Tour, 2018:
Link Light-rail

What was it like riding the Sound Transit system, circa 2018? Here's the author's account of riding the Link light-rail from Sea-Tac Airport to downtown Seattle:

Link's Tukwila Station sits high above 600 parking sports.

I walk up to the ticket kiosk at the Sea-Tac Airport station and buy an all-day pass for $6. Most of my fellow riders merely tap their ORCA cards on one of the electronic readers.

As we wait on the platform, an automated voice announces, "The northbound train to Seattle will arrive in two minutes." The bright white-and-blue train arrives on time and we file in through the automatic doors. There are plenty of seats, facing both to the front and to the rear.

The ride is powered by overhead electric wires—slightly reminiscent of the region's old trolley days, except this ride is quiet and surprisingly smooth. A voice from the loudspeaker intones, "Entering Tukwila International Boulevard

Station—doors to your right." The ride so far is on elevated tracks, high above the busy freeway traffic down below.

After we cross the Duwamish waterway and Interstate 5, the tracks descend to street level, right down the middle of Martin Luther King Jr. Way. We glide past junkyards surrounded by barbed wire—but also past rows of tidy new townhouses, advertising their easy access to Link.

The diverse nature of the neighborhood is illustrated by the names of the establishments we pass: East African Grocery, Café Huong Que, Abdul's Fast Food, Filipino Community Center, Abu Bakr Mosque, and Refugee Women's Alliance.

Link glides quietly above the Duwamish River.

Once or twice, we stop at a stoplight—we are sharing the road with auto traffic. For the most part, however, we zip quietly down the avenue to our various stops. The Beacon Hill station is underground—we enter the tunnel right before we get to it. When we emerge on the other side of Beacon Hill, we come out past the Old Rainier Brewery and see an expanse of Link railcars lined up at the massive Link maintenance base, right across the street from the brewery.

We head straight up 5th Avenue South at street level. Safeco Field (currently T-Mobile Park) and Century Link Field loom on our left. We enter the Seattle Transit Tunnel and wait for about a minute for traffic to clear. The tunnel is still shared with buses. The overhead voice reminds me that I am at Pioneer Square Station, my destination, and I exit into the perpetual twilight of the transit tunnel, along with a crowd of bustling commuters.

Passengers disembark from Link in the Pioneer Square Station in the Downtown Seattle Transit Tunnel. As of 2019, the tunnel was still serving both buses and trains.

But drivers will still be sitting in big traffic jams, most likely in the old familiar places. A 2017 list of the worst traffic bottlenecks in the U.S., compiled by the American Transportation Research Institute, had some dismal news for the region. Puget Sound was home to five of the 21 worst traffic bottlenecks in the U.S.:

- No. 4: Auburn's SR 18 and SR 167 interchange
- No. 10: Seattle's Interstate 5–Interstate 90 interchange
- No. 16: Tacoma's Interstate 5–Interstate 705/SR 16 interchange
- No. 18: Federal Way's SR 18–Interstate 5 interchange
- No. 21: Seattle's Interstate 90/Interstate 405 interchange

Other interchanges in Everett, Lynnwood, and Tacoma also made the Top 100 list—or should we say, the Worst 100 list?[7] Despite the rise in rapid transit, these bottlenecks kept getting worse, probably for two simple reasons. The region had more commuters than ever and most of them still drove to work, either because they wanted to or had to.

Sound Transit had never touted its system as a cure for auto congestion. Rather, it allows people the choice of avoiding it. "The one thing we are quick to say is that light-rail will not make congestion decrease," said Rogoff. "Because remember, we've got a million more people arriving in the region by 2040. … One of the concerns we all have is that it's actually going to get considerably worse in certain corridors before we can deliver the transit alternative."

Sound Transit does not claim that rapid transit will eliminate Seattle's notorious traffic jams, but it will give commuters an option around them.

However, as more lines open, light-rail will give far more people the option to simply opt out of the freeway rat race—all for the price of an ORCA card. And in the long run, that may someday alleviate some of the region's appalling freeway jams.

Finally, if history is any indicator, Link itself will fundamentally change the way the region develops and grows—for the better, in Constantine's view. "We didn't build freeways to serve some latent demand out there; we built freeways and created the land use patterns," he said. "And I think [they] are negative and unsustainable … patterns in a lot of ways. The creation of a high capacity, fixed guideway transit system is about creating a better, more sustainable, more environmentally responsible, and frankly more equitable, community. Not just transportation, but all the land use that goes with it."

Constantine said this was already happening in 2018. "The money to build is flowing to the places where transit is going to be, at Northgate, in Roosevelt, all up and down the line. … People recognize that this is where their customers want to be. Whether the customers are purchasing a home or leasing an office, these are the places that are going to be the most attractive and have the capacity to accommodate the most people and economic activity. And that's exactly what you would want to have happen."

In the old model, he said, the way housing affordability worked in King County was that "you drove until you qualified." In other words, you drove to Auburn, or all the way to Enumclaw, until you could find a house you could afford. "Everything you saved in terms of rent or mortgage you paid back in terms of lost transportation money—and hours — every day," said Constantine. "And being able to short-circuit that whole thing by getting housing [and] jobs that are also close to efficient and inexpensive transit, is a major breakthrough for equity." He was referring to social—not real estate—equity.

Constantine believes that rapid transit will help preserve another precious Puget Sound commodity: open space.

Crowds gather for a Sounder train at the Auburn Station stop.

When you give people more options for living in walkable, transit-oriented communities, "you're reducing the incentives for sprawling development." Of course, some people will still want to live on an acre in the woods. But that land is getting scarce. Some of the people who now live out in the rural fringes, might, he said, "happily trade for a place that is closer to transit, maybe a little more manageable … and now that trade can take place."

Meanwhile, the old question of whether transit should be centered around one hub in downtown Seattle or scattered around several metropolitan hubs, has been rendered moot by recent, shall we say, developments. Places such as Bellevue, Redmond, Federal Way, and even suburbs as far out as Issaquah have already become centers for development and the Link plan not only recognizes that expansion, but facilitates it. "We're going to expand the urban core," said Rogoff. "…[We're] making the transportation actually match the development patterns that have already happened. Bellevue is growing great guns. You can see it by the skyline."

Constantine said the Sound Transit 3 plan reinforces the idea that "it's not just downtown Seattle, although by historical accident, downtown Seattle is in the middle of all that." A company can have its corporate headquarters in downtown Seattle, Bellevue, Everett, Tacoma, or other major hubs and reliably bring in thousands of employees every day, said Constantine. In another sense, Link explodes the boundaries of downtown altogether. If a person can zip from downtown Seattle to downtown Bellevue in minutes, it creates, in essence, one big, seamless downtown.

After decades of playing catch-up to cities such as Atlanta and Portland—two places that received federal money that might have gone to Seattle—the Puget Sound region will soon have resources to match. In fact, Sound Transit will soon easily surpass Atlanta's MARTA system, said Rogoff, mainly because the original MARTA did not include all of Atlanta's surrounding counties. In Portland the MAX light-rail system currently surpasses Link in serving suburbs, but by the time Link reaches Lynnwood, Federal Way, Bellevue, and Redmond, Link will have caught up.

Link cars line up at the maintenance base in the SoDo neighborhood of Seattle.

These comparisons are not just a matter of civic pride, but of serious economic import. Seattle is competing economically with cities around the U.S. and beyond. "We're competing with Singapore … regions in Japan … [and] Barcelona, and if we can't get our workers to and from work, if we can't get goods and services moved around the region, we become definitively obsolete," said Nickels. "My frame of reference is, how do we make the region economically competitive with the great regions across the globe?" In Nickels' estimation, the Sound Transit 3 plan will do just that. "When it is done—and I hope I live to see it—we will have a regional system equivalent of the BART system [in the Bay Area]," he said.

The political road from Frank Osgood to the ORCA card has been more bone-rattling than the Toonerville Trolley, and that story has lessons not only for transit, but also for civic endeavors of every stripe. Rogoff summed up one of those lessons as: Don't just talk, act. "There's no question that the region spent literally a half-century talking about stuff, rather than executing it," said Rogoff. The rights-of-way alone are "painfully more expensive now" than they were in 1968. The region's taxpayers will be paying a steep price for decades. And if that's not painful enough, think about the right-of-way costs of 1911, the year of the Bogue Plan. Current taxpayers are essentially paying billions of dollars for what could have been purchased for a song if Seattle had approved the earlier plan. "You're welcome, 1911," said Constantine wryly.

Constantine describes Seattle's contentious civic culture using metaphors borrowed from A.A. Milne. He said Seattle has always been engaged in a tug-of-war between the "Tiggers" and the "Eeyores." The Tiggers, epitomized by Jim Ellis, were the civic boosters, the big thinkers, the people ready to carve out a new future. The Eeyores were the people with low expectations and little tolerance for risk, epitomized by numerous mayors, naysayers, and voters throughout the region's transit history.

"The Eeyores tended to win all the time, during my upbringing," said Constantine. "That's what happened with Forward Thrust. And I've always been in the former [Tigger] camp." He believes that the region has finally matured and accepted that change is coming, like it or not, and new residents will keep pouring in. Sound Transit's ballot successes signaled the public's desire to shape that change, not simply be swallowed up by it. The Tiggers, in other words, finally prevailed.

The Mercer Island Reporter *foresaw in 1995 that some heavy lifting might be worth it.*

This happened, in large part, because a few people simply refused to let the idea die. Nickels and Constantine both grow emotional simply talking about it; transit consumed so much of their public lives and meant so much to them. Nickels chose transit as his signature issue at the very beginning of his political career and never let up. "I thought it was nuts that we didn't have a mass transit system, just nuts," said Nickels. "I still believe that the 25 years from the defeat of Forward Thrust in 1968 and 1970, until we got back on the ballot in 1995, is the greatest failure of regional leadership in our history here."

When Constantine thinks about his transit legacy, he thinks about his grandfather, a high school football player from Everett, who was recruited around 1919 to play football for the University of Washington. He was the first in the family to go to college, and he could not have attended if not for the fact that the Seattle–Everett interurban allowed him to get from Everett to the UW campus quickly and cheaply. "And to think that nearly a century later, we were finally getting the train back to the same spot," said Constantine. When Constantine rides Link, he not only thinks of his grandfather, but also of the riders seated around him. "Every time I ride on it, I look around and I could not be happier that [this] is an expected and accepted part of their daily experience," he said.

Former Sound Transit board chair Dave Earling thinks about his grandson, Joe, and what lies in his future. Earling was standing near Sea-Tac Airport with his grandson recently when a Link train whooshed overhead. "I pointed at it and I said, 'Joe, I did that.'" These were words that many others—engineers, transit employees, construction workers, and electricians—could state with equal pride.

In an emotional ceremony on October 16, 2017, Sound Transit celebrated the most important person—by nearly universal consensus—in the agency's history: Joni Earl. On that day, Sound Transit christened the vast hall at their headquarters the "Joni Earl Great Hall at Union Station." Earl would remember it as an "amazing, very special" day. The tributes to her echoed off the hall's vast dome and those tributes continued in the months to come. Rogoff used the words "essential and elemental" to describe Earl's importance. Constantine said that the opening of the University Link was "an incredible testament to her tenacity and permanent impact on the region." Bob Drewel, who navigated the Dark Days alongside her, said, "I am strongly of the belief that, absent Joni Earl, we wouldn't be talking about Sound Transit today."

Ticket for the Joni Earl Great Hall dedication ceremony.

In 1993, when historian Walt Crowley predicted that metropolitan Seattle would continue in its same sad pattern of doing "too little, too late," he also predicted that future generations would be harsh judges. Sound Transit chair Paul Miller addressed a similar issue in a 1999 speech; yet by that time, he was able to frame the issue more optimistically. "We've asked how history will judge us," said Miller. " [We] will be remembered by what we as an agency and we as a community can achieve. I believe that at the end of the next century, Union Station will stand as a tribute to a generation that stopped talking about the transportation problems that threaten our region, and acted upon them."[8]

The story of Puget Sound's transit system has now come full circle after 134 years, with the old street rail systems dismantled and a new light-rail system pounded into place. As if to bring even more historical symmetry to the story, two small but fitting elements have been carved into the transit picture. A new extension to Seattle's modest streetcar system, the Center City Connector, is under construction on First Avenue, the former Front Street—the same street where Frank Osgood first proposed building Seattle's original streetcar line in 1884.

Meanwhile, on the waters of Puget Sound, the King County Water Taxi service sails Elliott Bay 21 times a day between West Seattle and Pier 52 in downtown Seattle, and six times a day between Vashon Island and Pier 52. This Greg Nickels brainchild was inaugurated in 1997 as the Elliott Bay Water Taxi. These passenger-only ferries now carry about 600,000 people per year, the old-fashioned way: the Mosquito Fleet way.

Timeline of Transit Votes

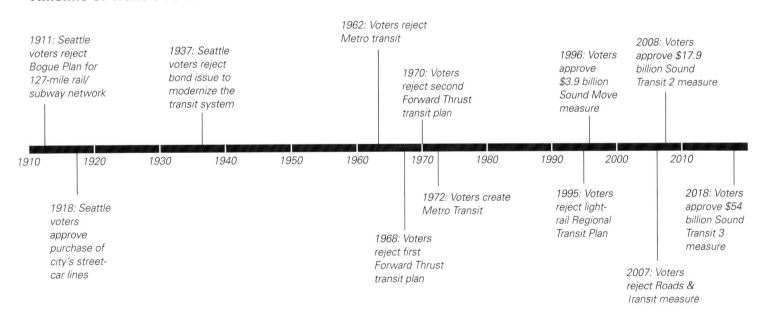

1911: Seattle voters reject Bogue Plan for 127-mile rail/subway network

1937: Seattle voters reject bond issue to modernize the transit system

1962: Voters reject Metro transit

1970: Voters reject second Forward Thrust transit plan

1996: Voters approve $3.9 billion Sound Move measure

2008: Voters approve $17.9 billion Sound Transit 2 measure

1910 1920 1930 1940 1950 1960 1970 1980 1990 2000 2010

1918: Seattle voters approve purchase of city's street-car lines

1972: Voters create Metro Transit

1968: Voters reject first Forward Thrust transit plan

1995: Voters reject light-rail Regional Transit Plan

2018: Voters approve $54 billion Sound Transit 3 measure

2007: Voters reject Roads & Transit measure

A Transit Tour, 2018:
The Sounder Commuter Train

What was it like riding the Sound Transit system, circa 2018? Here's the author's account of riding the Sounder commuter train from Everett to Seattle:

I drive into a large park-and-ride lot, which doubles as Everett's Amtrak and Sounder station. This is the northern terminus of the Sounder commuter train. I find an automated kiosk and buy a Sounder ticket to Seattle for $5, which, for a train ride, seems like a bargain. (It *is* a bargain—Sounder service is highly subsidized.) A train is waiting on the track, purring quietly. I enter one of the open doors.

The sleek white-and-blue cars have two decks. I go up the narrow stairs to the upper deck and take a seat. They are well-cushioned and grouped in four-seat configurations, two seats facing two. Some of them have small tables in the middle, where passengers have propped their laptop computers. I look out the window and see a commuter carry his bike onto the train.

An automated voice warns, "Doors closing," and soon we are rolling smoothly and quietly out of the station. Within minutes we emerge on the Everett waterfront, where we get a view of the Navy Shipyard. We hug the Puget Sound shoreline and head south. We will, in fact, hug the shoreline all the way to Seattle. Sounder is clearly an apt name. In some places, I feel as if I am looking straight down into the waters of the Sound. I see a bald eagle take off from a driftwood log, right below my window. Later, a seal sticks a flipper out of the water, as if waving to us as we glide by.

"Do not lie down or place your feet on the seats," intones an automated voice over the loudspeaker. None of us is doing any such thing, but a few commuters are napping upright in their seats. Most are looking at their phones or listening on headphones. Most people stay seated for the entire trip, but a few get up and walk down the aisles, headed for the restrooms. Unlike a bus, Sounder cars have restrooms.

At the first stop, Mukilteo Station, a few more commuters climb aboard. A freight train rumbles by on our left. Beachcombers walk the sands to our right. In a few spots, I see evidence of mudslides on the steep bluffs next to us—hazards which have been known to disrupt Sounder schedules during the rainy seasons.

The whistle blows as we approach Edmonds Station. A crowd pours into the car and soon most of the seats are filled, including the other three seats in my four-seat pod. I ask a man sitting across from me whether he takes Sounder often, and he says, "As often as I can. I love it." He works downtown at a financial firm.

We go right past Golden Gardens Park, near Ballard, where we see a woman in a wetsuit, swimming in the salt water. As we approach downtown, we enter a tunnel, which takes us under downtown Seattle. This is not the Seattle Transit Tunnel used by Link light-rail. This is the Great Northern Tunnel, a far more venerable passageway, used by the railroads in Seattle since 1906.

We emerge from the tunnel directly into King Street Station near Pioneer Square, where we all disembark. Because we are still below grade, we climb up a large staircase to a walkway up and over the tracks. The entire trip has taken 59 minutes.

Sounder commuters jam King Street Station in Seattle in 2018.

Acknowledgments

This book owes a tremendous debt to the transit historians who came before, especially the late Walt Crowley, whose book, *Routes: A Brief History of Public Transportation in Metropolitan Seattle*, served as a reliable guide to Seattle's transit history up to 1993. The first half of this book recounts the story of Seattle's early transit days, often using Crowley's book as a hard-to-improve-upon blueprint. I also had access to Crowley's original *Routes* manuscript—which was far more detailed than the much shorter published version. Crowley was the founder of HistoryLink, an endeavor ably carried on by his widow, Marie McCaffrey. This book would never have happened without McCaffrey's vision, from concept to execution.

This book also owes a massive debt to Leslie Blanchard, author of *The Street Railway Era in Seattle*, and Warren Wing, author of *To Tacoma By Trolley* and *To Seattle by Trolley*. These books tell the definitive stories of the region's early trolley days, and I leaned on them heavily. For a thorough history of the early politics behind the street railway systems and the power industry, I found Richard C. Berner's three-volume *Seattle in the 20th Century* indispensable.

I believe that journalists are, in fact, the world's first-draft historians, and I found myself time and time again seeking out their accounts. Jane Hadley's stories in the Seattle PI, and the stories of *Seattle Times* writers David Schaefer, Susan Gilmore, Alex Fryer, Ross Cunningham, Andrew Garber, Daniel Beekman, and, especially, Mike Lindblom and Bob Lane, were invaluable. Lane's fact-filled book of early Metro history was also crucial. I would also like to thank Josh Cohen, a reporter for *Crosscut*, who provided valuable groundwork on *Sound Transit*'s story. Thanks, too, to the journalists from the early trolley decades —mostly unknown and non-bylined—who gave me a feel for the wild and raucous streetcar era.

The latter chapters cover a story not yet found in books: the Sound Transit story. We owe many thanks to Bronwyn Dorhorfer, Sound Transit's unfailingly cooperative and knowledgeable research librarian, for helping us navigate a bewildering wealth of materials in the Sound Transit archive. She was also instrumental in helping us find photos, charts and maps to help illustrate this story. Geoff Patrick, Sound Transit deputy executive director of communications, also helped us every step of the way. In our search for photos and graphics, we also received expert help and cooperation from Phil Stairs at the Puget Sound Regional Archives in Bellevue, Lisa Labovitch from the Everett Public Library's Northwest Room, and Jeanie Fisher from the Seattle Municipal Archives. We'd like to give special thanks to David Koch, digital media editor at HistoryLink, for all of his work tracking down visual assets for the project.

The final third of the book relies heavily on oral history interviews I conducted with many of the major players in the dramatic Sound Transit story, including Greg Nickels, Joni Earl, Jared Smith, Bob Drewel, Bruce Laing, Anne Fennessy, Ron Sims, Dave Earling, Peter Rogoff, and Dow Constantine. All of them gave generously of their time and candor. Without their stories and perspectives, this history would have been lifeless and incomplete.

For more information on the region's transit, including essays on the Queen Anne Counterbalance and Trackless Trolleys in Seattle, please visit HistoryLink.org.

Previous page: Sounder train service would continue to grow over the next two decades. Shown here in 2018 with Mount Rainier in the background.

Sponsors

Platinum Level:

LMN Architects

Parametrix

WSP USA

Gold Level:

HDR

HDR

McMillen Jacobs Associates

McMillen Jacobs Associates

Silver Level:

David Evans and Associates, Inc.

EnviroIssues

HEWITT

KBA, Inc.

KPFF Consulting Engineers

Shannon & Wilson, Inc.

Bronze Level:

Anne Fennessy and David Moseley

PRR

VIA Architecture

Sources

The sources for this book can be roughly divided into three main categories: Books, interviews with the author, newspaper accounts, and other resources. This is a list of the most indispensable sources:

Books

Bae, Christine; Manish Chalana; Jeffery Ochsner, editors. *Back to the Future: A History of Transit Planning in the Puget Sound Region*. Seattle: College of Built Environments, University of Washington, 2013.

Berner, Richard C. Three-volume history: *Seattle 1900–1920, Vol. 1; Seattle 1921–1940, Vol. 2; Seattle Transformed: World War to Cold War, Vol. 3*. Seattle: Charles Press, 1991, 1992, 1999.

Blanchard, Leslie. *The Street Railway Era in Seattle*. Forty Fort, Pennsylvania: Harold E. Cox, 1968.

Clark, Norman H. *Mill Town: A Social History of Everett*. Seattle and London: University of Washington Press, 1970.

Crowley, Walt. *Routes: A Brief History of Public Transportation in Metropolitan Seattle*. Seattle: Municipality of Metropolitan Seattle,1993.

Crowley, Walt. "Routes: An Interpretive History of Public Transportation in Metropolitan Seattle" (This manuscript, prepared for Metro Transit in 1993 and available at the Seattle Public Library, was Crowley's much longer unpublished manuscript, from which the ensuing book was condensed.)

Hunt, Herbert. *Tacoma: Its History and Builders,* Vol. 1. Tacoma: S.J. Clarke Publishing Co., 1916.

Lane, Bob. *Better Than Promised: An Informal History of the Municipality of Metropolitan Seattle*. (This booklet was published by the King County Department of Metropolitan Services, 1995.)

Wing, Warren. *To Tacoma by Trolley: The Puget Sound Electric Railway*. Edmonds: Pacific Fast Mail, 1995.

Wing, Warren. *To Seattle By Trolley: The Story of the Seattle–Everett Interurban*. Edmonds: Pacific Fast Mail, 1995.

Interviews

Dow Constantine
Bob Drewel
Joni Earl
Dave Earling
Anne Fennessy
Bruce Laing
Greg Nickels
Peter Rogoff
Ron Sims
Jared Smith

Readers may assume that direct quotes from these individuals come from these interviews, unless otherwise specified.

Newspaper Accounts and Additional Resources

Finally, the book draws heavily from contemporary newspaper accounts, including the *Seattle Times*, the *Seattle Post-Intelligence*r, the *Everett Herald*, the *Puget Sound Business Journa*l, the *Seattle Weekly, Crosscut,* and other regional newspapers and magazines. The book also draws from many other sources, including HistoryLink.org, the online Encyclopedia of Washington State History, as well as the archives of Sound Transit, King County Metro, the City of Seattle, and the Northwest Room of the Everett Public Library.

Credits

All images courtesy of Sound Transit Archives except where indicated:

Cover

Washington State Archives,
AR-07809001-ph005135
Kevin Scott/LMN Architects
Seattle Municipal Archives, 10813
Glenn Landberg, Sound Transit
Kevin Scott/LMN Architects

Front/Introduction

1   MOHAI
2   Kevin Scott/LMN Architects
6   Washington State Archives
7   Seattle Municipal Archives, 145040
8   Puget Sound Maritime Historical
    Society
9   Kevin Scott/LMN Architects

Chapter 1

10   Seattle Public Library
11   MOHAI
12   MOHAI
13   Seattle Municipal Archives, 77291
14a National Archives
14b Blanchard Book
15   Tacoma Public Library
17   Seattle Public Library
18a Seattle Municipal Archives, 2864
18b Blanchard Book
19a MOHAI
19b Everett Public Library

Chapter 2

20   Washington State Archives,
     AR-07809001-ph005135
21   Seattle Municipal Archives, 8660
22   Lawton Gowey
23   University of Washington Special
     Collections
24   Shoreline Historical Museum

25   To Tacoma by Trolley, The Puget
     Sound Electric Railway, Warren W.
     Wing (Pacific Fast Mail, Edmonds,
     1995)
26   MOHAI
27   Matt Hinz
29   Washington State Archives,
     AR-28001001-ph002340
30   Seattle Public Library
31   University of Washington Special
     Collections
32a Pacific Northwest Railroad Archive in
     Burien
32b Blanchard Book
33   Seattle Engineering Department
34   MOHAI
35   MOHAI
36   University of Washington Special
     Collections
38/39 Seattle Municipal Archives, 12660

Chapter 3

40   MOHAI
41   MOHAI
42a Tacoma Public Library
42b Blanchard Book
43   Courtesy Bert and Elizabeth Prescott
44a Paul Dorpat
44b *The Seattle Times*
45   Washington State Archives
46   MOHAI
50b Blanchard Book
51   Washington State Archives
52a University of Washington Special
     Collections
52b Washington State Archives
53   Blanchard Book
54a Seattle Municipal Archives, 11119
54b King County Museum Collections
55   MOHAI
56   Washington State Archives
57a MOHAI
57b Washington State Archives

Chapter 4

58   Washington State Archives
59   MOHAI
60a Washington State Archives

61a MOHAI
61b MOHAI
62   Seattle Municipal Archives, 77092
63   Seattle Municipal Archives, 43556
64a *The Seattle Times*
64b Washington State Archives
65a Washington state Archives
65b Tacoma Public Library
66   Everett Transit
67   Steve Morgan
68a University of Washington Special
     Collections
68b Wikapedia Commons: copyright
     Steve Morgan
69   Washington State Archives
70   MOHAI
72   University of Washington Special
     Collections
73   Courtesy Ellis Family
74   University of Washington Special
     Collections
75   Washington State Archives
76a Seattle Municipal Archives
77   Detroit News Photographers, Thorpe

Chapter 5

78   Washington State Archives
80a MOHAI
80b King County Executive
81   Washington State Archives
82a HistoryLink from Group Health
     Cooperative
82b RTA
83   Seattle Municipal Archives, 1802-16
85a *The Seattle Times*
85b Seattle Municipal Archives, 175430
86a Washington State Archives
86b Seattle Municipal Archives, 73021
87a Seattle Municipal Archives, 33297
87b King County Archives
88   Washington State Archives
90a Washington State Archives
90b Trimet
91   *The Seattle Times*
92a Washington State Archives
92b Washington State Archives

Endnotes

Chapter 1

1 "Coast Salish Canoes," from the Jamestown S'Klallam website, http://www.jamestowntribe.org/history/hist_canoe.htm.
2 Crowley, p. 4.
3 Larry E. Johnson, "Puget Sound's Mosquito Fleet," HistoryLink.org, essay 869.
4 Crowley, p. 5.
5 Ibid., p. 6.
6 Walt Crowley, "Streetcars First Enter Service on September 23, 1884," HistoryLink.org, essay 2688.
7 Blanchard, *The Street Railway Era in Seattle*, p. 5.
8 Hunt, p. 431.
9 David Wilma, "Tacoma Street Railway Inaugurates Service on May 30, 1888," HistoryLink.org, essay 5065.
10 Rudyard Kipling, *From Sea to Sea and Other Sketches: Letters of Travel*, Vol. 2, New York, NY: Doubleday, Page & Company, 1913, p. 43–46.
11 Blanchard, p. 17.
12 Crowley, p. 7.
13 Ibid.
14 Blanchard, p. 9.
15 Crowley, p. 8.
16 Ibid., p. 1.
17 Hunt, p. 474.
18 Blanchard, p. 25.
19 Ibid.
20 Ibid.
21 Crowley, p. 8.
22 Blanchard, p. 43.
23 Ibid., p. 42.
24 Clark, p. 30.

Chapter 2

1 Crowley, p. 8.
2 Blanchard, p. 57.
3 Ibid., p. 25.
4 Crowley, p. 9.
5 Blanchard, p. 60.
6 Crowley, p. 9.
7 Hunt, Vol. 2, p. 203.
8 Wing, *Tacoma*, p. 63.
9 Ibid., p. 11.
10 "Service Begins Today," *Seattle Times*, September 26, 1902, p. 12.
11 Wing, Tacoma, p. 67.
12 Ibid., p. 37.
13 Ibid., p. 67.
14 Ibid., p. 126.
15 Blanchard, p. 53.
16 Wing, from the *Seattle Post-Intelligencer*, November 23, 1902, p.21.
17 Wing, *Seattle*.
18 Ibid., p. 137.
19 Wing, *Tacoma*, in an account written by Clinton H. Betz, p. 127.
20 Arthur Kramer, *Among the Livewires: 100 Years of Puget Power*, Edmonds: Creative Communications, 1986.
21 Wing, *Tacoma*, p. 19.
22 Blanchard, p. 77.
23 Ibid.
24 Ibid., p. 76–77.
25 "Tacoma Horror," *Seattle Times*, July 5, 1900, p. 5.
26 Daryl C. McClary, "43 passengers die in a trolley car accident in Tacoma on July 4, 1900," HistoryLink.org, essay 7477.
27 David Wilma, "Two Passengers Die in an Interurban Streetcar Accident in Rainier Valley on April 30, 1910," HistoryLink.org, essay 3087.
28 "Death on the Interurban," *Seattle Times*, September 3, 1902, p. 4.
29 Blanchard, p. 96.
30 Crowley, p. 11.
31 Ibid.
32 Blanchard, p. 81.
33 Crowley, p. 12.
34 Bogue, "Plan of Seattle," 1911, p. 131, http://www.bettertransport.info/pitf/BoguePlan1911.htm.
35 Ibid.
36 Ross Anderson, "We Get a Second Chance to Fulfill Bogue's Vision," *Seattle Times*, February 24, 1995, p. B4.
37 Blanchard, p. 81.
38 Clark, p. 113.
39 *Moody's Manual of Railroads and Corporation Securities,* Issue 21, Part 2, p. 365.
40 Blanchard, p. 87.
41 Ibid.
42 Ibid.
43 Ibid., p. 92.
44 Ibid., p. 93.
45 Ole Hanson, letter to the Seattle City Council, June 24, 1918, posted on HistoryLink.org, http://www.historylink.org/File/20468.
46 Blanchard, p. 90.
47 Berner, Vol. 1, p. 266.
48 "City-Owned Cars Run on Schedule," *Seattle Times*, April 1, 1919, p. 10.
49 Blanchard, p. 95.
50 Crowley, p.14.
51 Berner, Vol. 1, p. 268.

Chapter 3

1 Wing, *Tacoma*, p. 68.
2 Hunt, Vol. 2, p. 272.
3 Tacoma Public Utilities website, https://www.mytpu.org/tacomarail/about/history.htm.
4 David Wilma, "Tacoma Municipal Railway Streetcar Service begins January 2, 1919," HistoryLink.org, essay 5803.
5 David Wilma, "Tacoma Public Utilities," HistoryLink.org, essay 5025.
6 David Wilma, "Tacoma Municipal Belt Line Railway Sheds Passenger Service on January 1, 1947," HistoryLink.org, essay 5117.
7 Crowley manuscript, p. 24.
8 Blanchard, p. 99.
9 Ibid., p. 101.
10 Crowley manuscript, p. 25.
11 Blanchard, p. 104.
12 Ibid., p. 106.
13 Crowley manuscript, p. 25.
14 Ibid.

15 Beeler report, 1937, p. 14.
16 Blanchard, p. 107.
17 Crowley manuscript, p. 25.
18 Ibid.
19 William Whitfield, History of Snohomish County Washington, Chicago and Seattle: Pioneer Historical Publishing Co., 1926, p. 400–401.
20 Blanchard, p. 108.
21 Dave Wilma, "Elmer Yates Remembers the Toonerville Trolley in the Rainier Valley," HistoryLink.org, essay 3085.
22 Crowley manuscript, p. 25.
23 Blanchard, p. 109.
24 Wing, *Tacoma,* p. 113.
25 Ibid., p. 128.
26 Ibid., p. 99.
27 Quoted by Frederick Bird, "The Seattle-Everett Interurban Railway," Snohomish County History series, on the Snohomish County website, https://snohomishcountywa.gov/DocumentCenter/View/9684.
28 Crowley manuscript, p. 31.
29 Blanchard, p. 46.
30 *Back to the Future,* p. 127.
31 "Council to Pass on Tram Request," *Seattle Times*, June 19, 1935, p. 2.
32 Crowley manuscript, p. 26.
33 "Settlement of Car Debt Looms," *Seattle Times*, June 18, 1935, p. 1.
34 *Beeler Report*, 1935, p. 3 (report and revisions on file at the Sound Transit archive).
35 Ibid., p. 4.
36 Ibid., p. 36.
37 "Seattle Railway Rejuvenation Plan Is the Work of Experts," *Seattle Times*, January 17, 1937, p. 3.
38 "Car Men Fight Modernization," *Seattle Times*, October 4, 1936, pp. 1 and 12.
39 "Seattle Railway Rejuvenation Plan Is the Work of Experts," *Seattle Times*, January 17, 1937, p. 3.
40 *Beeler Report*, January 18, 1937, p. 4.
41 "Dore Questions Car Plan Vote," *Seattle Times*, January 28, 1937, p. 22.
42 Blanchard, p. 125.
43 "Two Die, 60 Hurt in Crash," *Seattle Times*, January 8, 1937, p. 1.

44 "6,000 Cheer and Jeer Dore And Langlie in Car Debate," *Seattle Times*, March 8, 1937, pp. 1 and 10.
45 Ibid.
46 Ibid.
47 "Dore Asks Council Foes to Resign," *Seattle Times*, March 10, 1937, p. 1.
48 Crowley manuscript, p. 28.
49 Kramer, p. 40.
50 Blanchard, p. 131.
51 "Transport System to be Ready Within Year," *Seattle Times*, September 3, 1939, pp. 1 and 7.
52 Blanchard, p. 132.
53 "Seattle Streetcars End Service Record of 57 Years," *Seattle Times*, April 13, 1941, p. 10.
54 Ibid.
55 Crowley manuscript, p. 30.
56 "Tacoma to Ride on Rubber Tires," *Seattle Times*, December 31, 1937, p. 11.
57 *Life Magazine*, July 11, 1938, p. 63.
58 Ibid.
59 Ibid., p. 65.

Chapter 4
1 "Modern Facilities of Seattle Transit System's Huge New Terminal Keep Buses Rolling," *Seattle Times*, January 11, 1942, Sunday Rotogravure section, p. 4.
2 "Stagger' Work Plan to Affect Every Family," *Seattle Times*, July 19, 1942, p. 17.
3 Ibid.
4 Ibid.
5 Berner, Vol. 3, p. 61.
6 "Ride Rationing Considered by Transit System," *Seattle Times*, November 24, 1942, p. 1.
7 Metro website, "About Metro," "Milestones, the 1940s," http://metro.kingcounty.gov/am/history/history-1940.html.
8 "Transit," *Seattle Times*, June 8, 1947, special section, p. 5
9 Ibid.
10 "Dime Fares on Trolleys Go in Effect," *Seattle Times*, June 22, 1947, p. 1.
11 Crowley manuscript, p. 31.

12 "Firm Modernizes Name," *Seattle Times*, June 1,1941, p. 10.
13 *Back to the Future*, p.6.
14 Crowley manuscript, p. 41.
15 Lane, p. 39.
16 Crowley manuscript, p. 58.
17 Ibid., p. 41.
18 Ross Cunningham, "Toll-Tunnel System Urged to Ease City's Traffic Jams," *Seattle Times*, December 21, 1953, pp. 1 and 4.
19 "If City Folk Would But Use Their Heads," *Seattle Times*, December 23, 1953, editorial page.
20 Ibid.
21 Crowley manuscript, p. 41.
22 "Tacoma Transit Employees Offer to Buy Bus System," *Seattle Times*, July 29, 1954, p. 1.
23 "Employes Buying Tacoma Transit Co.," *Seattle Times*, December 1, 1954. p. 1.
24 "Tacoma to Offer $750,000 for City's Transit Company," *Seattle Times*, August 16, 1960, p. 11.
25 "City Owned Transit Buses are Driving Tacoma to Brink of Bankruptcy," *Seattle Times*, June 25, 1964, p. 60.
26 "Everett to Ask Vote on Transit Purchase," *Seattle Times*, September 10, 1969, p. 31.
27 "Everett Will Buy 16 Used Buses," *Seattle Times*, November 25, 1969, p. 14.
28 "City Owned Transit Buses are Driving Tacoma to Brink of Bankruptcy," *Seattle Times*, June 25, 1964, p. 60.
29 Ibid.
30 Crowley manuscript, p. 38.
31 Ibid., p. 40.
32 Bob Lane, "Bare Bones Service Now Being Provided," *Seattle Times*, September 17, 1972, p. E4.
33 Crowley manuscript, p. 42.
34 *Back to the Future*, p. 24.
35 Crowley manuscript, p. 45.
36 Ibid., p. 46.
37 Walt Woodward. "United Plan for Seattle," *Seattle Times*, November 3, 1965, p. 1.

38 "A Bold Community Action Plan," *Seattle Times*, November 3, 1965, p. 9.

39 "Balance is Key to Transit Plan," (with map), *Seattle Times*, October 6, 1967, p. 4.

40 Ibid.

41 "Forward Thrust Tools—Voters Should Buy Whole Package," *Seattle Times*, February 11, 1968, p. 10.

42 "King County Demos OK Part of Thrust," *Seattle Times*, February 6, 1968, p. 29.

43 Information for this profile came from: Cassandra Tate, "Ellis, James Reed (b.1921)," HistoryLink.org, essay 7833; "Official Test of Light Rail," *Seattle Times*, October 8, 2008, p. B7; "Thrust Defeat Laid to Economic Lag," *Seattle Times*, May 20, 1970, p. D1; Larry Coffman, "Thrust's Jim Ellis," *Seattle Times*, *Pacific NW Magazine*, February 11, 1968, p. 1.

44 Ad in the *Seattle Times*, February 8, 1968, p. 2.

45 Crowley manuscript, p. 51.

46 "Even Losses Hearten Thrust Backers," *Seattle Times*, February 14, 1968, p. 8.

47 Crowley manuscript, p. 55.

48 "Chamber's Transit Stand Hit," *Seattle Times*, April 16, 1970, p. 12.

49 "Thrust Defeat Laid to Economic Lag," *Seattle Times*, May 20, 1970, p. D1.

50 Ibid.

51 "Thrust Opponent Cites Distrust," *Seattle Times*, May 20, 1970, p. D1.

52 Crowley manuscript, p. 56.

53 Ibid., p. 57.

54 ibid., p. 56.

55 Cassandra Tate, "Ellis, James Reed," HistoryLink.org, essay 7833.

Chapter 5

1 Lane, p. 39.

2 Crowley manuscript, p. 60.

3 Ibid.

4 Ibid., p. 61.

5 Lane, p. 39.

6 Crowley manuscript, p. 64–65.

7 Ibid.

8 Ibid., p. 65.

9 Ibid, p. 66.

10 Bob Lane, "Bus Plan Hinges on Voters," *Seattle Times*, September 17, 1972, p. E4.

11 Crowley manuscript, p. 67–68.

12 Ibid., p. 68.

13 Bob Lane, "County-Wide Bus System: A Go Signal," *Seattle Times*, September 20, 1972, p. A1.

14 Ibid.

15 "Two Election Comebacks," *Seattle Times*, September 20, 1972, p. A12.

16 Crowley manuscript, p. 70.

17 Ibid., p. 71.

18 Lane, p. 37.

19 Ibid.

20 Crowley manuscript, p. 71.

21 Ibid.

22 Ibid., p. 72.

23 Ibid., p. 73.

24 Lane, p. 40.

25 Crowley manuscript, p. 75.

26 Bob Lane, "Bus Order Dies for Lack of Bids," *Seattle Times*, January 21, 1975, p. B4.

27 Ibid.

28 Lane, p. 41.

29 Crowley manuscript, p. 86.

30 Don Glickstein, "Aubrey Davis (1917–2013)", HistoryLink.org, essay 8179.

31 Crowley manuscript, p. 87.

32 Community Transit website, https://www.communitytransit.org/about/about-us.

33 Pierce Transit website, https://www.piercetransit.org/about-pierce-transit/.

Chapter 6

1 Crowley manuscript, p. 90.

2 Ibid., p. 89.

3 Lane, p. 72.

4 Crowley manuscript, p. 93.

5 Ibid., p. 99.

6 Ibid.

7 Lane, p. 73.

8 Julie Emery, "Streetcar Desire Turns to Real Thing on Waterfront," *Seattle Times*, May 30, 1982, p. B1.

9 Crowley manuscript, p. 105.

10 "Waterfront Trolley: A Dream Come True," *Seattle Times*, *Pacific NW Magazine,* May 18, 1982, p. 3.

11 "Olympia Digest," *Seattle Times*, April 4, 1981, p. A9.

12 George Benson, "The Waterfront Streetcar—The Steep Grade from Idea to Reality," 1992 speech, reprinted in HistoryLink.org, essay 7271. 9 Crowley manuscript, p. 101.

13 Lane, p. 73.

14 Crowley manuscript, p. 105.

15 Ibid., p. 102.

16 Lane, p. 73.

17 Frank Chesley, "Charles Royer," HistoryLink.org, essay 8265.

18 "Performance Measure Summary, Seattle," 1990, Texas A&M Transportation Institute, Urban Mobility Information, https://static.tti.tamu.edu/tti.tamu.edu/documents/ums/congestion-data/seattle.pdf.

19 Crowley manuscript, p. 107.

20 Ibid., p. 108.

21 Ibid., p. 110.

22 Lane, p. 75.

23 Crowley manuscript, p. 115.

24 Ibid., p. 112.

25 Rick Anderson, "Bus Tunnel Users Find No Refuge From Soggy Seattle," *Seattle Times*, November 14, 1990, p. D1.

26 *Back to the Future*, p. 55.

27 Ibid.

28 Ibid., p. 56.

29 Crowley manuscript, p. 130.

30 Ibid., p. 131.

31 Crowley manuscript, p. 144.

32 Peyton Whitely, "Regional Transportation—A Hopeless Situation," *Seattle Times*, October 28, 1990, p. A17.

33 Crowley manuscript, p. 159.

34 "Sound Transit Board honors transit champion, State Representative Ruth Fisher," Sound Transit news release, February 23, 2006.

35 Revised Code of Washington, RCW 81.112.

Chapter 7

1 Crowley manuscript, p. 149.
2 Ibid., p. 148.
3 David Schaefer and Keith Ervin, "A Long Road to Opposition: Kemper Freeman Jr. vs the RTA," *Seattle Times*, March 6, 1995, p. A1.
4 "Make Progress, Not Tracks—Scrap Glitzy Rail Plan; Be Bold With Buses," *Seattle Times*, April 25, 1993, p. A22.
5 Dave Earling, "Why Rail Works," *Open Spaces: Views From the Northwest*, Vol. 3. Issue 3, 2000, p. 23.
6 David Schaefer, "RTA Ready to Unveil New Plan," *Seattle Times*, January 11, 1996, p. A1.
7 Josh Cohen, "Sound Transit," HistoryLink.org, essay 8002.
8 "RTA: Let's Get Started," *Seattle Times*, November 3. 1996, p. B6.
9 David Schaefer, "Voters Back Transit Plan on Fourth Try," *Seattle Times*, November 6, 1996, p. A1.
10 "RTA Goes From a Dream to High Expectations," *Seattle Times*, November 8, 1996, p. B6.
11 Jared Smith, interview, December 21, 2017.
12 "'Sound Transit' to Be the Name for Regional Transit Authority Services," Sound Transit news release, August 15, 1997.
13 "Seattle's Historic Union Station to Become Sound Transit Headquarters," Sound Transit news release, June 18, 1998.
14 Walt Crowley, "Seattle's Union Station Re-Opens As Sound Transit Headquarters," HistoryLink.org, essay 7751.
15 "First Public Ride of Sounder commuter train," Sound Transit news release, February 16, 2000.
16 John Zebroski, "A Commute That Brings a Smile," *Seattle Times*, March 1, 2000, p. B3.
17 Information for this profile came from the author's interview with Greg Nickels, and from Phil Dougherty, "Nickels, Gregory James (b. 1955)," HistoryLink.org, essay 20452.

Chapter 8

1 O. Casey Corr, "Chugga, Chugga, Clank: A Not-So-Sound Transit Plan," *Seattle Times*, July 28, 1999, p. B4.
2 Josh Cohen, "Sound Transit," HistoryLink.org, essay 8002.
3 "Sound Transit Board Achieves Historic Milestone by Selecting Route for Central Link Light-rail," Sound Transit news release, November 18, 1999.
4 David Schaefer, "Tukwila Makes Its Pitch to Reroute New Rail Line," *Seattle Times*, January 17, 1999, p. B2.
5 Alex Fryer, "Showdown in Rainier Valley—Despite One Group's Signs, Some Others Favor Street Level," *Seattle Times*, October 4, 1999, p. A1.
6 Andrew Garber, "Sound Transit Told to Tighten Purse Strings," *Seattle Times*, September 8, 2000, p. B4.
7 Lance Dickie, "On Track So Far," *Seattle Times*, October 8, 2000, p. C1.
8 Emory Bundy, "Emory Bundy Responds," *Open Spaces: Views From the Northwest, Vol. 3*. Issue 3, 2000, p. 23.
9 Andrew Garber, "Price Puts Tunnel on Hold," *Seattle Times*, November 17, 2000, p. A1.
10 Ibid.
11 "Beyond the Tunnel," *Seattle Times*, November 20, 2000, p. B6.
12 "Revised Budget and Schedule Proposed for Link Light-rail," Sound Transit news release, December 14, 2000.
13 Greg Nickels interview with Josh Cohen, 2017.
14 "Sound Transit Executive Director Bob White Submits Resignation," Sound Transit news release, January 23, 2001.
15 "Light-rail Cost Soars $1 Billion," *Seattle Times*, December 13, 2000, p. A1.
16 "Chief Operating Officer Named Acting Sound Transit Executive Director," Sound Transit news release, January 25, 2001.
17 Josh Cohen, "Sound Transit," HistoryLink.org, essay 8002.
18 "Federal Aid in Jeopardy for Light-rail," *Seattle Times*, March 30, 2001, p. A1.
19 Ibid.
20 Chris McGann, "Sound Transit Concealed Light-Rail Costs For Years," *Seattle Post-Intelligencer*, May 4, 2001, p. 1.
21 "Sound Transit Costs Story Incorrect," *Seattle Post-Intelligencer*, May 10, 2001, p. 1.
22 "Sound Transit Launches Tacoma Light-rail," Sound Transit news release, August 22, 2003.
23 Rachel Tuinstra, "Sounder Train Opens Everett-Seattle Route," *Seattle Times*, December 22, 2003, p. B1.
24 Alex Fryer and Mike Lindblom, "Light-rail Plan Clears Major Hurdle With Feds," *Seattle Times*, July 8, 2003, p. A1.
25 Ron Sims interview.
26 "Federal Transit Administration Approves $500 Million Light-rail Grant," Sound Transit news release, October 24, 2003.
27 Mike Lindblom, "Groundbreaking Today for Light-rail," *Seattle Times*, November 8, 2003, p. B1.
28 Two HistoryLink essays provided the bulk of the information for the monorail sidebar: "Monorail (Seattle)," by Walt Crowley with Phil Dougherty, essay 2524; and "Elevated Transportation Company: Extending the Monorail," by Tom Carr, essay 2534.

Chapter 9

1 Eric Pryne, "Scaling Back of Light Rail Upheld," *Seattle Times*, March 5, 2004, p. B1.

2 Susan Gilmore, "Light-rail's South End Falls Short," *Seattle Times*, September 1, 2002, p. B1.

3 "Light-rail Goes to Airport," Sound Transit news release, December 21, 2004.

4 Eric Pryne, "Bus Tunnel Error is Costly in Shutdown Today," *Seattle Times*, October 13, 2005, p. A1.

5 "What, Whys of $82.7 Million Tunnel Project," *Seattle Times*, September 23, 2005, p. A15.

6 Susan Gilmore, "Bus Tunnel Shuts Down Tonight for Two Years," *Seattle Times*, September 23, 2005, p. A1.

7 Paula Becker, "Seattle's South Lake Union Streetcar Begins Service on December 12, 2007," HistoryLink.org, essay 8421.

8 Mike Lindblom, "Audit: Light-rail Contractor Didn't Set Culture of Safety," *Seattle Times*, February 10, 2007, p. B1.

9 "Sound Transit Seeks Public Input on Three Options," Sound transit news release, July 13, 2006.

10 "November 2008 Mass Transit Ballot Measure Provides Express Bus Expansion, Speeds Up Light-rail by Five to Seven Years," Sound Transit news release, July 23, 2008.

11 Mike Lindblom, "Light-rail Foes Launch Preemptive Strike," *Seattle Times*, July 10, 2008, p. B2.

12 Mike Lindblom, "Road vs. Rail: 2 Spar over Transit Options," *Seattle Times*, October 23, 2003, p. B8.

13 Sandi Doughton and Mike Lindblom, "Seattle Hops On Board," *Seattle Times*, July 19, 2009, p. A1.

14 Tim Newcomb, "How to Build Train Tracks Across a Bridge That Won't Hold Still," *Popular Mechanics*, November 29, 2017.

15 Nicole Tsong, "Light-rail Squabble Fractures Bellevue Council," *Seattle Times*, January 12, 2011, p. A1.

16 Mike Lindblom, "New Sound Transit Chief," *Seattle Times*, November 20, 2015, p. B1.

17 Daniel Beekman, "Light-rail at UW," *Seattle Times*, March 20, 2016, p. B1.

18 Ibid.

19 "Board Applauds Legislature and Governor's Support for full ST3 Funding Authority," Sound Transit news release, July 1, 2015.

20 "ST3 Plan Would Cost Typical Adult $169 Annually or $14 Per Month," Sound Transit news release, July 8, 2016.

21 Mike Lindblom, "Long Road Ahead for $50B Transit Plan," *Seattle Times*, March 25, 2016, p. A8.

22 "Reject Sound Transit 3," *Seattle Times*, October 20, 2016, p. A15.

23 Sara Bernard, "The Lovers and Haters of ST3," *Seattle Weekly*, October 19, 2016.

24 Mike Lindblom, "Sound Transit 3 Leading," *Seattle Times*, November 9, 2016, p. A7.

25 Mark Higgins, "The Election's Silver Lining," *Seattle Times*, November 1l, 2016, p. A15.

26 Laura Bliss, "On Tuesday Night, Transit Was Victorious," *CityLab*, November 9, 2016.

27 Information for this profile came from: the author's interview with Joni Earl; Jane Hadley, "Earl Put Agency Back on Track," *Seattle Post-Intelligencer*, July 7, 2003, p. A1; Hannelore Suderman, "What I've Learned Since College: Joni Earl '75," *Washington State Magazine*, Spring 2010, p. 47.

Chapter 10

1 Mike Lindblom, "Soaring Land and Construction Costs Push Light-rail Into Federal Way Over $2.5 Billion," *Seattle Times*, July 26, 2018.

2 "System Expansion: Building More Connections," Sound Transit flyer, 2018.

3 "Board Sends Major Light Rail Expansion Plan to November Ballot," Sound Transit news release, June 23, 2016.

4 Mike Lindblom, "Transit Use Up in Central Seattle," *Seattle Times*, February 15, 2018. p. B1.

5 "Greater Seattle Leads the Nation in Transit Ridership Growth," King County Metro news release, February 22, 2018.

6 Julia Martinez and Emily Parkhurst, "On the Right Track," *Puget Sound Business Journal*, November 24, 2017, pp. 14–15.

7 "2017 Top 100 Truck Bottleneck List," American Transportation Research Institute website.

8 Walt Crowley, "Seattle's Union Station Re-Opens as Sound Transit Headquarters on October 16, 1999," HistoryLink.org, essay 7751.

Index